REBIRTH

Letting Go of the Past

REBIRTH

Letting Go of the Past

Arnold Henry

TO: Varnia Henry
Thanks for the support

Piton Books

Some names have been changed in this book to protect the privacy of the individuals involved.

REBIRTH: Letting Go of the Past by Arnold Henry

ISBN: 978-0-9940272-2-1

Published 2015 by Piton Books, www.pitonbooks.com, Chestermere, Alberta, Canada. All rights reserved. No part of this publication may be reproduced, stored in a retrieval system, or transmitted in any form or by any means, electronic, mechanical, recording, or otherwise, without the prior written permission of Piton Books.

The Cataloguing-in-Publication Data is on file at Library and Archives Canada.

Printed and bound in the United States of America

For my son, Amarion Stephen Henry,
and my future wife, Stephanie Paige Beninger,
who has given me a chance
to make things right.

The New Dream

TABLE OF CONTENTS

Warm-Up

First Quarter
Persevere

Second Quarter
Accomplish

Third Quarter
Satisfy

Fourth Quarter
Tendency

Bonus Chapter

Warm-Up

Introduction

When my mother first held that eight-pound-five-ounce baby boy, I wonder if she thought I would become the man she dreamed I would. Through her eyes, have I lived the legacy she envisioned? Often times, I felt like she only saw me as her confused little boy. Maybe I was just her six-foot-seven dream chaser still hanging on to the end of the ropes. I know she is proud of who I became, but were the expectations of her first-born fully met? Does she really know me?

A year ago, if anyone had asked me where I thought I would be in 2014, I would simply reply, "I didn't see myself being here." Am I even supposed to be here?

We all have our own lives to lead. I want to live the rest of my life believing that tomorrow is never an option. One thing I have learned since my first book is that I am responsible for all of my past decisions, which have led me to the point of potential failure or success.

There are so many untold stories buried deep inside me. I have often contemplated spilling these stories to people, even those who look up to me. Will I be viewed differently? Whatever others may think of me, I know myself best, and I know what I expect of my future. Being criticized for my way of life used to be my biggest fear—until I realized the same people God created are destroying the world. By pretending to be the higher power, we are creating Judgment Days on Earth. Instead of pointing fingers, we can learn from each other's actions and implement our knowledge by sharing with the generations to come. We don't have to wait to die to live in paradise. Do we?

My time here is a blessing that no evil can take away from me. My greatest gift to this world will be created in the form of a reproductive cell. All the dripping of my blood, sweat, and tears will be showered upon the seed I will watch grow. I have been given an opportunity to start over, to pass on the knowledge sustained through my mistakes. My legacy will continue with new dreams waiting to come true.

The past trials I endured prepared me for future victories. The winding, gloomy, and secluded roads I travelled took me on a path of self-discovery; I gained from my pain. No one really knew the real me until I decided to find myself in the memories of my yesterdays. The journey didn't go according to what was scripted, but the story will live to tell a new tale. A new dream was born, and I feel more alive than I have ever breathed, the strongest and liveliest I've ever felt. If walking all these miles is what I had to do to make everything right, then I would do it again without taking any shortcuts. The lessons needed to be learned in discovering the man I seek to become. Will I be given a second chance to do it correctly? Or, will I run out of time?

Before I move forward in my pursuit of being born again, I had to turn my back on the events I wasn't able to change—I had to let go of the past.

The Only Father I Knew

I was not alone, I mean, it has been set in stone,
But now I'm a strong believer,
It took my life to flash before my eyes to see a clearer picture.
I was young and stupid,
Drunk-driving home after five straight hours,
Of pouring vodka down my throat.
Swerving into lanes of oncoming traffic,
I swear to ya'll, He cruise-controlled my Honda Civic,
It was like magic how I escaped death as if I were psychic.
Still, today, I count all my blessings.
If a car crash had taken place,
I would not have made it.
A blessing in disguise, and, to make up for the lost time,
Now I pray three times a day,
Always giving thanks for all His patience.
For the Lord is my Shepherd, my provider, my protector,
Who has always been there for me.
And even though we never met eye to eye,
I felt His love on the first day,
My mother's smile stopped all my cries.
I was lost, but now I'm found at the end of the road,
I was blind, but now I see the cross where Jesus died for me.
When you single mothers have to deal with deadbeat fathers,
Just get on your knees and pray to the heavenly Father.
He is the one true man to never leave your side,
I learned that through my mother's toughest times.
She could have easily rejected her children.
But through her faith and relationship with Him,
She remained strong and self-driven.
I call her my living-proof Christian.
Surely, goodness and mercy shall follow me,
All the days of my life.
Psalm 23, verse 6, I live by faith, not by sight.
So, whenever I get the opportunity to be in the spotlight,
I thank the Almighty above for blessing me everyday with life.
But that's just life, I'm gonna follow Him,
Until my body resurrects,
In the everlasting life.
I shall not be led into temptations, so I carry the cross,

Arnold Henry

Around my neck to my death like Jesus Christ.
My faith, I exercise.
So many religions; so many lies.
They call him by so many different names,
But there is only one Matthew Chapter 6, verse 9,
And yet still …
Family has always been important to me.
I say this because I never knew my father's family.
I barely know my grandmother, and, before I was born,
I had already lost my grandfather.
It took me 16 years to finally meet my oldest brother,
Who introduced me to three other older brothers.
And through my words reaching on a different island,
Now I know I have an older sister.
You can replace your friends, but family stays forever,
Uncles, aunts, cousins, I wish I knew them better.
You can choose any religion, but Jesus is still saviour,
And at the end of days—get it?—Judgment Day,
We are all brothers and sisters,
But why am I complaining?
No disrespect to the British people,
But my mother is my royal queen.
She lifted me higher through every single thing.
And when she wasn't strong enough,
She got on her knees, prayed, and lit a candle for me.
I'm so blessed, I'm about to sneeze, and, for these reasons,
I'm still hanging on to my dreams,
'Cause who Jah blessed no man curse,
But, more importantly, I live to practice what I preach,
From the readings in the Bible's verse.
But don't get it twisted 'cause I'm not perfect,
I know God is coming, so I'll wait 'cause I know he is worth it.
All I'm trying to say is, through all my triumphs and tribulations,
I was not alone, so I thank God for the friends and family who've,
Been there for me since the age of birth.

$$1 + 1 = 3$$

First Quarter

Persevere

Chapter 1

The End of the Beginning of My Dreams

Again, I knew then that it was over—after making it so far—from a Caribbean island, to a continent of opportunities, to freezing my butt off in the wintry country of Canada.

I was a boy trapped in a man's body, where losing myself was easier than defining the man I am destined to be. I was living through the same impassable struggles of my past. The path's direction is different now, but the bumpy routes to my dreams haven't changed. *Will things ever get better?*

I ended up on a road with a dead end—my dead end on Sept. 9 2011, at 9 p.m.

My eyes were focused in the rays of the headlights of the silver Honda Civic I was driving. There was one thing that constantly banged on the back door of my mind—*swimming with the fishes ... fuck my life ... I'm going swimming with the fishes. If fish could speak, what would they say to my lifeless body floating, streaming down the Bow River?* Perhaps, they would say, "Stupid human ... so young ... what a waste of life."

At that point, I was certain destiny was calling me; I heard it say to me, "Are you ready to take these last few breaths with me? Arnold, I promise, this is where all your troubles end." My hands trembled as I swerved onto a muddy trail that led me underneath a bridge, where I stopped the car. Destiny whispered in my ears, "Arnold, you're almost there." I was persuaded by the gentleness of the voices in the air and comforted, as if someone's soft hands were embracing mine.

I had no idea how I ended up near that bridge. I tried to search my memory and recap my last destination, but the only entities that I uncovered were fate's directions. It must have been fate, because I barely knew the city of Calgary.

I turned off the engine and switched off the headlights. I inhaled and then exhaled. When I felt brave enough to leave the car, chills crawled up my spine as I noticed the moon reflecting off the river. I walked alongside the shadows of the demons surrounding me. The sounds of the wicked, chilly winds tried to pull me into the moving water.

How do I say goodbye to everyone who has supported me throughout my 26 years of life?

My thoughts were taken into consideration as I pulled out my BlackBerry and logged onto my Facebook account. My eyes browsed the screen of my cellphone, simultaneously paying attention to the passersby and joggers in my peripheral vision. They must have found it strange to see a car parked near the riverbank with a tall, black man wearing casual clothing and flip-flops. *What should I write for a status update*, I asked myself. *Swimming with the fishes* had already made its way through my mind's door.

Scrolling through my author fan page on Facebook, I noticed two of my updates that I wrote on Sept. 7. The first one, which I posted at 2:09 p.m., read: "This is my second autobiography and the lowest point I've ever reached is being written as I currently breathe! Thanks for the ones helping me go through with this tough time! I will survive!"

The other update, posted seven hours later, said: "I will not be on Facebook for a very long time. I'm going through some struggles. I'm seeking motivational and inspirational quotes from you to help me go through these tough times! I'll be reading them on a weekly basis! Thanks for all your support."

Although people didn't have the slightest clue about what I was going through, their comments made me believe they actually cared for me. *Do I have a purpose for which to live?* I braced myself against the car and read some more comments. My eyes were so teary it was as if I was already submerged in deep waters. One particular comment made me cry a river. It began: "Footprints in the sand ..." It is an old poem that portrays an example of the love of our Lord, and His grace and mercy for never leaving our sides during our most difficult times. He has always—and will always—walk with us. The missing footprints in the sand illustrate that God carried us when we didn't have the strength to walk on our own. He never gives up on us.

If God were an earthling, I would have dialled his cellphone number so that he could reassure me that this nightmare would soon come to an end. Or, I could have simply got on my knees and prayed. But I knew for a fact, there was one person's voice I needed to hear say certain reassuring words. It was like reliving my book, *Hanging On To My Dreams*, all over again—like my past was haunting me.

Why do I still have thoughts about contacting her? I asked myself, thinking, *I will never learn.* I took one more look at the most recent photos that she uploaded on her Facebook page—it was the only publicly posted activity on her wall. *She was out to ruin my reputation with these images of physical abuse,* I thought.

I don't give a damn about the court's orders, I said to myself as I dialled the area code, 403, with a shaky thumb. *What? She picked up?*

"Hello?" she said with a curious tone.

I choked for words while triple-checking to ensure that I hadn't blocked my cellphone number. *She picked up, and my number was not blocked.*

REBIRTH

After releasing a deep breath, I spit out words at a hundred miles per hour while I walked in circles on the riverbank. "I cah do dis anymore … I cah live in dis life," I cried out. The sounds of my gasps intensified as I struggled for oxygen. "I want to end it all … right now!"

"Where are you?" she asked cautiously. I was trying to figure out if it was a good idea to divulge my location, while drying my tears, when the sound of police sirens pulled my attention to the other side of the river. I felt my heart had burst out of my chest, as if someone had connected a punch to my back. Paranoid, I asked with a harsh tone, "Did you call the cops on me again?" While waiting for her to reply, I stood at attention and thought to myself, *maybe it is about time I end this nightmare.*

Or, maybe, I should start where I left off at the end of my last book.

"We're going to Nationals! We're going to Nationals!" my teammates, coaches and I screamed, hopping around in a huddle, dancing behind the closed doors of the locker room.

"Yeah!" I shrieked one last time, as if I was releasing five long years of struggles in America. As I sat down to gather my thoughts and unlace my sneakers, I was still in disbelief that we'd pulled off back-to-back tournament wins during epic battles against two nationally ranked teams in our conference. *I love my team … they are, indeed, my brothers.*

"The season is not over," Coach Mosley reminded us, bringing each one of us safely back to reality. I nodded in agreement, and so did all the heads across the room. Coach continued, "Let's have a productive spring break, make sure you go to the gym, stay out of trouble, and return to school, ready to fly to Missouri for the National Tournament."

Since I was already in the south of Florida, I decided to visit my aunt in Fort Lauderdale for our spring break. My time spent with family wasn't as fun as expected since everyone was at work, and I mostly spent my days inside watching the March Madness college basketball tournament. I headed back to the Edward Waters College (EWC) campus one week later. I'd taken that time off to stretch my legs on a couch and to think of our team's upcoming challenges at the National Association of Intercollegiate Athletics (NAIA) Men's National Basketball Championships. After all, before our 2007-08 season had begun, Coach Mosley preached to us, "… and we want to go the Nationals and win it all." While I reflected on our head coach's words, I knew that we had every right to compete for that title. As a team, we had overcome all the obstacles set before us—from starting the season with a full 13-player roster, to downsizing to eight players, to conflicts with coaches, to a murder allegation. Accomplishing our No. 1 goal—winning the national championship title—would be the perfect ending to a dramatic basketball season and my college career.

A week later, as a team, we were aboard our first flight. We were on our way to the NAIA 17th Annual Division II Men's Basketball National Championships. We stayed at a hotel in the city of Branson, Missouri. The tournament was held at the College of the Ozarks' Keeter Gymnasium, located in the neighbouring town of Point Lookout. Our arrival to the city was welcoming, especially when we saw a road sign that read, "Go! Edward Waters College Tigers!"

A chubby male host full of cheerful high spirits, whose primary aim was to ensure that we felt at home, greeted us. Branson was a small community, but driving the main road full of flashy venues and billboards, it was evident that the place could be very entertaining. It was almost like a miniature Manhattan, Las Vegas, and Dallas all in one, although it looked more western than anything. This observation proved correct when all 32 national basketball teams were gathered for a ceremonial dinner and show at Dixie Stampede, a dinner theatre owned by Dolly Parton. I sat inside the arena with my teammates and coaches, and I feasted on a whole rotisserie chicken, hickory smoked barbecue ribs, vegetable soup, corn on the cob, and baked potatoes, while sipping on lemonade out of a cowboy boot-shaped cup. For entertainment, we all watched the modern-day Wild Wild West show that featured Indians and cowboys, horse riding competitions, pig races, and other activities, which gave us a glimpse of the western American life of years ago. It was quite an opening act. I was certain that, years later, all the basketball players and coaches in attendance would still be keen to reminisce about that warm welcome.

The following day, March 12, 2008, was just as memorable because we were facing our first opponent of the tournament—the seventh-seeded Eastern Oregon University Mountaineers.

The game tipped off at 5:45 p.m. with no sign of our home fans or cheerleaders in the bleachers, which was expected coming from a poor and smaller school that only had the funds to fly out the team and coaches. Most of our opponents were in the same position. The crowd was mostly made up of basketball fans from the surrounding areas of Taney County, and, possibly, coaches and players who came out to scout teams. It was our first time facing any team from the west side of America. The only basic thing we knew about Eastern Oregon was that they were a bunch of white boys.

I won the jump ball, and we went on to score the first seven points of the game. Initially, we felt like it was going to be an easy win. However, one time out would change the course of the game, and, in turn, make us smell defeat. By halftime, the Mountaineers were leading the game, 38-16.

REBIRTH

The locker room was speechless with towel-covered heads and all eyes staring at the floor.

The second half of any game is always an opportunity for the losing team to redeem itself, but we were looking like we didn't belong. Two of our starters, Jean Metelus and Johnny Nelson, fouled out of the game, and our starting shooting guard was also in foul trouble. We shot 38 per cent from the field, while they shot 60 per cent. To sum it all up, we were humiliated, annihilated, and demolished—93-62.

I tried my best to carry the team to victory with a contribution of 13 points and 12 rebounds, but the game of basketball will forever remain a *team* sport. Four of the Mountaineers scored in double figures, for a total of 64 points, which was a better performance than our overall final score. I will have to live the rest of my life knowing that my final college basketball game was a 31-point deficit defeat.

What was next for me? Could this possibly be the end, or the beginning, of a new chapter in my life? Was it time to let go of my hoop dreams? Before deciding what to do with my life, I posted a Facebook status, "Should I pursue a professional basketball career right now or should I graduate first then fulfil my dreams?" I wanted the opinions of my friends and family.

The majority of my Facebook friends' replies suggested that I think about life after a possible injury in the early stages of a professional basketball career. They asked: "What would you fall back on?" One person wrote, "Once you graduate with a degree that is an accomplishment that can never be taken away from you. Basketball is not promised tomorrow." My friends' comments were taken into serious consideration. My dreams were now put on the back burner as I cooked up the recipe to educational success.

All I ever wanted was for my dreams to feel so alive that I would never have to dream again. Was that too much to ask? It was a life lesson to know that a dream is only a dream if you haven't been awakened by its reality.

Chapter 2

My Immediate Family

"Standing at six-foot-10, from Castries, Saint Lucia, Aloysius Henry," roared the announcer. Hearing these words called out from an announcer gave me goosebumps. My younger brother, better known as Marvin, didn't show an interest in basketball when we were younger. Back then, he was the marathon runner. Now, I literally had to look up to him. To me, he was my big little brother, and, in some ways, it felt as if he was the oldest of our mother's children and my dream was to grow up to be just like him. I was envious of the three inches he had on me. Whenever I got the chance to stand next to him, I had the feeling that I was a seed buried in shaded dirt next to a coconut tree. The ball was now bouncing on his side of the court. For him, it was the real start of his journey.

In the spring semester of 2008, I was wrapping up my college basketball career, while my brother was living up to his potential and proving that he could excel in sports as he entered his freshman year in college. A few months earlier, he had successfully completed a preparatory school year at Maine Central Institute, where he accepted a full basketball scholarship from the Three Rivers Community College in Poplar Bluff, Missouri. In my opinion, my brother could not have been in a better situation; he was about to be coached by the legendary Gene Bess, who was the first college basketball coach to win 1,000 games. In the year that my brother got signed to Three Rivers, Coach Bess was also known as the all-time winning junior college coach. My brother's new head coach was reputably the best.

In my biased opinion, Marvin was good enough for a National Collegiate Athletic Association (NCAA) Division I school, but, unfortunately, he didn't qualify academically for college admittance. His next two years of junior college were an opportunity for him to get prepared for an advanced level of education and basketball. This was a reminder of the importance of making education a priority—it eliminates categorizing an individual into less fortunate situations, and obtaining sports scholarships were no exception. As the experienced, older brother, I saw it as my duty to guide him along a positive path. I couldn't say the same for my youngest sibling, Marva, my 16-year-old sister who was looking like a full-grown lady. She had stretched in height, had relaxed, long black hair that extended down her shoulders, and had a busty and curvy physique. She resembled a lighter-skinned version of what I imagine our mother looked like at an early age.

Marva was still living in our same green wooden house in Saint Lucia, while finishing her final years at secondary school. But here's the heartbreaker—she was living alone in the house, with no family to support her or supervise her whereabouts. There was no telling if she was living her life with constructive intentions. Even though I had no part to play in that matter, I still felt accountable for leaving her behind, knowing that both of her big brothers were balling in America.

How could my mother be so senseless? How could any mother be so foolish? To cast aside the responsibilities of your teenage child was just as bad as abandoning him or her at birth. *Didn't my mother realize that Marva still needed a mother figure in her life, especially during her peer-pressured teenage years?* I knew for a fact that, at 16, if I were living alone in a house in the rough environment where I grew up, I would have made many harmful choices. I probably would have skipped school, consumed plenty of alcohol and/or drugs, and maybe even ended up in prison or dead. Seeing my mother's hard work and struggles had been an inspiration for me to excel in life. Her guidance, too, was a direction that only led to success. I believe that my baby sister needed that same inspiration, guidance, and continuous bonding more so than the boys. I felt like she wasn't working toward a dream like her brothers.

In our small family circle, I was noticeably more of the momma's boy; Marva was really attached to her father, Lucius; and, Marvin was sort of in-between, as commonly expected of the middle child. When it came to defining my immediate relations closest to my heart, they were the ones considered to be my Day 1 family, minus Lucius, of course. The grudges I held against him were too powerful to overcome at the time.

Being away from Saint Lucia, I was out of the loop when it came to family drama, and I didn't have a clear understanding of how Marvin and Marva took my mother and Lucius's separation; neither did I bother to care nor to ask—too sensitive a topic for that. My basic understanding was that Lucius had moved out and now lived in a house near the shore where he kept his fishing boat. I still don't know what day and year the two of them parted ways. I believe the separation had to do with infidelity. For me, it just felt like it was way overdue. I had hoped the separation would come the day after their wedding, but that was wishful thinking on my part. Maybe for Marvin and Marva the separation was difficult, but who knows? My immediate family never spoke from the heart.

I still remember the disturbing phone conversation I had with my mother while I was in America.

"Mario, I really do not know what to do," my mother wept to me over the phone. She still calls me Mario and speaks to me in proper English, like she spoke to the tourists at the hotel where she used to work.

"Wha' you mean?" I asked.

"I got offered a job, but I really do not want to leave Marva alone in the house, by herself."

"Wha' kind of work? Where you goin'?" I asked, realizing that she was holding back on some of her concerns.

"I met a man who wants to fly me to Antigua to take care of his children. You know, like a babysitter." In the back of my mind, I'm thinking, *but what about Marva, the child you conceived?* On the other hand, it was almost impossible for my mother to find a well-paying job in Saint Lucia while recovering from a leg injury. Rather than sharing my real thoughts with her, I just listened.

"Well, I eh too sure wha' to say, Mummy. Jus' now I go have to com' dong cause my student visa go expire in May."

"How long you will be coming home for?" she asked.

"I eh know. I go com dong after dis spring semester."

"But Mario, you finish your degree?"

"Awa, I tink I have one year left. Buh, eh mind dat. I go com dong and fly to Barbados to renew my visa."

"So what about your basketball?"

"Well I tink it's best if I finish my degree. I only have one year left."

"I hope you get that visa, eh."

"Mummy, doh worry. I go make sure I have all de documents before I leave de States."

That was one of the last phone conversations I had with my mother before she decided to pursue the job in Antigua. No attention was paid to everyone's not-so-sure-if-that-is-a-good-idea feelings about moving. It almost seemed like my mother was bitter toward Marva and wanted to run away—as if my mother wasn't strong enough to handle a teenage daughter going through puberty. But I highly doubt that was the case. My mother would never leave her children behind for her own pleasures. I understood the Antiguan man was once a guest at one of the hotels where my mother worked. I still find it hard to believe that a babysitting job would pay the bills, unless the father was some kind of highly recognized man in his country. However, my family believes certain things are better left unsaid. And we never bothered to ask—

14

which is why so many mysteries in my family remain unsolved. For instance, *who should be blamed for the complications of my family? Did my father, Tobias, ever love my mother? Was he a player? Was I fortunate to be brought up from a one-night stand? Did he lie to my mother about his wife and four sons? Or, did my mother carelessly proceed with having sexual relations with a married man?* Even as an adult, every time I've picked up the phone to search for answers, family bonding seemed pointless. I want to know more about my father's family. *Who am I? Where do I find my roots?*

At times, I've felt like randomly calling Maury Povich, saying, "Sir, I have an issue. Can you please help me determine if Tobias is a *father* or not?" I secretly hoped to be on international television, seated next to Tobias, as Maury says, "The results are in ... when it comes to the life of Arnold Henry, Tobias, you are not a father to him." It wouldn't be a personal attack. I just wanted him to know that he has been a horrible father to me, or for him to be aware that he has a son out there who would appreciate a father figure in his life. A father's love was what I was lacking. All I wanted was a male role model to say to me, "That was a great game you played today," or, on bad game days, "Let's go to the court to work on some moves." These father-son-lonesome feelings were buried deep inside me. At least I still had a close relationship with his eldest child, Kervyn, who was now married and, at that time, a father of a handsome, healthy boy. I had to include Kervyn in my circle because he was my family more than Tobias ever was.

My mother, Marvin, Marva, and Kervyn? Really, that's it? While living in America, realizing the closeness of my teammates and their families, at times it made me feel like an intruder to my own kind. I believe that I am a loner, roaming the world, trying to dig up my roots, only to find out they don't exist. In my mind this is true because I was the only child conceived by my mother and biological father. Possibly, it is time to let go of my past and recreate a whole new world, or maybe my own family. But how can I when questions remain unspoken and unanswered?

I supposed that it was time to be brave and do some inquiring.

Chapter 3

Appreciating My Position

"Boi, Marva have mun in da house now ih," Marvin told me during a phone conversation. For some reason, my heart raced as if I was in danger.

"Wha'you mean she have mun?"

"De girl checking a 22-year old patna from up North. Somebody tell me de mun is an ole, papicho fella."

"Oh for real? You mean he eh good for her?"

"Yeah gason. I hear de mun does sleep over home and all."

A man six years older and she is still in secondary school, the voice in my head kept on repeating the fact. I was now indecisive about staying at my Saint Lucian home during my summer vacation. I kept on wondering what my first reaction would be if Marva introduced me to her *"boyfriend," a.k.a. child molester, a.k.a. cradle robber.* There was only one way to find out.

At first, I felt like purchasing a direct return flight from Florida to Barbados, so that I would avoid picturing my baby sister with a vagabond—that's Saint Lucian for someone who has no life. I really did not have many options; plus, I had insufficient funds for a return flight and the fees for renewing my student visa.

The school year had come to an end. If I had been part of the graduating class of 2008, like my roommate, Travis, then I would have pursued a professional basketball career instead of having to renew my student visa for another year. I needed to complete my bachelor's degree in computer information systems. I had attended five schools in five years, and I felt like I had been through enough schooling for a doctorate. Some of my college credit hours were unacceptable at Edward Waters College because they were non-transferable.

I bought a one-way plane ticket with the money I'd saved up from my on-campus tutoring job. I hadn't been back to Saint Lucia since January, 2006. There was no storage on EWC's campus, so I had to pack all my belongings and take them with me when I travelled: three suitcases, a backpack, and a carry-on. I had just enough space for my laptop, webcam, digital camera, 10 baseball caps that colour-coordinated with my 10 pairs of basketball sneakers, all my casual clothing, including NBA jerseys, practice gear, and brand-name jeans and T-shirts, as well as all the other items I had acquired throughout the past five years of living in America.

REBIRTH

On the afternoon of May 4, 2008, I was aboard a plane next to a window seat adoring the natural beauty of Saint Lucia. I was so excited that it felt like it was my first time on an island. It was easy to spot our lush tropical rainforest, the World Heritage Site—the Pitons—as steam rose from the Sulphur Springs and waves crashed against the coastline.

It was a hot, sunny, beautiful day on my paradise island. Upon exiting the aircraft, the heat from the sun made me feel unfamiliar with my territory, as did the security from the Hewanorra International Airport. The security officers made me feel out of place and too Americanized. "How long do you plan on staying in Saint Lucia?" I looked at the woman who held onto my passport, wondering, *Ki koté fanm sa sòti?* Maybe if my Kwéyòl thoughts were outspoken, then she would have felt like a real dèkdèk. *Am I being judged by the way I am dressed?* Was it because I had my do-rag and Yankee baseball cap covering my braids?

I simply replied, "I am a born and raised Saint Lucian. You're holding my passport. I will stay for however long I want." She rolled her eyes over the pages of my passport and scrutinized it as if it were counterfeit. I felt as if she didn't believe me because of the way I spoke. Was I already sounding too American?

"Why you have so many items in your bag?" she asked.

Really? "I am a student in the United States," I replied. "I am home for the summer."

"Open your bags," she demanded.

I sucked my teeth. "Bétiz," I muttered. For a moment, I felt like I was targeted to undergo maximum-security measures. I remember the days when visiting home felt like I was visiting home. Nowadays, violence had risen and was just as bad as the rest of world. After my bags went through inspection, I was allowed to enter my native country without further issues. By then, I was sweating balls. But it was good to walk on my hometown's soil again.

"Check da mun," Dudley mentioned upon his first glance at me.

"Hey guys, how's it going?"

An outburst of laughter by Dudley and his girlfriend made me feel like I could be a comedian without reciting any jokes. "Gason, eh mind dat, I still have it," I corrected myself, quickly conversing with a Lucian dialect.

Even though I hadn't seen Dudley, one of my best friends, for a long time, it felt like I had never left. He hadn't changed much; he was the same ol' tall, lean, smiley-faced Dudley. He made me feel welcomed back, as if I had been away at war. In Saint Lucia, when you obtain your driver's licence, we say, *he or she legal on de road.* Dudley was now legal on the road and I appreciated the ride, otherwise, a taxi would have been costly. His girlfriend sat in the front passenger seat while I sat in the back. She was same girl he had when I first left Saint Lucia in 2003. I think they were in love.

"Mama, Saint Lucia really change eh," I kept on repeating as the fresh, moist winds hit my face through the open car window.

"Dem days nuff crime happening. All mun have guns now," Dudley said with exaggeration.

"As long as dey eh look for trouble wif me, den I safe." Seeking trouble was the last thing on my mind. I was looking forward to a relaxing summer vacation and living like a tourist, with a vacation filled with seawater baths, beautiful scenery, eating local dishes and fresh fruit, visiting great friends, and attending the Jazz Festival and events from the Carnival season. I intended to recapture the memorable moments I had missed due to my college basketball career.

"Oh yeah," Dudley said, distracting my tourist-life thoughts. "Boi, if you see Tenny now, you go say you eh know mate."

"Uh huh? Wha' happen to mate?" I asked, bringing my ears and attentiveness closer to the front of the car.

"Gason, da mun turn jumbie."

"Serious ting? You mean de mun living and begging on de streets?"

"Yeah gah. I hear is woman dat make de mun go crazy like dat."

"Dats sad," I whispered and thought, *no one is guaranteed a successful life.*

Tenny was a basketball teammate at Entrepot Secondary School. We had graduated together. He wasn't as close a friend as Dudley, but he was associated with another circle of friends who were all involved in our school's basketball team. I often wonder how Tenny's friends could have allowed him to get to that low point. *Was no one there for him?* Then, I reflected on my life, thanking God for Himself, great Saint Lucian friends like Dudley, Kendell, Java, Bobdole, and Ali—who had an encouraging presence during my teenage years.

"Look him over deh!" Dudley shouted as we drove on the busy streets of the city of Castries, near the market area.

"Who, Tenny?" I asked, "Where you see da mun?" My heart felt like it was being pulled to the ground and stepped on—my heart felt crushed. Every day, I see homeless people and drug addicts with rugged clothing, walking through life with bare feet, living off the generosity of strangers, but it was uncomfortably illuminating to see someone I know personally in that position. *We could have been walking his dusty paths,* I thought to myself as I remembered the quote,

REBIRTH

"Before you criticize someone, you should walk a mile in their shoes." I was in no position to judge my former teammate—nothing in the future was promised—a simple mistake played by my part can lead me down Tenny's miserable path. At least he knew how to survive on the streets, which I found impressive. A struggling college basketball career stood no comparison to life with rock-hard, blistering feet, unpredictable skies as your shelter, and having to boldly stretch out your arms, living like a parasite. At the end of the day, basketball was just a sport.

The acceleration of the car allowed Tenny to fade away; however, images of Tenny will forever be stuck in my memory. I see it as a reminder of what could be if I took my life for granted. Or, maybe, Tenny's situation was misunderstood and he was living the life he wanted. Whatever the case may be, I didn't want to be in his position; I wanted more, especially since I didn't have much to give to a starving person. At that point in my life, all I had to offer was hope.

Marchand, the area where I was brought up, seemed to be deteriorating. Infrastructure looked mouldy, houses seemed out-dated, and most of the youths were posted up on their blocks as if standing watch for other rival gang members. It looked like we were driving through a warzone. I shook my head at the increasing number of nappy-headed boys sitting on the street corners with joints in their mouths. This was the same generation of kids I saw playing in underwear and diapers when they were younger. *Where are these children's parents? This can't be our future generation,* I thought and shook my head.

My life could have been so much worse. I was appreciative for my position thus far.

Chapter 4

Catching Up

"Look at Mario!" a few of my neighbours shouted from the distance as I approached my green wooden home. Dudley followed, assisting with my luggage. It must have been the biggest excitement they'd had in a long time. The same quiet yard with walking path reminded me of the days when we played cricket. *So good to be back in my neighbourhood,* I thought to myself. Being back in Da Yard allowed me to reflect on my youthful days and it almost felt as if my most favourite childhood friends, Jermal and Jovan, were welcoming me back. But Jermal and Jovan still lived in New York City. I was actually being greeted by the toddlers I left behind—now teenagers—who still remembered my face. I waved and smiled to acknowledge them.

Stepping into the house, it no longer felt like home sweet home; my mother's absence was to blame. Inside, my eyes landed on Marva, who was seated on the living room sofa, next to a male stranger who looked to be the same age as me. A strong scent of perspiration crawled up my nose, or was it the stench of sex? Their first reaction to my entrance was to stand at attention, as if I'd just intruded on their private time. *What were they doing?* The television was on, so I assumed they were watching it, or was the TV watching their R-rated show?

"Hey Mario, dat's my boyfriend, Shervy," Marva said with a panicky tone. It seemed like Marva had forgotten about my flight. The innocence on Marva's face caused me to hesitate to meet her lover eye to eye. He was just as tall as me with an uncombed afro. I nodded my head then stretched out a fist to initiate a peaceful gesture. But what I really wanted to do was to connect my fist with his jawbone for being with my baby sister. He returned a pound to my fist and I forcibly masked my hatred toward him with a quick smile. No further words were exchanged. Before I headed to my old room, I cut eyes at Marva, and, before my eyes could gaze at Shervy's unshaven face, it landed on his feet.

The room was so silent that we could hear Dudley's blabbering voice from outside. I believe he intentionally left my luggage at the front doorstep and stood outside, chatting with the new additions to the neighbourhood, Kendell's parents, to avoid the foreseeable tension.

"See you later," I said to Marva after carrying all my bags inside. Then, I stormed out of the house. "Oye, Dudley, let's move." At that moment, I wanted to be somewhere that would relax my aggravated mental state. The house didn't seem to belong to our family anymore; it felt like it was under Marva's possession, and I was just a visitor. I was under the impression that my home was broken beyond repair, and Marva was the only one left.

Dudley drove all the way to the north of the island to Reduit Beach. *Just what I needed*—the sounds and breeze of the Caribbean seas. It just happened to be the day for Jazz on the Beach, the first day of the 17th anniversary of the Saint Lucia Jazz Festival. The festival began May 2nd and ran for nine days. The annual, internationally recognized event is held at several locations around the island. Our yellow sandy beaches are walked on by tourists from around the world, and the instrumental sounds that reverberated through the speakers this particular year weren't only local artists, but were regional and international artists as well—even Wyclef Jean was part of the lineup.

"Look dem fellars over deh," Dudley pointed toward the direction of one of the tents where beverages were being sold.

"I didn' even know you was comin' dawg," Kendell said with a surprised tone, as he snuck up on me backed by his circle of friends. We pounded fists. "Wham to you deh?"

"I safe deh ih," I replied after noticing Dudley dismissed himself to buy some drinks for the group. "Where Java?"

"Oh, look da mun coming deh."

"So, I hear we neighbours now, eh?" I asked as his older brother approached us with a drink in his hand. Java and I bumped fists.

"Yeah mun, since da other day," Kendell responded. Java nodded. By their reactions, the brothers weren't as thrilled as I was to be neighbours. It seemed like they were withholding information. *Hmm.* I was a bit confused. I started to space out, staring at the horizons of the beaches.

My childhood friend and former classmate, Kendell Clarke, had always been an easy friend to talk to; he was like my personal counsellor with whom I had shared most of my problems and vice versa. Back in our teen days, whenever I was on the way to play basketball on The Summit, I always extended an invitation to them. Java and Kendell were like brothers to me. Somehow, our friendship had dismantled during the years I spent overseas. I believed a true friendship should be able to travel through the roughest oceans and come back stronger than the first day it was built. In reality, I've learned a few of my so-called friendships were myths.

The principle behind the Clarkes being one of our newer neighbours was a touchy subject for me. To tell you the truth, I didn't have any issues with Kendell and his family's presence being only two steps from my home. In my mind, I didn't have to travel far to hang out with trustworthy friends. The whole reasoning for my disheartenment toward this matter was the fact that my grandmother had disrespected my mother and our family by selling the piece of land upon which our home was built. As a result, the Clarkes had, in effect, become our landlords. That day was an eye-opener for my siblings and me, as we realized our maternal grandmother was the most selfish being on the planet. She could have easily divided the land and sold the other half, but she wanted more money.

For as long as I could remember, my grandmother had always lived in London, England. During a rare trip to Saint Lucia, she decided to visit our home for business and to discuss the possibility of selling her rental property; literally, our house was her business—the only home that my mother had ever known for more than 55 years. I had sensed some bad news when she treated me like a stranger. The 20 pounds that she usually handed me stayed in her purse. She wore an old-fashioned granny dress, smelled like a foreigner, and had lost her Saint Lucian slangs. The mother and daughter held their *business meeting* at the kitchen table. When grownups sat at a dinner table, we kids understood that we were to be nowhere in sight, but could be close enough to eavesdrop. Their conversation quickly escalated into a heated debate. My grandmother complained to my mother, yelling with a broken English accent, "Why you extended the house? I never said you could do that." (In the late '90s, Lucius had added two rooms, a bathroom and a restroom to our original two-bedroom home with kitchen and living room, and we used a nearby homemade outdoor bathroom and pit toilet to shower and go No. 2).

"I needed more room for my children," my mother calmly explained. I looked at Marvin as he mirrored my expression of disbelief. We were young, but we knew exactly what was happening.

"I had plans with that piece of land," my grandmother added. Her lack of consideration for her own grandchildren made me feel like spitting in her face.

"You can leave now! Get out now!" my mother yelled back at her. Their conversation ended with my mother yelling at the top of her lungs until my grandmother was out of sight. Her defence for her children inspired me to love and appreciate my mother even more.

Later that year, the last strand of respect I had for my grandmother slipped away when I found out she had put the property up for sale. Because our house was built on that piece of property, this meant the purchaser of the land would become our landlord. My grandmother might as well have handed her own daughter and grandchildren the eviction notice. After never having to pay for rent, my struggling mother now had to pay the Clarkes a monthly charge for her own home. However, things could have been worse or unfriendly.

After witnessing my grandmother's actions, I thanked God that my mother never turned out to be the same egotistical bitch.

"Oye, wha'you drinking?" Dudley shouted, bringing my attention back to 2008.

"Anyting gason!" My response was jaw dropping. They had never seen me consume alcohol.

"What? You drinkin' dem days?"

"Yeah mun. Since de day," I replied. Back in our high school days, the boys on our block used to pitch in to buy bottles of liquor, and I would be the only one sipping on their non-alcoholic chasers. These were the years when our friendships were unquestionable. Now, a few years later, it was like I was being introduced to a new circle of friends. I had so much catching up to do.

Chapter 5

All Gone

"Good morning, Marva," I said, attempting to fix breakfast in the early morning, complete with hangover.

"Good morning, Mario," she replied, stirring the hardboiled egg in the pot on the fire.

"One ting, I hope your boyfriend not sleeping here eh," I warned Marva.

"I know, Mario," she said, lying through her teeth. There was sort of a discomfort as I lectured my baby sister; having been away for so long was starting to get to me. Shervy had already left on my return to the house from Jazz on the Beach. I knew he was living there. I could smell it. Our neighbours were my eyewitnesses, and Marva probably thought they weren't the gossiping type. Unbeknownst to her, I had eyes and ears all over Bishop's Gap.

After eating the most important meal of the day, I decided to unpack some of my essential items for easier access. "Look, a bottle of perfume. I bought it for you in America. Hope you like da smell," I said, handing the bottle to Marva on my way to the living room.

"Thanks," she said with a smile. I didn't know what she would like, so I was hoping that the fragrance's fresh crack coconut scent would make her feel refreshed. Our conversation didn't last long. I think I was still holding a grudge from the boyfriend situation. I just couldn't find the emotions and words to illustrate my disappointment. I don't know if it was my big brother overprotective nature, their age difference, or my belief that Shervy wasn't the right guy for my baby sister. Ultimately, it was her decision, so I tried my best to respect her desires.

Although I wasn't in agreement with everything pertaining to Marva, she did portray some levels of responsibilities. At least she wasn't walking around with a big belly. Despite the house having some roof and wood damages from the outside, my baby sister was still keeping the inside clean. The creaky carpeted floors were swept; furniture was dusted; and, there were pots on the fire. I saw lots of my mother's qualities written all over Marva.

The following day fell on a Monday, or rather, a business day. This was a reality check, as I was the only college boy amongst my closest friends. I couldn't call on Dudley or Kendell to go to The Summit to shoot some hoops. They were too busy with their daily jobs:

REBIRTH

Kendell worked at a bank and Dudley worked at a brewery. I looked at the mountaintop from our house's side window and predicted a long, boring summer vacation with limited basketball.

The clock on our house's partition showed nine in the morning, and Shervy was already knocking at the front door. *Doesn't he have a job? Didn't he realize that I just arrived and I might need to spend time with my only family at the house?* I saw nothing but a fool's kind of love in these two. I rolled my eyes at the sight of him and sighed. I needed to stay away as much as possible to keep from vomiting. Hopefully, he was catching on. I then proceeded to get myself fresh and clean to head to town.

Oh boy, I didn't miss these cold showers. We never owned a solar water heater. I remember the best time of day to bathe was on a sunny afternoon because the pipes, which ran outside and then into our house, would soak up the heat from the sun and warm the water. On the flipside, on stormy nights, we would jump in and out of the shower quicker than a cat being thrown in a bucket of water; it was that cold.

It was important for me to dress like a chick magnet whenever I stepped outside. I was a single, carefree young adult who was ready to scratch some wishes off my bucket list. I was poppin' my collars wearing T-shirts. Some might say that I was showboating, and that I went to America and forgot where I came from; but, in the words of a Saint Lucian who could careless, I'd say, *mwen pa mélé*. Small-minded people tend to be the shallow thinkers. My style, I called it balling, walking with an air of overbearing self-confidence, feeling fly and cooler than the lonely side of the bed. Even my underwear had to colour-coordinate with my pants, shirts, sneakers, and caps.

"Marva, I goin' to town," I said as I left the house. I did a slow take as I realized Shervy was wearing yesterday's clothes. Every time I saw this guy, bad vibes of energy filled the room. I really needed fresh air.

Flashbacks played in my mind as I travelled the same paths I used to go to school, to buy bread, to go to church; the road that took me beyond my youthful days. Nothing new came from the street corners, though. The same families greeted me as I walked down the streets. The same small, convenient stores were open for business. I was about to head for the bus stop, when I stumbled upon a group of boys playing card games near the side of the road. The jealous look in the eyes of these nappy-headed boys was obvious as I walked by. They stared at me as if I was a tourist who was creeping on their turf.

"Oye, Mario, you must make me hold dat cap and dat sneaker before you go back foreign," a familiar face from the group shouted.

25

For a moment, I felt like a model walking the runway. They stared me down from head to toe, as if I was a mannequin in a clothing store window display.

"Yeah mun, I go give it to you before I leave," I said in a joking manner as I waved away the smoke from the joint that was blown in my face. Some locals tend to believe that you inherit riches from the soil while living in America. To an unacquainted passerby, these boys may come off as scary. But I wasn't intimated by their presence. In fact, these were the same boys I grew up with. It was such a disillusion to see how they were choosing to live, that they had stooped to the thug life. I often wondered how these young guys were able to afford everyday living expenses. They weren't the type of crowd I like to associate with, so I kept on walking.

Instead of being bored out of my mind between the working hours of nine to five, I visited the work offices of family and friends. Not everyone had known of my arrival on the island. My first priorities were visiting the people I cared for the most, such as my oldest brother, Kervyn. If I ever needed a man to look up to, he would be the first. Still, to this today, he's the one who presented me with the best gift ever: my 16th Christmas was the day he introduced himself to me.

On the day of my visit, our brief conversation ended with me asking him to keep his ears open for any new job postings. I thought it was a great idea since he had a career in information technology. But, honestly, my hopes were quickly drowned when I was told the unemployment rates were steadily rising. Being jobless in my own country gave me a glimpse of the likelihoods after graduation. The depression was everyone's excuse. If Americans thought they had it bad, they just needed to buy a litre of apple juice for nearly 20 Eastern Caribbean dollars, and then they'd realize a store like Walmart is heaven to a struggling Caribbean family.

Things were rough in Saint Lucia. Even the price of a loaf of bread was above 25 cents. My mother used to say that bread was as cheap as 10 cents back in her earlier years. I only hoped that my savings were sufficient to live throughout the weeks on what I was beginning to think of as Not-So-Paradise Island. To the tourism industry, Saint Lucia was still a cheap destination, but the struggles were real for its citizens.

Since Kervyn was too busy to socialize, I was working on building a new relationship with another older brother, Segun Tobias. Before I left the island in 2003, Segun was still studying medicine in Cuba, so we never actually had the opportunity to get acquainted. All his time and hard work spent abroad had paid off. Now, he was a doctor, working at Victoria Hospital, the main hospital in the city. Most people called him Dr. Tobias. Hearing this title tagged to my brother's name made me feel so proud to call him family. On Segun's weekends off, he would pick me up and we'd drive to the north of the island to party for the night. I was grateful of his efforts to make up for the lost time, which gave us a chance to bond as brothers.

A new and exciting month was approaching, and things were looking up. I tried my best to keep my hands out of my wallet, yet I was having a hard time doing so because June 1st was the official opening of Carnival. The Carnival season would last for more than a month, with various competitive shows such as: Calypso, Groovy, and Power Soca events; the Carnival Queen Show; Steel Band Panorama, King and Queen of the Bands; and, J'Ouvert. Carnival concludes on the third Monday and Tuesday of July with two days of Masquerade or Parade of the Bands—formerly dedicated to February, my birth month. My mother used to say that I was known as a bacchanal baby. If you wanted to enjoy the true spirits of Saint Lucia's tradition, you had to join the crowd. In other words, you couldn't just watch from the sidelines. My intentions were to live for the moment. All these upcoming events would keep me away from the awkwardness at home.

On my way out of the house one morning, Marva and I got into an argument. I can't even remember what caused it, but what I do recall being so frustrated that I ended our confrontation by shouting, "I doh want Shervy coming over here anymore!" My baby sister thought she was a big woman who took no orders from anyone. Never had I seen Marva so irritated. To avoid seeing any further reaction from her, I jetted out of the house. I ended up in the north of the island, where I met up with two women I'd met over the weekend while partying with Segun. Their companionship was just what I needed to relax— engaging conversations, some drinks, and a long walk on the beach. But as nightfall approached and I was heading home, my cellphone rang, displaying an Antigua area code.

"Mario, what happened to you and Marva? Why you telling her that you don't want Shervy coming home?"

I sighed. "Mummy, don't worry with Marva. We got into an argument. It was nothing serious."

"I don't want any trouble please, Mario. Marva have been seeing the boy before you came down. I met him and he is a good fella. He even helps Marva when she wants something," my mother said with a warning tone.

"OK … OK," I said, flagging down a bus before boarding.

"If you don't see Marva at home, it is because she will be sleeping at Shervy mother's house tonight. She called to ask me."

"OK, Mummy, I goin' home now. Talk to you later."

Aboard the public bus, I recited an apology in my mind, *Marva, sorry about earlier. I didn't mean what I said.* Immediately, that thought was erased from my mind when I realized that I have the right to be upset. She was still in secondary school; no man should be coming over to see her. *How can Mummy approve of Marva going to Shervy's mother's house for the night? What about Lucius? Does he even know about his youngest daughter's whereabouts?* Rumour had it that Lucius was on lockdown with a stripper from Colombia. He must have forgotten about his responsibilities as a parent because it seemed like he was more interested in saving the whore. *Yuck!* A coincidence, maybe, remembering that he was once lost at sea, and found by Colombians. It was such a tragedy when he was brought back to Saint Lucia. I wonder if he beats the living crap out of his new-found love like he did my mother.

When I paid the bus driver, my watch was showing 10 p.m. I walked up the Bishop's Gap road and when I passed by Marchand Church, I noticed that the nappy-headed boys still standing on the corner, as if they were on neighbourhood watch. "Mario, nice kicks … dats da new Jordan 23s?"

I turned around for a quick second without coming to a halt. "Yeah mun," I replied, backpedalling briefly. That quick glance at their silhouetted group made me realize they were all staring at my sneakers. I sped up until I was out of sight.

Oh wow, Marva, really isn't home? I asked myself, seeing the darkness in my home from the distance. Before I keyed my way through the front door, I realized the window was open. Strange. Marva was probably asleep.

"Marva," I shouted, hoping she'd answer. "Marva?" The only response was the creaking of the floors as I planted my feet. "Marva!" *Why would she leave the window open if she isn't home?* I switched on the florescent light in the living room. My first glance landed on the computer desk, which, all of a sudden, seemed naked. I gasped for air; the atmosphere felt contaminated, and it was becoming hard to breathe. "No, no, no!" I shouted.

I reached for my cellphone. I was sure the operator on the receiving end of the call suffered ear damage when I yelled, "Someone robbed me!"

Chapter 6

They Took Everything!

"Calm down, sir!" the female officer said in response to my outburst.

"Wha' you mean calm down," I responded, still pacing back and forth in the house. "I need da police assistance right now!"

"I need you to relax. What happened?"

"They took everything! Someone robbed me."

"I'm afraid we cannot come out tonight. We do not have any officers at the station."

"Are you kiddin' me? I live Bishop's Gap. Two-minute walk from da Marchand station," I shouted. "Someone stole all my stuff. They took everything."

"I understand but we cannot do anything until tomorrow morning." I hung up my cellphone, just as I was on the verge of smashing it to the floor. The rooms in the house rotated around my confused mind. *Who could have robbed us? Nappy-headed boys?* No one has ever dared try to rob my mother's house. Obviously, I was the main attraction to the thieves' eyes. *But how did they enter?* Since the useless, Marchand police officers decided to take a mini-vacation, I felt it was my duty to get into a *CSI* state of mind.

I scrutinized all possible areas of entry; there were no signs of force. The front window was left open but its screen was still perfectly in place, which made it doubtful that was the thieves' entrance. And above all, my neighbours could have easily spotted someone trying to break and enter there. Tiptoeing through the living room, past the kitchen to the entry to my bedroom, I noticed the back doors were wide open. The darkness coming from the backyard made it difficult to trail any evidence. I latched the door, careless about the perpetrator's fingerprints. Only my belongings had been stolen. I noticed that my passport was still on my dresser, wiped the sweat on my forehead, and whispered, "Thank God." I stumbled to the ground with an overwhelming feeling of exhaustion, as if I had just completed a marathon. *My laptop, my laptop,* I whined, *all my files, pictures, documents from school ... they're all gone.* Everything was gone, except the items belonging to my mother and my sister. I felt targeted. The trust I had for anyone in my community had now vanished.

Still lying on the floor, I dialled the one person who I trusted the most. "Oye, Dudley—" I took some time to gather my thoughts, "... someone robbed me."

"Uh huh? Where?"

"I just reach home and they took every ting. All my sneakers, clothes, my laptop, webcam, camera … every ting."

"Doh worry yourself. I go check you tomorrow before I go to work," Dudley said calmly, as if he figured he'd be able to retrieve the stolen items.

Midnight. The wall clock was the only thing I could see. Sleep was slowly creeping on me. Before I had a chance to enter into dreamland, I was startled by a loud knock on the front door. "Oye, Arnold!" The clock's hands now showed seven in the morning. I was surprised to have slept the night away so easily.

"Yeah," I shouted, on my morning breath, slowly coming to my feet. I opened the door to an energetic Dudley.

"So dem men robbed you, eh?" Dudley asked, as if he had a lead to solving the crime. He was all dressed up in his work clothes.

"Dem men? Who you tink rob me?" I asked curiously.

"Probably dem men by de road. Boi, dem days every house in your area getting rob. You didn't know?" Dudley's comment triggered a hint; there was no hesitation as I headed to the closest front door of a nappy-headed boy, Miguel, who was actually the youngest son of my godmother. Dudley followed suit, ready to engage in physical combat.

"Oye, did you see anyone breakin' an enter at my home?" I asked as if I expected him to snitch.

"Nah, I eh see dat uh. But wha' dey teef?"

As I answered his question, I was staring him down, hoping he would offer me some details about the theft. "My sneakers, clothes, laptop, camera … every ting I com' dong with." He looked to the ground.

"Serious ting? Well, if I hear anyting, I go check you."

I wasn't buying it. The guilt expressed on his face boosted my suspicions.

"OK, thanks," I said, retreating to another house.

Dudley gave him an evil stare. Even though it wasn't Dudley's fight, he looked like he was ready to kill for me. On the way to the roadside, we sought assistance from all our neighbours. Nothing. And more nappy-headed boys were questioned; still nothing.

Dudley and I returned to my house and continued to investigate for clues. A knock on the front door brought our attention to the living room. It was Kendell. "Oye, my mother just show me you got rob deh," he said. His No. 1-suspect-facial-expression looked more promising than Dudley's.

"You know someting?" I asked.

30

REBIRTH

"Gason, I tink is your sister that rob you ih."

"Nah mun. I eh tink so. My sister, Marva? My sister will never rob me, gason. Dat eh true."

"Well, yesterday, as I was walking home from work, I saw her and her boyfriend walking down Arundel Hill. When she check is me dat deh, she jumped, looked away and started walking faster. They were both holding bags looking like yours."

"No, Kendell," I said, shaking my head. "What? Serious ting." That's when it hit me, and I started to recall events from the previous day. Dudley and Kendell continued talking, but I couldn't hear them.

My own sister robbed me? Did she rob me because of what I said? Was it a coincidence that Marva chose to sleep at Shervy's home the night I got robbed?

I figured they had everything planned out. From our verbal dispute, to the front window being left open, to there being no signs of forced entry, to Marva using our mother as an alibi. It was an inside job. It all started to make sense.

"Good morning, Marva. Where did you put my stuff? Kendell saw you," I accused her over the phone.

Without hesitation she replied, "What stuff?"

Kendell grabbed my cellphone and asked, "Marva, I didn't see you yesterday with bags in your hands?" Dudley and I could hear Marva raising her voice at Kendell.

"Kendell, you see me with Mario tings?" Marva shouted.

He rolled his eyes.

"So, Marva, you calling me a liar?" Kendell asked.

"Eh take me for your shate eh, Kendell," she shouted back. Disgusted by Marva's lies, Kendell handed the cellphone back to me.

"Marva, I want all my stuff back," I said, calmly. "Where did you put it?"

"Mario, I don't have your things." She hung up.

I tried calling her back, hoping it was a dropped call, but she didn't pick up. I gave up after my third try, and I started to believe Kendell's accusation.

"I have to go get ready for work," Kendell said as he left the living room.

"Let's go by Shervy's home," Dudley said aggressively.

"You know where he living?" I asked.

"Yeah."

Although it seemed pointless, I locked up the house on the way out.

31

Java, who probably heard the news from his younger brother, Kendell, decided to join us as we climbed into Dudley's car. I felt protected; plus, Dudley had his machete in the car. "Call Katia!" Dudley advised me, roaring the car's engine to life and pulling off fast as if we were in a car chase. Katia was not only a good friend of mine, she was also Dudley's cousin. She worked for the Special Services Unit (SSU) of the Royal Saint Lucia Police Force. "Tell her what happened and then tell her to pull up in Monchy with her boys and big guns," Dudley advised.

A 15-minute drive north brought us to the inland village of Monchy. It was easy to find Marva and Shervy because they were sitting at the bus stop. I figured they were probably trying to move the drama away from Shervy's mother's house. Dudley, Java, and I hopped out of the car like we meant business. "Marva, where my tings?" I asked ignoring Shervy's presence.

"Mario, I do not know," she replied with that innocent-looking face; her eyes never glanced at any of us.

"But Kendell saw you!" I shouted, clenching my fist.

"Marva, you have nothing saying!" Shervy screamed, startling Marva.

"Boi, who the hell you think you are? I eh talking to you. Talk again and you go see if I eh chop you," I threatened. "Where my tings?"

Marva ignored my questions, which made everyone believe that Shervy controlled her like a puppet. "You eh talking? OK, de police on their way."

Chapter 7

Interrogation

Two pickup trucks arrived on the scene with about eight SSU officers, all dressed in camouflage attire. Some of them were carrying guns as long as my leg. Seeing Shervy's reaction started to build a smile on my face. However, I tried to display a straight face, as the officers were about to place my sister under arrest. She was seen as a criminal in my eyes.

"Where are your brother's things?" the lead officer asked Marva. The other officers assumed their positions, backing up their commander as he came to a halt in front of Marva and Shervy.

"I eh know noting," she replied, looking at her boyfriend as if he had something to add. Shervy looked away.

"You don't know nothing," the officer repeated sarcastically. "Well, let's go down to the station."

The officer assisted them to the backseat of the truck. I thought they would have surrendered by then, but given their I-will-never-back-down attitudes, it was difficult to know what to believe.

I tried to picture Marva as a criminal; it was impossible. My own sister wouldn't rob me. *What have I done to her? Is she corrupted, brainwashed? Where did my sweet, innocent baby sister go?*

By the time I arrived at the station, Dudley had already gone to work and Java had returned home. If I needed them, they were only a phone call away. The lead officer needed evidence for my accusations, so after placing Marva into an interrogation room and Shervy in a cell, we went to my home. It was evident to the officer that the robbery was staged. His brief investigation led us back to the interrogation room where Marva was handcuffed to the chair that she was sitting on. The officer and I both sat at the table across from Marva.

I fired the first question. "Marva, we know you took my tings. So where you put it?"

From the minute we walked in, her eyes never stopped glancing at the police station's tiled floors; she ignored us, acting as if she was the only person sitting in the room. I looked to the officer.

"You can return the stolen items or spend the night in jail," the officer said. Again, silence ensued. If I had clenched my jaw any harder, some teeth would have popped out of my mouth.

"Marva!" I shouted, irritated by her silence.

My cellphone rang. "Oh, excuse me. Dats my mother." The corner of my eyes spotted Marva gazing in my direction as I exited the room.

"Mummy?"

"Mario, what I'm hearing there now? You call the police on Marva? I knew you coming down was a bad idea." Others who were standing nearby could have heard my mother's rage.

I stepped outside the station and then responded, "Buh Mummy, she teef my tings. Yesterday, Kendell saw her with my bags when he was walking up the Marchand Road from work."

"So Mario, how you know if Kendell not mistaking?"

"Buh Mummy, only my tings they teef. Nutting of yours or Marva was taken. Only my tings. And no damages was done to your house. Marva is de only other person with keys to de house."

The tone in my mother's voice suddenly made a transition from angry to worried. "So what the police doing with Marva? Where's Shervy?"

"We jus' deh trying to ask Marva where dey put da stolen items," I replied. "Shervy is in da cell." A loud sigh was transmitted through my end. "Mummy, doh worry. I eh go press charges on dem."

"OK, cause you have to remember she is your baby sister eh."

"I jus' want my tings back," I said, ending the call.

The investigating officer walked up to me as I hung up the phone. "I can tell she has your stuff," he said. "She looks guilty. But someone has to break her down. Want to go in there by yourself and give it a try?"

"Yeah, I go try my best."

I walked back into the room, bringing the chair closer to Marva before sitting down; she never moved. Her head still down, as if she was embarrassed to look into my eyes. It was a hot summer day in Saint Lucia, but the room felt cold—cold-hearted.

"Marva, I jus' want my tings back," I said, trying to hijack her stare.

"Marva, please. I'm your big brother. I always think of you when I in America. Did you tink I left you? No, everyday I tink of making a better life for you, Mummy, everybody." Water flooded my eyes, and the glare from the sun coming into the room shone on the tears streaming down Marva's cheeks.

"You don't care about me! You and Marvin just left me in Saint Lucia," Marva wept, her lips trembling. My heart raced in response to her words. "You'll don't care about me."

"Buh Marva, you have to remember, I left because I had an opportunity to play basketball and get a free education. I did it for our family. Because we suffer for too long. I promise, tings will be better once I finish college. I just have one year left." I tried to lean down to catch her stare.

"Marva, I love you," I said as she quickly glanced at me. These last three words unleashed a fountain of tears down her cheeks. She instantly rested her head on the desk to cover her eyes. Her cries made me feel like I needed to extend a hug. I've felt the pain of feeling abandoned, after all, and everyone that was close to her was now living in foreign countries. I ended up masking my emotions with pride. "Marva, please," I begged and I noticed the truth was at the tip of her tongue. "Come on, Marva. Jus' tell me where my tings are."

With her head still placed on the table, she mumbled with caution, "So let's say, if I knew where your things are … you going to press charges on Shervy?"

I quickly wiped the smile off my face before she saw it. I assumed that she was more worried about her boyfriend's safety than her own. I replied, "No … no! I promise. I just want my tings back."

She raised her head. "Bring Shervy in here first."

I didn't think twice; I was outside the room, explaining to the officer what had just taken place. "I tink she is going to talk," I said, "but she want to see Shervy first."

I walked up to the cell where Shervy was being held and displayed my smarts. I said to him, "Marva just snitched on you. She wants you to come in and tell me where you put my tings. I already made a deal with her dat I eh go press charges on you." Shervy was a magnificent actor, he didn't flinch, wince or show any sign of worry. My fingers were curled up in my palms as I looked through his eyes. The officer handcuffed him and escorted him out of the holding cell. Shervy followed me into the room where Marva was, and she seemed to relax in his presence.

"So, where my tings?" I asked Shervy.

"I don't know where your tings is boy," he replied, gazing at Marva as if she was the one who asked him the question. When their eyes met, it was as if they were talking, each knowing what the other was thinking.

"Marva, you know where your brother tings is?" Shervy asked.

"No, I don't know where his tings is," Marva responded, still staring at him. I rolled my eyes, thinking, *it was such a bad idea for her to see Shervy.* How can Shervy have so much power over Marva? Before the rage within became visible, I bolted out of the room.

"They not talking," I said to the officer. "I already know that she has my tings. She asked me if she knows where my tings were if I was goin' to press charges on Shervy. I just have a feeling it is dem who teef my tings."

The officer agreed with a nod. "That boy has her wrapped around his finger. Don't worry. We will keep them in separate rooms until they start talking."

Chapter 8

The Truth Shall Set You Free

I sat unaccompanied on the wooden cushioned chair in my living room. My body was spent from the long day of investigating. The house was quiet, yet I was hearing echoes of my baby sister calling my name, *Mario, Mario, Mario.*

Marva was about to spend a night in jail because of me; I was jeopardizing any future relationship with my only sister. *What if my accusations on Marva and Shervy remained alleged?* I would be known as the fool, especially after announcing to everyone that Marva and her boyfriend robbed me. My accusations had ruined her reputation in our community. All my neighbours, too, were in shock, not by the allegation that she was a thief, but because of the thought that she had stolen from her own flesh and blood. No one seemed bothered that a brother called the police on his sister. Rumours made their way to me that Marva was friends with the nappy-headed boys. There was no telling what kind of other crimes they've committed. Again, for the number of years I lived in my mother's house, not once had a thief attempted to break and enter. All of the other nearby houses had been threatened, but never before was my home. I shook my head.

The following morning, I was awakened by the ringing of the home phone.

"Hello, good morning," I said with a slight excitement, hoping it was good news from the officer.

"Good morning. Mario?" The unfamiliar tone in the lady's voice sounded with curiosity.

"Yeah? Speaking," I said, trying to match the caller's voice with a face.

"First of all, I am Shervy's mother. Secondly, I am so sorry of what I'm hearing this morning."

"Oh, wha' goin'on?" I asked with hesitation, not knowing whether I should trust this person.

"I spoke to Shervy and Marva. And I am so disappointed. They have told me where your things are."

I felt like my eyebrows connected, forming a wave of wrinkles across my forehead. "You do?"

"Yeah, but I have a question for you," Shervy's mother said.

"I listening." I was now fully awake as I glanced out the window that was left opened on the night of the robbery.

"Are you going to press any charges?" she asked.

"To tell you da truth, I told dem yesterday dat I jus' wanted my tings back. But dey wasn't talking for nutting. Dat night dey spend in jail could have been avoided. So, no, I eh go press no charges on dem. I jus' want my tings back. Dat's all."

"OK, thank you," she said with a sigh of relief. "Thank you so very much. I haven't met you yet but I sense I can trust you."

"I have a lawyer who will be going to retrieve your belongings from the third person's home."

Maybe that third person is you, I thought to myself. "OK, well once I get my tings, den they are free to go," I reconfirmed.

As promised, I met with a decent-looking man on a street corner, close to the Marchand Police Station. Noticing the bags in his hands, I felt like I was about to cross the finish line in first place. I was able to lift my cheeks again after seeing that everything was in placed, especially my laptop. For all I knew, the lawyer wasn't a lawyer, but I wasn't willing to entertain my suspicions. I expressed my gratitude and then carried all the bags to the police station.

"I have all my stuff. You can let dem go now," I advised the officer, who I had previously informed of my whereabouts.

"You sure?"

"Yeah, dat's my baby sister in dere. I cah press charges on her. I still love her," I replied.

"What about the boy?" the officer asked.

I thought about his mother. "Jus' let him go, too. I believe he learn a lesson from all dat."

Before Marva and Shervy were released, I rushed home. I couldn't face Shervy, especially with the absurd thoughts swirling in my mind. I was envisioning squeezing Shervy's neck until he was unable to breathe.

On my short walk home, a few heads were turned. I was asked, "So Marva dat tiff your tings, for reel?" And as I nodded, jaws just dropped.

When I returned home, I immediately locked all my bags in my bedroom. *I'm not going to take any more chances with these two,* I thought. Then, I made some phone calls, first to my mother and then to all my helpful and worried friends. My mother was more concerned with Marva's release than with the fact I had found all of my belongings.

A few hours later, my cellphone rang, displaying an unknown number. "It is Shervy's mother again," the familiar voice said. "I just want to say thank you again. Shervy is with me right now and he also has something to say."

"Wait, what?" I questioned, trying to interrupt, but she had already handed the phone to Shervy.

"Sorry for teefing your tings," he said softly. His words weren't at all convincing. I'd assumed that his mother's involvement inspired him to lift the phone to his ear, and to whisper a few words of gibberish. No matter how tough a guy acts, thugs always respect their mothers. "I hope one day you will forgive me," he ended.

I, too, had many things to say to Shervy—violent, harsh, and threatening words filled with the hope of fulfilling them one day. However, the thoughts of a hard-working mother persuaded me to co-operate in a friendly manner. "It's all good. I forgive you," I said. By my quick response, he probably thought that my sentiments were insincere. I immediately hung up the phone. *Ugh, I never ever want to see or hear from this lame excuse for a man again.* Marva and her boyfriend were dead to me.

Now, I felt insecure in my own yard. I just wanted to go back to America; however, the summer was far from coming to an end. After all, it was only June. *How can I feel comfortable living here?* Still, the bigger question was: *How would I react when Marva came home? What will be the first words spoken?* Perhaps it would be best to act like nothing had happened, or to just pretend she didn't exist.

When Marva's father, Lucius, heard of his youngest daughter's actions, he surprised me with a visit, and apologized on her behalf. *As if his words meant anything to me. Why did Lucius believe his presence would make a difference?* I hadn't seen him in over five years. His beard was trimmed, revealing sharp cheekbones; his grey hair was braided down his back, making him look like an old ass, a struggling thug. Being around Lucius left a bitter, disgusting taste in my mouth. Facing him then in front of the house, with no one in sight, brought on the urge to throw a couple of punches.

"I doh have much on me buh here five dollars," he said to me with a sympathetic tone.

"It's OK. I doh need it," I responded, holding my head up high.

Staring into his eyes, my only thought was that I would never be forced to say the word *Daddy* ever again—to anyone—unless I was teaching my own child to say that word back to me.

Chapter 9

Not Again

I grew suspicious when Marva didn't return home. For peace of mind, I was thinking of calling her to ask her where she was. She was still only a 16-year-old secondary school student. Soon after, my mother called to try to calm my nerves, and said Marva was staying at Shervy's mother's house for the remainder of my vacation. This news made me feel more comfortable staying at my home, especially because I really didn't want to see her or Shervy again. Now, I could really begin enjoying my stay in Saint Lucia.

I started to feel like a one-man family. *Wasn't this what I wanted?* The wooden partitions of the house projected images of my past like an old film projector. My family was broken and dysfunctional. I felt like the main cause and the odd one out. *What if I was never born? How did I even get here? I was the first born, so why should I be the one to feel like I don't belong?*

Marva's statement in the interrogation room kept on popping up in my mind: *You don't care about me! You and Marvin just left me in Saint Lucia.* My guilt made me feel as if I were the person to blame, well, at least for a brief moment. Being her big brother, it was my duty to call her at least once a week and make the effort to put family first. I never called like I should have. Still, that didn't give her the right to steal from me. *My sister robbed me.* That just didn't sound right to me. If someone were to ask, I'd rather say, some bitch robbed me. Right there and then, Marva was no longer my concern.

On that day when I chose to disown my baby sister, stresses became unbearable. The only therapy was to pick up a basketball and hit the court. It helped reduce some of the tension. Like old times, I bounced my ball and ran up the Entrepot Hill to The Summit, expecting to play for hours. But, as they say, that was then, this is now. Nowadays, you have to beg these working boys to even touch a basketball. My youthful traditions and comrades had fallen victim to the world of grownups. I did not blame them—not everyone had professional basketball dreams.

The court was now fully fenced with a better, smoother surface. Bleachers were mounted on the sidelines to encourage an audience. Still, the youth on the island seemed to have lost their interest in that sport. Gone were the years when it was a privilege to play next. Now, the court was empty, begging for anyone's attention. I guessed the next generation had zero intentions of pursuing college basketball dreams like the Henry brothers. Still, I thought the government's effort to fix the court in an attempt to generate more players was worth a try.

Lonesome days on the court became like a boring rerun episode of a once-loved TV show. I used this time to reflect on my basketball career, thinking back to the first time I stepped with a pair of church shoes onto The Summit, all the way to being back on the same court wearing a pair of Nike sneakers. I will never forget where it all started.

I looked up to the blue skies, while reflecting on my journey. The life-changing, dream-shattering incident that occurred on Dec. 13, 2004, constantly invaded my glorious thoughts. I kept on reminding myself that things could have been worse—a lot worse.

A police vehicle drove down the hill bringing to my memory a former teammate, who was arrested for murder. His name was Josh; he called me "Saint Lucia." Before the school year ended, I sent him a letter, letting him know that he was in my thoughts and prayers. I told him all about our basketball season at Edward Waters College, and how he would have been a great asset to the team. He responded with much hope and inspiration at the thought of being free some day. In that same letter, he requested an invitation, after his release, to Saint Lucia for a relaxing vacation. He also wrote that he hoped to play professional basketball in Europe some day if the jury delivered a not guilty verdict. Josh also informed me that his mother was the only person who kept in touch while he was going through the hardest time of his life. Neither Coach Mosley, nor any other coaching staff, showed him any concern. To me, this was a perfect example of the notion that when you're no longer needed by someone, you become expendable. In simplified terms, when you're gone, you're gone—just like in death. Later, I learned Josh was found guilty of manslaughter at his trial and given the maximum 25-year sentence. I will be in my 50s when he is released.

A gust of wind brought my attention to a black, piece of cloth tied to a nearby light pole. This meant The Summit was mourning the loss of a friend and basketball player. *Oh yeah, Kern!* It was back in January, 2006, when I'd received the devastating news of an accident that led to Kern's death. It happened on the same day of my return flight to America. When I signed online to MSN Messenger to let my Saint Lucian friends know that I had made it back to America safely, I received shocking news. The news made life's tomorrows seem unfair, short, and unpredictable. All my friends' MSN statuses read, "Rest in peace, Kern." My heart dropped, as if it had just slipped out of the hands of someone standing at a mountain cliff. I instantly messaged

Kendell, Java, and Dudley, searching for answers. Kendell was the first to respond.

"Oye, wham to you deh?" he asked.

"Kern, die for true?" I asked.

"Yeah gah, he died in da early morning. He was in a car crash and broke his neck as the car hit da tree."

Kern had been a good friend and a talented basketball player who was fanatical in his love for the game. He had helped me become a better player when we used to play friendly matches on The Summit. If he were alive today, he would be worthy of a college basketball scholarship. I was saddened that I could not make it to his funeral. Like they always say, he's in a better place, where angels sleep.

My thoughts faded away as the wind stopped. I walked to the side of the court overlooking downtown Castries and other communities. From my position, I was trapped in an airspace that peacefully lured me into reminiscing about my beloved sport. The sight of the open green grass brought my attention to two events that were missing from my world: track and field, specifically shot put and discus. I dropped the basketball and walked down to Mindoo Phillip Park—the place where my love of sports began.

During my walk, I remembered being informed by one of my first coaches of an upcoming track-and-field event. It was the 24th edition of the National Individual Track and Field Championships, being held on June 22, 2008, at the George Odlum National Stadium, located in Vieux Fort at the south end of the island. I saw a great opportunity for me to relive moments when I dominated the shot put and discus throws. My state of mind returned to the hard training days of the past. As I approached the Mindoo Phillip Park, I wondered if my throwing techniques were as good as they once were. I intended to pick up where I left off despite the non-existence of my old Cuban coach, Noup. Noup was the man who had empowered me to release my inner strength and excel.

I stepped into the weight room at three in the afternoon, the usual start time for training. The newer and younger athletes made me feel uneasy, as if I had just walked into unfamiliar territory. Some of the same coaches were still seen, being supportive to the up-and-coming runners, jumpers, and throwers. But my presence was not welcomed in the weight room. No one remembered or cared that I had once represented Saint Lucia on a regional basis. In fact, as I tried to pick up a dumbbell, a coach who was very familiar with my face asked me to leave the premises. For a moment, I felt like I was not in Saint Lucia. *Is that the treatment we get as athletes? How can we grow as a nation with leaders who can't lead?* My temper started boiling up in the back of my mind. I wanted to be heard. I was also on a verge of throwing a tantrum, but I quickly realized that I had to be the bigger person. Instead, to release that anger, I ran a few fast laps around the playing field and wiped away my tears before coming to a halt. I had had enough emotional outbreaks for one day. It was time to go home.

I felt lonely walking to the house, like I was stepping in paths where nothing or no one existed. I was hurt and shocked by the attitudes of my people, especially those who had watched me evolve as an athlete. As I was keying my way through the front door, my instinct led me to believe there had been an upheaval. I cautiously crept through my quiet home. My heart raced. I felt a sense of déjà vu, like I was walking into the same event that took place only a week ago. Just like a military step, my feet did a right face toward the computer desk. My eyes bulged. My mind shouted, *What the fuck! Not again!*

Chapter 10

Just My Luck

"No! No! No!" I shouted. The scene of another robbery invaded my sense of safety. A vibration of shock streamed through my veins. *Marva?* I wondered. As I placed the cellphone to my ear, I stood motionless, staring at the computer desk where my laptop was once hardwired into the wall. "Hello, Marva, where are you?" I asked with a furious tone while pacing the length of the living room.

"I'm at Shervy's mother's! What you want?" A sound of resentment was projected through her voice.

"Did you come home?" I carefully asked her.

"No! Now leave me alone—"

She hung up. Calling the police never crossed my mind; I gathered from the first incident that they were a hopeless lot. Even our city's Crime Investigating Department wouldn't have been any assistance, because they didn't have the advanced technology like the crime shows we see on television. Someone was watching my every move, and, this time, the robbery was conducted in broad daylight. I was ashamed to approach my neighbours with the exact same issue. It might make them think I'm an attention seeker.

I had hoped to catch the thief in the act, but the broken back door signalled their form of escape. The padlock I used to lock my bedroom door had been hammered down. The thief, or thieves, even had an opportunity to take a leak because the toilet seat was up and they forgot to flush! *Hmm, sounds like they were prepared. Marva?* Hints suggested that the same culprits robbed me. The bent aluminum window louvres in Marva's room seemed to have led them inside the house. How could someone be small enough to fit between the louvres? From the outside, the thief had gained ground by piling bricks upon bricks. *Hmm, forcibly entry. Marva?* The exact same items were stolen, with a few other things such as my underwear and dirty clothes added for good measure. They took the damn laundry basket, too. *Hmm, an act of framing someone. Marva?* As much as I tried to leave my sister out of my thoughts, the evidence kept on leading to her. *She definitely learned from her mistakes,* I thought, *this time she made it look like a real robbery.*

Before stepping outside, I fixed and straightened the aluminum louvres, shutting them tight, and then slid Marva's wardrobe in front of it. Attempting to search for clues that would lead me to the burglars, I uselessly locked the front door. *They could always find a new way in,* I thought to myself. As I approached the roadside, I became suspicious of others from my community, weakening my thoughts of Marva's guilt. She was now the least likely suspect. I walked down the road, near the church, until I spotted someone familiar. Everyone probably noticed the distressed look on my face. My fists were clenched, and I was ready to strike. I questioned a neighbour and a long-time friend.

"Did you witness any unusual behaviour today?"

"Nah, wha' happened?"

"You happen to see Marva today?" I asked.

"Nope. Haven't seen her ever since you came around. Buh wha' happen?"

I exhaled noisily. "Someone robbed me again!"

"Uh-huh? Well, I just reach home from work and I did not see nuttin'. Buh I suspect is dem fellas by de road," he said, pointing to the nappy-headed boys.

"Dem fellas robbing everyone home when we go to work. A few weeks ago, someone robbed me and I know is them. One day I go jus' go mad and chop dem."

The usual nappy-headed boys were sitting on their block, smoking their joints. It was difficult to read the faces of suspects who are so used to disobeying the eighth commandment. Questioning them was irrelevant at that moment. To be on the safe side, I reported the second robbery to the Marchand Police Station. The officers found it unbelievable that I was robbed twice in a week. Eventually, word of mouth spread and everyone on the streets heard the news. But no one came forward as an eyewitness; no more Kendell to save the day either. This showed the typical scenario of how our people are never able to unite and take down a common enemy. You realize how big the world is when you're not able to find what you're looking for. I started to believe that my stuff was gone forever.

The month of June was just my luck. I was experiencing cold times, rather than the heat of summer. *Time to return to America,* I thought. And that was just my plan. On June 17, 2008, I headed to the downtown areas of the city to have a passport-sized photo taken of me for my student visa. Walking on Brazil Street across from the Derek Walcott Square, I noticed Tenny sitting near a corner store, stretching his arms out for money. My initial thought was that I should keep walking, but I really wanted to talk to my old team- and schoolmate. He was wearing torn, brown short pants and a plaid shirt, and he smelled like he hadn't showered in years. "Tenny, what's up man?" I asked before I sat on the dirty pavement next to him.

"Hey, Arnold," he said with a straight face. I was hoping that he would be as amused as I was to see one another after five years.

Wow, at least he remembers my name. "Long time, dawg," I said. "I remember like it was yesterday we were playing basketball for Entrepot Secondary School. You eh remember those days, gason?"

"Yeah," he said, staring at the pedestrians across the street like a lion preying on his next meal.

I began to wonder if I should stop talking. I continued anyways, "I remembered when—"

"Arnold, you eh have no change for me to buy some food deh, mun?" he begged. His head never rotated.

I sighed and then grabbed $20 out of my jeans pocket. "Here, take this," I said. He quickly snatched it out of my hand.

"Thanks," he said, dismissing himself.

"You're welcome," I said, waving my hand in the air.

"Wow, Tenny. All you want is money. At least I tried to catch up. Oh, my poor friend," I whispered as I dusted my backside.

We cannot change others unless they are willing to change themselves.

That same day, a light-skinned man, wearing casual clothing, confronted me. He was staring me down from head to toe with a vicious look in his eyes.

As he walked past me, I said, "What you looking at?"

"What I looking at?" he repeated multiple times, while steadily approaching me. He acted like he couldn't believe I would ask such a question. We were now eye to eye.

"Pick up that bottle you throw in the gutter now! That is littering!"

"Man, get out of my face," I shouted. I took a quick gaze at the pop bottle before looking down again at this undersized alpha male. *How did the bottle end up there?* Either way, I wasn't putting my hands in the dirty gutters that separated the street and sidewalk. Back then, I didn't drank soda pop, so there was no way I owned that bottle.

He reached to the back of his pocket. "Here is my badge! Now pick it up!"

"I don't care if you da Po Po. I didn't do shit."

"Pick it up, or I will have to place you under arrest."

"Arrest? For what? You're power tripping."

"For littering," he said.

"Man, get outta my face. You crazy!"

I slowly began to walk away after noticing the officer dialling his cellphone. He followed me around as if I was walking a dog. I came to a standstill at a crossroad, deciding whether I should go right to the Derek Walcott Square, or left toward the Castries Cathedral. When I saw two patrolling officers in uniforms approaching, I picked up my pace in an attempt to get away from that senseless officer. From the corner of my eyes, I saw him pointing fingers at me, crying out for assistance from his comrades. The two officers caught up to us, and I was apprehended before I thought about sprinting. All of my pockets were searched and stripped, and so was my backpack. I was put in handcuffs.

"Why you arresting me? I did not do nuttin'," I repeated continually. Fighting to hold back tears, I noticed a supporting cast of people who had witnessed the scenario.

"De boy didn' do nuttin. Leave de mun alone," the bystanders shouted in my defence. Still, I was put in the back of the police pickup truck. Judging by the reaction of the locals, I was led to believe the arresting officer's acts were filled with corruption. He must have had little man syndrome or something.

"There is no higher power above God," I said to him. "What you doin' is illegal." Before I was assisted into the vehicle, a friend of mine appeared from across the street and shouted, "What's your mother's number? I will tell her what's going on!"

Sobbing, I yelled back, "It's OK. My mother is not on the island."

As soon as the truck drove away from the scene, the tears began streaming down my face. I sat between two officers dressed in camouflage attire. The officer who accused me of wrongdoings, Corporal Vincent Peters, was in the front seat. They smelled like pigs, and that's no lie. Even though I was taller and bigger than them, I felt bullied. I harshly voiced my words of distress to all of the officers in the truck. At some point, Corporal Peters shouted, "Shut up!" I thought I was about to receive the stock of an AK-47 to my jawbone. His threats and gestures did not stop me from practising my freedom of speech.

The truck stopped at the Marchand Police Station. I quickened my pace to escape the sight of my friends in the community. *A free ride home,* I was thinking. Inside, my assumption was inaccurate. *Free lodging for the night was more likely.* A familiar face asked me, "Aren't you the one who was just here reporting a robbery?"

"Yeah, and you should be trying to find the thieves instead of picking fights with innocent people," I said. "Why I'm arrested?"

The booking officer informed me that I was being charged with the following offences: littering; disrespecting an officer; resisting arrest; and, possession of a deadly weapon for having a pair of scissors in my backpack. *Was this a joke?* The rage building inside me was projected with an outburst of raw emotions. When I got to that point of annoyance, what was said needed to be said. Can I remember what I said? No. My behaviour at that time may have been deemed life-threatening to the police officers, and I believe they had no other choice but to lock me up behind bars after confiscating my belt and sneakers. It's a good thing that I restrained myself because, if I hadn't, I would have strangled a cop.

"Dats bullshit! Dis is a bullshit justice system," I shouted on my way to the cell. My volumne may have startled some of the prisoners. I felt like making the concrete walls my personal punching bag.

I was sitting amongst criminals. I'd been in this situation before.

Chapter 11

I Know Who Did It

I sat alone in the corner of the cell, trying to ignore the other prisoners, who were dressed in ragged clothes and looked like real jailbirds. The night was young. Four hours had gone by, and I was quiet as a landing feather, alone with my thoughts. *Arrested for littering?* Ever since I'd arrived in Saint Lucia, every weekend I heard of locals being killed by stabbings or gunshots. *Murderers were still walking the streets, and I had been arrested for littering?* Unbelievable, especially when I unintentionally kicked a random bottle that was dropped on the sidewalk by someone else. Even a two-year-old knows that's no crime. Corporal Peters was probably having a bad day and decided to take his frustrations out on me.

"When I getting out?" I asked an officer as he walked by.

"Corporal Peters already left. Maybe tomorrow."

"Tomorrow!" I shouted, breaking my calmness. I gripped the bars, shaking them to release some anger.

"Dats really bullshit. I didn' do nuttin'." The officer ignored my complaints, and left the room. I realized at that moment that it was Game 6 of the 2008 NBA finals: the Los Angeles Lakers vs. the Boston Celtics. Still making noise with the bars, I yelled, "Who winning? Who winning da game?"

"Sit down and stop all that racket deh. Looks like Celtics is about to win the championship!" he responded before leaving again.

"I knew you played basketball," a voice behind me said. I turned around and noticed everyone in the cell staring at me, no doubt noticing my tall stature, rather than my outburst.

I walked toward the corner and dragged my back against the wall until I was sitting on the dusty floors.

"Yeah, played in America," I said. They looked at me attentively, anticipating words of my experiences in the States. I told them a shortened version of *Hanging On To My Dreams*. One by one, eyes were shutting closed as I recited my experiences and transition from Saint Lucia to America. Then, I was looking at bodies asleep on the cold floors. I was unable to sleep; I couldn't help but think of whether my mother's house was safe. *What if someone robbed my home again?* I imagined the thieves would return with a truck and load up all my mother's furniture. These thoughts made it very tough for me to fade into dreamland.

"Arnold!" the officer yelled. I looked his way as he opened up the cell. "Time to go!"

"Wha's da time?"

"Eight a.m." My eyes squinted from the brightness in the checkout room. I did a double-take in the direction of the station's front door. Tobias, my biological father, was standing there. Everything I had on me when I was arrest was returned to me, and I was told that I had to appear in front of a judge in a few days.

"A judge? Really? For kicking a bottle?" I muttered.

"Well, it says here you are also arrested for possession of a deadly weapon, disrespecting an officer and resisting arrest," the officer said.

"But all that happen because—anyways, I go shut up," I said.

Upon leaving, my heavy eyes were tracing the floor of the police station until it met Tobias's shoes. He stood at the front entrance. At that point, I just wanted to cry and be hugged, but I knew that I had a better chance of touching the president of the United States of America than being embraced by my sperm donor. I muttered, "Uh, um, how you know am here?"

"Your mother called me," he said. "What trouble you get yourself in?"

I shook my head, fighting back expletives. *How dare you ask me that,* I thought.

"I didn' do nutting," I whispered, still looking at his shoes.

"You always finding yourself in trouble, eh," he said.

What the fuck, I shrieked to myself. My stare met his; I couldn't believe his words. In my mind, I continued to question the dude who stood before me: *Do you even know me?*

"The officer arrested me for kicking a bottle," I simply replied. Being able to look at Tobias up close, I noticed his gain of wrinkles and grey hairs; this made me realize I hadn't seen or heard from him since my visit to Saint Lucia in December, 2005. He was definitely an older man now. *Was I happy to see him? Um, how can I be?* He was never there for me when I needed him. At that moment, so many questions arose in my mind, begging to be asked. *Why you never called to check up on me? Why you never sent me one cent when I needed money for college? Why you never said you were proud of me?* Right there, face to face with my father, I felt like it was the perfect time to ask about his absences in my life. But it was easier to stutter the questions in the back of mind. I choked as I processed the thought of showing him that I cared.

Instead of expressing the years of grief without him, I feigned my respect by pretending to be paying attention to what was saying without actually listening. We briefly discussed my arrest, and then I pointed out my concern about returning to America.

"I need to get out of here. I need to go back to the States," I said. "Trouble keeps findin' me. I got rob twice, once by my sister and den by an unknown person."

As if he didn't hear me clearly, he asked me, "Why you came down in the first place?"

"I need to renew my student visa."

"Well, are you working on that?"

"I don't have the money yet to go Barbados. I thought I was going to find a job, buh I eh find nutting since I come down. Tings in Lucia rough."

"I will look into a plane ticket for you. For now, take care of your court case."

"I will. Thanks." It was the longest conversation I had ever had with Tobias. *Do I believe he cared?* No. It seemed like he just wanted me far away from him—and that's exactly how I felt.

Dudley was the first one I told about my arrest. He laughed at the charges brought about by the police officer. Knowing Dudley, he probably went on to use my petty allegations against me to get a laugh from our mutual friends; he was a clown, always turning flaws into jokes. I returned home, and felt lucky to discover that the little I had left remained untouched. I quickly made myself breakfast, watched highlights on ESPN of the NBA championship game, and took a shower. When I left the house, my mission was to leave Saint Lucia as soon as possible. I continued my attempt from the previous day to have my passport-sized photos taken in town.

After running my errand, I had lunch at a restaurant near the government buildings in Castries. I asked myself, *Where else do I need to go?* I was just about to take a bite out of my chicken stew when a tap on my shoulder changed my course of thinking.

"Oye Arnold, I have a vibe to show you," said Ed, a fat kid, who was younger than me but had attended the same secondary school.

"What you mean?"

"Here, take my number and shout me later," he said, quickly handing me a piece of paper before disappearing out of sight. I checked back to see if Ed was being followed but nothing looked suspicious. *What the hell?* I couldn't handle the suspense. Still seated at the restaurant, chewing faster, I called him immediately.

"Ed, wha'goin' on?" I asked.

"I know who robbed you."

"Huh? What? Who?"

"Tompie!" The food I was chewing on suddenly became hard to swallow.

"What! Tompie? Serious ting?" I shouted.

"Da day he rob you, he try to put your tings at my house. But when I check is your pictures in de wallet, I told him Arnold is my partner and I cah hold dem tings."

"So my tings not at your house?"

"Awa, he base it somewhere else."

"Oh, irie. Thanks dawg. I go check you later," I said, hanging up the phone. I'd heard enough. A pinch of hope was brought into my world. I kept on saying to myself, *I'm gonna kill dat little motherfucker. I'm going to get my things back ... I know I will.*

Tompie was the nickname of a guy I thought was a childhood friend and former track-and-field teammate. He was a short, skinny fellow, known for his fast speeds on the track, or at least that's how I remembered him. I learned that at any point in your lifetime, anyone who claims to be a friend could turn out to be a backstabber. Obviously, Tompie no longer considered me a friend since he had the audacity to break into my home and steal my stuff. *At what point in his life did he decide that being a thug was the righteous way to live?* I was still in disbelief when I reported him to the police.

The officer who was working on my case didn't have any trouble finding and arresting the lead suspect to the robbery because Tompie lived close to the police station and his hang out spot was only seconds away from his home. God only knew what I would have done if I had caught up to him first. I was ready for a bloody war.

Just when I thought it was going to be a closed case, we had problems getting in touch with Ed. All we wanted from him was a written statement, but he acted as if we had just asked him to write a book. He wouldn't pick up our phone calls. We assumed he didn't want to be classified as a snitch in the Marchand communities, which could have put his life at risk. He even ignored my offerings of a reward. Nevertheless, Tompie was detained that same evening. We were now playing a waiting game until my belongings were found.

Despite all the negativity, I had to remind myself that it was still my summer vacation. If you wake up with expectations to live another ordinary day, then you probably won't achieve as much as you could if you're not willing to live for extraordinary days. I wasn't allowing these hardships to ruin my fun. I was slowly taking care of my plans to return to America.

With the Carnival season in full swing, I was looking forward to the weekend to party and to competing in the 24th National Individual Track and Field Championships. Since I was denied access to the resources to be prepared, I didn't expect to dominate the throwing events like I once did. Typically, I wouldn't even party before a track-and-field event, but that approach was part of my competitive nature reserved only for basketball tournaments. I just wanted to get wasted and have a good time.

On Saturday, June 21, 2008, Kendell, Java, Dudley, and I were aboard a public bus on our way to Samaans Park to an event known as Cooler Fete, where attendees could bring coolers filled with their favourite beverages. The public showed up in large numbers, displaying the creativity of their coolers. Anything you can think of was used as an insulated box to keep drinks cool, from couches, to tires, to car trunks—to name a few. It was such an unforgettable evening, with real friends, great performances, and music by local Soca artists and deejays. The event ended in the wee hours of the morning, and everyone was tipsy on the bus ride back, cracking jokes until we were dropped off at our homes.

The gloomy, cloudy skies poured down rain as we exited the bus. My head was spinning and my vision was slightly blurry. All I needed was a bed and a big glass of water to sleep off it off. I also needed to rest before it was time to catch the 60-minute bus ride to the track-and-field stadium.

"Later, Kendell. Later, Java," I said to my friends as they headed home. Before I keyed myself through the front door, I whispered to myself, "Didn't I leave the living room lights on?" The inside was blacker than black. *Something isn't right. I know I switched on the lights.* I crept through the house and turned on the living room lights. I ran into the kitchen and switched on more lights. I looked left and right, searching for anything unrecognizable. I ran to the back of the house. "Hello?" I asked carefully as I grabbed a broomstick out of the corner. "Anybody there?"

Raindrops and the blowing of wind against the trees seemed to answer my cries. I took a deep breath and then charged to the back of the house, ready to swing at anything in my way, only to find out the back door wide open. I was too late.

Chapter 12

Seeking Revenge

Buh how Tompie rob me if he still in jail? I asked my drunken self, trying my best to hammer a nail through pieces of hardwood to deny further access through the aluminum louvres of my mother's bedroom. The window was more damaged than the thieves' previous entry through Marva's room. A bigger person, someone different, must've been the burglar. I thought that maybe it was Tompie's accomplice, trying to make it seem like he was an innocent man behind bars. I started to think there must be an advertisement on the streets for freebies at my home. If I were to leave Saint Lucia right then, I literally would have flown back to America with one backpack and a passport. I had just as much to my name as a homeless man roaming the streets. Getting robbed for the third time made robbery seem like a typical day in my neck of the woods. After doing a shoddy job at securing the house, my intoxicated state meant I could at least get some sleep.

Three hours later, I tossed myself awake and out of my mother's bed. The right side of my head was pounding, as if it had been hit with a bottle of liquor. I had a dream so real that I thought I was awake. A quick peek at the damages resulting from the latest robbery confirmed this was no dream. Three times in a row, my mother's belongings were untouched, as if the thieves knew exactly what belonged to me and where my things could be found in the house. *What more can they take from me?* I locked the front door, and set off to be reunited with shot put and discus throwing at Saint Lucia's 24th annual National Track and Field Championships.

Surprisingly, I was awarded two medals for first place in the shot put and discus men's events, with a throw of 12.71 metres and 35.89 metres, respectively, and walked away with the Men's Victor Ludorum trophy. At one point during the discus throws, I almost had my ass handed to me by a teenage boy who looked up to me as his role model. With two gold medals hanging around my neck, I continued to reminisce about what could have been if I had overlooked basketball.

When I had turned my back on track and field in August, 2003, a future with basketball looked more promising. *What if I never got that call? What if I never got that scholarship? Where would I be now?* I wasn't expecting a remarkable performance from myself that day at the 24th championships, but I still had the fire within me to compete, especially knowing I would be facing a younger group of athletes.

REBIRTH

When I was a teenager, someone said to me, "Arnold, I foresee you as a world-class discus thrower. An Olympian." Reflecting on what could have been is equivalent to wanting to know what our futures hold. The answer to these questions will always be the same: we will never know until we live to see it. There is no point regretting our past decisions because we are not living for yesterday's regrets. Had I chosen track-and-field, I'd probably be wishing I'd chosen basketball. Although this was proving to be a rough summer, I learned a valuable lesson: we all have the light inside us, ready to shine through on cloudy days.

That same evening, after a long day of participating in events and watching Saint Lucia's future athletic talents, I reported the third robbery to the police officer who hadn't been doing anything to solve my cases. I didn't know why I was wasting my time.

The following morning, I sought breakfast at one of the roadside convenience shops, where I noticed Tompie roaming the streets. I did a double-take. *Is this for real?* I crept slowly so that he wouldn't see me. With every step I took, my heart raced faster, as if I was sprinting after him. I asked myself, *Why is he a free man? Were my items returned?* Before his eyes met mine, I did a U-turn and headed straight to the police station.

"I just saw Tompie," I said, pausing to catch my breath. "Did he return my tings?"

"Well, your witness never came to give his statement," the officer said. "We have no evidence, so we had to let him go."

"What! I cah believe dis!" I shook my head, at Ed's negligence.

Every muscle in my body tensed as I walked in the direction where I'd just seen Tompie. *I'm going to kill him.* When I caught up to him, I hesitated to take quick actions. He was seated at his normal block, doing what he did every day—absolutely nothing. "Oye, where you put my tings! I know you have my tings!" He stood up with a bossy gesture, as if that would make him taller or bigger.

"Boi, Marva dat take your tings and you go and tell de police I teef your tings! Doh talk to me!" His act of pointing fingers at Marva only served to justify his guilt. I gave him one more opportunity to come clean.

"Oye, where you put my tings?"

He started to walk away.

"Boi, eh talk to me. OK, you tink you a bad man," I said, picking up two of the biggest rocks in sight. He started to run for cover as I held a grip. I was so heated at Tompie's lack of regard for our childhood friendship that I felt like I was boiling under a flame. His attitude was only adding kerosene to my fire.

"Boi, Tompie, where you put my tings!" I was screaming so loud my voice sounded like an emergency warning siren. I aimed for his head and launched the rock before he gained momentum over the force of my strength. The rock flew over his head and landed in front of his sprinting path. Tompie's speeds reminded me of how fast he was when we were on the same track-and-field team. I wasn't running after him; instead, I ran to pick up another rock.

Tompie quickly disappeared behind the Marchand Church. All of a sudden, he reappeared to the battlefield with as many glass bottles as he could hold. He fired at me. I was not backing away. Instead, I dodged his ammo, which would have been right on target if I had stood still. The shattering of the glass bottles brought out neighbouring residents. Their voices rooted for me, as if I was some kind of saviour with my actions representing their frustrations over all the times their houses had been broken into.

"If you want a cutlass, I go give you one to chop him up. I tired of all dem men robbing us," shouted a guy who lived opposite the church. Their voices were heard, but my eyes were focused on Tompie. He ran behind the church again. I stayed on the roadside to avoid a sneak attack. Again, he returned with more glass bottles, this time, launching them from the grounds of the church that was gated at its entrance. It was as if Tompie had opened a bottle depot business. He obviously hid these glass bottles in case of unexpected wars to protect his turf. There were no words exchanged between us, and still I showed no fear. I ducked, jumped, and stepped aside as glass bottles flew over the gated fence. After throwing one last bottle, Tompie ran away again.

The same investigating officer from the robberies had arrived on the scene. I assumed someone had dialled 911. I dropped the rocks before the officer saw me. "Tompie that started it," the community yelled in my defence. I realized they really did have my back.

"Where him?" asked the officer.

Feeling like I was being let off the hook, I decided to leave the scene. Meanwhile, the residents were slowly returning to their homes. Fearful that I might get hit with a bottle, I started walking backwards in the middle of the road. Tompie had returned with more bottles; however, I was at a distance where I could see him but he couldn't see me. Tompie approached the edge of the church's high grounds, while the officer was walking up the hill. They were now head to toe. I waved my hands to get the officer's attention and signalled to indicate that Tompie was right above his head. The officer slowly pulled out his gun, which was tucked in his trousers, and pointed it upward. Tompie poked his head down, only to be staring at the barrel of a gun. "Freeze!" the officer shouted. My heart was beating vigorously, anticipating a bloody scene.

Tompie hesitated to run. "I didn' do nutting," he said to the officer and then he attempted to take flight. Everything happened so quickly. The sound of a single gunshot echoed in the air. "Ouch!" Tompie screamed, but he still kept on running behind the church. My eyes opened widely. *What just happened?* I asked myself, placing my hand over my gasping mouth to hold my breath. At that moment, it seemed to be the sweetest revenge.

Summer In Saint Lucia, 2008

Second Quarter

Accomplish

Chapter 13

Emergency

The sound of the gunshot sent all the neighbours back to their homes. I returned too. Nobody wanted to be known as a witness. From the outside, my demeanour seemed calm, but, inside, anxiety was running high wanting to know what had happened. Five minutes later, I peeked outside the window of my home and then quickly rejected the thoughts of having to face the nosy neighbours.

I needed answers from the officer who pulled the trigger. I pulled out the number he had given me in case of emergencies and called his cellphone. "Wha' just happened?" I asked him. He sounded distressed. His words were so slurred that I could imagine the sweat on his forehead.

"I just got off the phone with ER," he said.

"The ambulance just picked him up."

"So da bullet hit him?"

"Yeah buh dey say da bullet passed through his flesh, missing his bone." I rolled my eyes. *Dammit.*

I believed the officer was trying to tell me that Tompie would only sustain a scare from the gunshot and flesh wound. That was disappointing to hear, as I thought that something more serious might have helped to end his career as a B&E artist.

For the next few hours, I was constantly looking over my shoulders because my troubles with Tompie were behind the shooting. Through my eyes and in my mind, all the nappy-headed boys in my community were gunning for me. And for that reason, for the first time in my life, I strapped myself with a knife and the intention to kill anyone who threatened my life. Although it was not the best solution, it gave me confidence to walk the streets. I trusted no one but the God before me.

That same morning, with ongoing fears of retaliation, I left home and travelled to Victoria Hospital to visit my brother, Segun, or maybe I should say, I had an unscheduled appointment with Dr. Tobias. First, though, there were some unexpected occurrences. Getting off public transportation, to my surprise, I noticed Tompie's affiliates guarding the surrounding areas like watchmen. They all stood under a nearby tree, which offered sufficient shading from the sun. When they noticed me, I ensured I didn't look happy. I felt the right side of my waist to confirm that my weapon was still in place. They noticed. The only time I lost sight of these nappy-headed boys was when I entered the hospital.

"Dr. Tobias, please," I said to the lady at the information desk. She directed me to his location. The scent of hospitals always makes me feel nauseous. It looked like it was shaping up to be a busy day, with a number of patients with stab and machete wounds. As I entered into an emergency room, guess who I saw sitting in a wheelchair? Yes, that's right: Tompie. He eyed me with a vicious stare. My heart picked up the paces for a few seconds but instantly calmed when I saw my brother. The gestures made by my mouth let Tompie know that I found something funny.

"Boi, you laughing?" he softly said. Luckily for him, I was not as violent as the thugs who were causing the current situations in our ghettos. Ignoring his comments, I walked past him and stood next to my brother.

I pounded my brother's fist. "Dats de mun dat teef my tings," I whispered to him.

"Uh-huh. Yeah, I see he just reach deh with a bullet in his leg," Segun said.

"I saw everything. He lucky I eh buss his head with a rock. I was so mad earlier, I woulda kill him. Buh dat good for him. It go teach him eh take people tings."

Despite the room being filled with bad blood, it was an honour for me to be able to witness my own flesh and blood wearing a white lab coat. Segun, the tallest of my older brothers, was almost the same height as me. But with his beer belly, I couldn't imagine him running up and down a basketball court even though he loved the game as much as me. I assume he fulfilled his ultimate dream by being a doctor. If I had to pick someone who was living proof that hard work pays off, Segun would be it. Had I grown up with him, I would have easily fed off his determination and perseverance.

While we're on the subject of dreams, later that day, I received an email from Cleo—or, better yet, a brilliant proposition from an old-time friend who was now living in New York City. Cleo, a short, petite, light-skinned woman with long, straight hair, was my counsellor during my teenage years in Saint Lucia. After an increase in my mischievousness at secondary school, my mother thought it was a good idea for me to speak to a professional about personal issues that were affecting my life.

Just like back in the days, Cleo had reached out to me to share some valuable information that would be beneficial to my development. Her email indicated that a connection of hers was able to generate opportunities for me to fulfil my hoop dreams sooner than I had expected. The news made me smile until my cheeks hurt. With that type of incentive in place, I booked the earliest appointment with the U.S. Embassy to renew my student F-1 visa.

I flew to Barbados on Thursday, June 26, 2008, courtesy of Tobias's gifted round-trip flight. I was issued a student visa to continue my studies in America. Even though I had only one year left to complete my undergraduate program, the visa wouldn't expire until 2013. By then, I hoped I would be playing professional basketball in Europe.

Chapter 14

The Return

Whenever I walk between the walls of my very first home, I'm always filled with this overwhelming feeling that I may never return. Being away most of the time was a major factor. *Will I ever return to my home after I leave?* That was a question I asked myself as I packed what little clothes I had left in preparation for my trip. No matter where I end up, I will never forget where I came from, I promised myself.

After packing, I decided to dig deep in my old bedroom for memorabilia from my younger years. While searching through my old wooden chest of drawers, I came across a few notebooks I hadn't seen in years. It felt like I had just found a hidden treasure box. I even stumbled upon a number of handwritten letters that I'd received from my pen pals, thanks to a program that was run through my primary school. The objective of writing these letters was to improve literacy, to learn about other cultures, and to build new relationships around the world.

Of all my pen pals, Jessica of Madrid, Spain, was one of my favourite. I had actually met her during a family picnic on one of Saint Lucia's beaches in Gros Islet when I was 11 years old. I spotted her in her pink bikini, swimming to the shore. She was probably the first foreigner I was attracted to, and, on that day, I told her how I felt just before she kissed me while we were in the ocean. Unfortunately, that one kiss was my first—and our last—because she was leaving the next day. As with a few friendships in life, we were pen pals for a short period of time, just less than three years. We wrote to each other with hopes to reunite someday. At times, I wondered if we would ever cross paths again, or, if she'd still remember me.

There was so much dust and cobwebs covering my old journals, it made me sneeze a few times. After dusting off the front cover, I flipped to the front page and spotted my very first journal entry. As I read through each word with teary eyes, I remembered the day like it was yesterday.

Today's Date: April 25, 1995

Dear Diary,

I really hate here. He beet me again. I doh do anyting. I just wanta play with friends outside. I doh know why Mummy marry that man. He big evil man. All he do is beat me up. Am scare of him. Am never happy in home. How can I call it home? I doh want to live here. Mummy doh say nutting at all. I feel like runnin away and never come back. Mayb Mummy go miss me and leave evil man.

I wish had a real father. Somebody I call Daddy and be happy. I doh know why my real father never come visit me. I wish I coud live with him. Maybe I will be happyer. I have 4 older brothers but I never see dem. I wonder if dey know bout me. Sometimes I wish I was not alive because am in so much pain. I doh feel loved by anyone. Am feeling lonely. Am so sad. I cah stop crying.

I hate life.

I shut the book, wiping away my tears. Reading these words I wrote all those years ago made me feel as if I was stuck in a dark room watching a horror movie. I didn't want to relive these years, but still I decided to take all of my journals back to the States.

I wound down my last few days on the island by preparing for my return to American college life. With the ongoing investigation into my stolen belongings, as well as the anticipated retaliation from Tompie, I thought there would have been a war zone. But things died down after I stopped trying to get back what had been taken away from me. Even though my outburst may have been deemed irrelevant, seeing Tompie limping around with an injured leg gave me some satisfaction. Whenever we crossed paths, he wouldn't dare look into my eyes. It was pathetic how pitiful his demeanour came across now. We went from being teammates and friends to enemies for life.

In regards to the charges I was facing, there was a mandatory court appearance. I was highly aware of it, so I attended to obey the law. In the courtroom, the judge called on the arresting officer and me. While standing next to Corporal Peters, I was acutely aware that I was towering over him and that was very funny to the other police officers and alleged criminals. More amusement surfaced when the judge stated that I was arrested for littering. I wasn't too sure if the law officials and the officer's colleagues were laughing at our height difference, or the petty charges I was facing. But I'm sure that if I was sent to jail for these petty charges, I would have been the laughingstock of the prison. Furthermore, after my *not guilty* plea, the judge seemed to take the matter much less seriously than the police did the day they put me in handcuffs. I was allowed to leave after I was given a later date to reappear. *A later date to appear in front the judge?* I had no intention of being an example to their justice system. *I need to get out of here,* I said to myself as I left the courtroom.

REBIRTH

I became paranoid with thoughts of facing more bad luck, and made the final decision to leave Saint Lucia a little sooner than I thought I would. With financial assistance from Brittany, a potential girlfriend who lived in a city near Chicago, Illinois, I booked a one-way ticket to New York City. The beginning of the fall semester at Edward Waters College was in two weeks, and Brittany was hoping I would be able to come for a visit. Throughout my years in America, social media had kept us connected on friendly terms. Since we were both single, we thought it was the perfect time for us to meet in person.

The evening before my departure, I ensured that I said my goodbyes to the people who helped me survive the summer. These people provided me with a plate of food when I needed it the most, and extra support when I needed a shoulder to lean on. Apart from my support people, I tried to keep my return to the United States a secret for the simple fact that I had four criminal charges against me. After my experiences this summer, I felt robbed of all my positive childhood memories by the bad-minded people in Bishop's Gap. Places away from Saint Lucia began to feel more like home. Aboard the plane, I was sweating nervously until the pilot announced we were clear for take off.

When I arrived in America, my first childhood best friend, Olvin Cyril, picked me up at John F. Kennedy International Airport. Olvin was no longer the yellow, fat kid I knew growing up. He had lost a tremendous amount of weight and was now a father to a beautiful baby girl.

"What's up, son?" he asked.

"Boi, tings in Lucia rough. I had to leave," I replied, carrying my only piece of luggage to the trunk of his car.

"Yeah, I know how it is," Olvin said as he drove off in the busy streets of Manhattan, heading for Brooklyn. "So, how dem fellas robbed you?"

"Oh, you hear about dat. Gason, I eh even feel like talking about that cause dem fellas teef all my tings. And I know who did it, too."

"Sorry to hear about that, kid. Buh who dat rob you deh?"

"First, it was Marva, then gason you know Tompie? Well, we used to call him Coco-boy. He is Jonathan little brother."

"For real? Marva and da mun? Gason, wasn't dat your patna? And I cah believe your own sister do you dat."

"Yeah gah. Anyway, what done is done," I said. "I have better things to worry about now. I'm happy to be back in da States. I have one more year to complete my degree. And I just hope I will be able to play pro basketball after."

"That will be sick, son."

Staring out the car windshield, I was lulled into a daydream as I looked out at the buildings across the bridge. *Land of opportunities, right?*

Since Olvin had a full house, I accepted an offer from his cousins, Jermal and Jovan, to stay with them for the remainder of my time in NYC. I slept on a mattress in their living room, my usual resting place whenever I visited them. Jermal and Jovan now owned their home and lived on the same quiet block as Olvin, which made it convenient for me to visit Olvin and his family on a daily basis. Being back in America helped to release some of the stress from the summer holiday. First, the cost of living was up to par with my budget. Secondly, I had many friends living in the city that had heard of my situation and were willing to help replace some of my everyday essentials. Although I was mostly handed monetary donations from everyone else, the most appreciated of them all was what I received from Aunty Monica. She provided me with some polo shirts, socks, white vests, shorts, and a few pairs of underwear. I never understood how I was so privileged to have this type of kindness in my life. Aunty Monica was Lucius's sister. Although I was now a young adult, Lucius still lived in my childhood memories. Despite the monster of my childhood, I tried to look at the positive outcome of my yesterdays, one of which was Aunty Monica.

A few days later, I took New York City's transit from Brooklyn to Manhattan. I was headed to an appointment to see Cleo and meet with the man who claimed to have a prosperous opportunity for me. I was punctual for the appointment, and walked into a small, busy office. "Hey, Cleo, so nice to see you," I greeted her, bending over to embrace her tiny body.

"Wow, you making me feel so short. You have grown so much from the last time I saw you," she joked, continuously measuring herself against me as if I were a walking measuring tape. But I was in no mood to be bothered with the entertainment. I was all about business.

"So, is he here?" I asked.

"He is just finishing up a business meeting. He will be with you shortly." Seated in a nearby room, I clasped my hands on my knees to reduce the constant shaking of my legs. I daubed my bandana on my forehead to minimize the sweat. *I hope this is it. I hope he has the answers.* Cleo had relayed so much information about this guy to me, that I was forced to be optimistic about my future in professional basketball. It seemed as if she was making him out to be some kind of

God. She told me that he was a self-made millionaire with numerous connections to established, high-end individuals.

"Here he is! The man of the hour." My train of thoughts was interrupted by a smooth voice coming out of a plump, black man with a clean cut. As I stood, I shook hands with an average-height gentleman dressed in business attire. "Mike Brown," he said with a big, welcoming smile. "And you must be the basketball superstar, Arnold Henry."

"Yes, sir, a pleasure to meet you." We walked into his office where we sat down so that I could listen to his proposal. Cleo was present, looking like a proud spectator.

"So, here's the deal. Cleo may have told you a little bit of my work."

Real estate agent, entrepreneur, owned property, millionaire, blah, blah, blah, I thought to myself. I nodded politely at Mike, hoping that he noticed my heightened interest.

"Throughout my business ventures, I've connected with people all over the world: businessmen, athletes, sports agents, etc. I believe my next step is to *get* into the world of sports."

Oh, no, wait a minute. So, he has no experience? "So, I will be your first client?" I asked.

"Yes, of course," he answered with great confidence. "It is a win-win situation for us."

He continued to elaborate, "I've prepared this contract for you. You can read it now, if you like."

I picked up the sheet of paper, carefully reading the agreement.

"Basically, I will represent you for three years," he said. "And during that term, if I assist you in finding a professional basketball team, my payoff will be 10 per cent of your salary and 20 per cent for endorsements."

Really, that's it? That's what brought extreme excitement out of Cleo? I stared at her momentarily. She nodded with excitement. I wanted to roll my eyes at her, but two pairs of eyes were waiting for my response.

I sighed. Then, I inhaled and exhaled a couple times before I quickly attempted to look for any signs of loyalty written on Mike's face. *Do I even have a better option right now?* I read through the one-page agreement once more.

"OK, where do I sign?" I asked. Cleo applauded with the loudest excitement, as if I'd already landed a big basketball contract.

After jotting down my signature, a handshake confirmed the deal.

"Welcome aboard," Mike said. "I have your number, so we will keep in touch."

I thanked Cleo for her contributions and then I was off to Brooklyn to enjoy the last few days of my time in NYC with my friends.

Staying with these two brothers always brought back remembrances of our juvenile years in Saint Lucia. Indeed, our days spent together were times I would cherish forever, especially when we were up to no good, being mischievous, and annoying the neighbours in Da Yard. Whenever we get together, it's as if someone must start a sentence with, "Do you remember the time when ..." This helped us to summon up the reasoning for our never-ending friendship. Now that we were young adults, it was even more important to protect our bond. Friendships are often put to the test, but Jermal, Jovan and I were falling apart as a result of outside forces. Let me explain.

On the last night before I flew to visit Brittany, an altercation arose between Jovan, his girlfriend, and me that almost caused a fist fight. The uproar started after I had spent an entire afternoon shopping for things I'll need for my last year in college. I returned to Jovan and Jermal's to pack for my flight. I went looking for my laundry, and, when I spotted Jermal at the computer in the dining room, I asked him, "Where's my clothes?"

"Mario, I don't know," he replied, with a smirk that made his cheeks chubbier than when we were kids. I went upstairs.

"Jovan, you seen my laundry?"

"No," Jovan replied with a face that showed no remorse. Jovan's overweight, black girlfriend, who lay next to him on his bed, did not look in my direction. *Weird.* The only possible place left to search was outside the back of the house. I exited through a sliding door, stepped into their backyard, and looked left. No laundry in sight. Then, I looked to the right, only to find a black bag. Inside, I noticed that my white clothes—that were supposed to be dry—were still wet and had been placed outside in a black garbage bag with my coloured clothes that were supposed to be in the washing machine. My white clothes were dyed, and my coloured clothes looked like unfinished graffiti. I stared at the garbage bag. I retraced my morning: *No one was home. I emptied the dryer, placed the dry clothes in the nearest laundry basket, put my washed white clothes in the dryer, and put my coloured clothes in the washing machine.* That's exactly what I recalled. My clothes were now ruined. The longer I stared at the wet clothes in the bag, the tenser my muscles became. The tight feeling in my chest was worse than all the times when I was robbed.

"Who da fuck did dat!" I shouted to Jermal because he was the only one I noticed upon going back inside.

"Boy, I eh know," he shouted, keeping his eyes on the computer screen. I sensed a slight look of guilt on his face.

"Dat's so fucked up! Who did dat to my shit? Are you fucking kidding me?" I screamed so loud, I made the neighbour's dogs start barking. Then, I heard footsteps running down the stairs.

"I did it!" Jovan's girlfriend admitted. She stood behind her man, who was trying his best to keep her from getting any closer to me. *Why wasn't I surprised?* She was already my No. 1 suspect because I didn't think my childhood friends would have done me so wrong.

"You're a fucking bitch! Why the fuck you did dat shit?" All eyes opened wide around the room. Jermal stood up like he was ready to attack me if I was to strike in his brother's direction. I held my ground.

"Who you calling bitch?" the obvious asked.

"You, you fuckin' bitch! You ruined all my damn clothes," I screamed in her face, waving my index finger near her forehead, ensuring that I emphasized the word once more.

"Oye, Mario, stop calling my girl a bitch," Jovan said loudly over his yapping girlfriend.

"Fuck you, Jovan. What she did was a bitch move! Ever since I've been here, I notice dat girl is not for you! She is controlling, bossy, and she think she owns your mother's house!"

"But Mario, you put her clean clothes in the dirty laundry basket," Jermal tried to defend with a calm tone.

"Fuck you, Jermal! You said you did not know shit, so shut the fuck up." I was so upset that I was yelling and cursing at everyone. "And you think I did dat shit on purpose?"

"Get the fuck out!" Jermal demanded, pointing to the front door.

"Fuck it! Fine," I shouted, bouncing shoulders into Jovan's chest as I walked into the living room where my bags were sitting. "I hope you marry that bitch!" I shouted at Jovan sarcastically.

I packed quickly, as if I was running late for my flight, and the noise in the house lessened. The only sounds came from the zipping of my bags and stomping of my feet. Jermal, Jovan, and Jovan's girlfriend had stayed back in the dining-room area. A few minutes later, I slammed the front door shut before the waterworks ran down my face. I walked two houses away, and before anyone could see me and mistake me for a homeless person, I hid in a dark corner, holding my one piece of luggage and a black garbage bag filled with wet clothes. I hoped that the darkness would obscure my appearance—not that anyone knew who I was on these Brooklyn streets—but it was still disconcerting for me. While dialling numbers from my cellphone with teary eyes, I was shocked and saddened at the possibility of the end to a great friendship. No other's heart should have this much weight to sink the number of years it took to build a friendship. My mind kept on repeating, *over a girl? A fat, ugly-ass girl with such a bad attitude?* It seemed to me like Jovan was fooled by love, or blinded by deception. Looking from the outside, there was nothing appealing about her. But that was just my opinion.

"Olvin, can you check your mother for me?" I asked desperately since I had limited places to go with such short notice.

"What's going on, son?"

"I need somewhere to stay for the night, please."

A couple of giant steps later, after I placed my wet clothes in the dryer, I was seated with Olvin at the kitchen table. I explained the fight I just had with his cousins. It seemed as if he was on my side since he showed annoyance toward Jovan's girlfriend. When my clothes were dry, I separated them, disposed of those in terrible condition, folded the rest, and packed them into my one piece of luggage.

Before midnight struck, I was asleep on the couch. When my alarm clock rang, I was reminded of my trip to Chicago. Olvin worked for JetBlue Airlines at JFK airport, so, on his way to his early start at work, he dropped me off at my departure gate.

When will this summer end?

Chapter 15

No Room

Wherever I seek love, I am willing to find a way to get there. I was no stranger to long-distance relationships, and catching a flight to the American Midwestern was no exception. For the past few months, I'd found more interest in a young mulatto lady by means of instant messenger. I wasn't willing to limit my options in women to my local city, so I decided to explore a different setting. Maybe my love waited for my arrival. I spent the last week of my summer vacation at Brittany's house in Elgin, Illinois, about 35 miles northwest of Chicago. What I found very admirable about her was that she took care of her little sister as if she were her own daughter.

Brittany was a sweetheart, but during my visit, I quickly learned that everything that tastes sweet has the same potential to turn bitter. At one point, she left me at her house to be with another dude. I got suspicious when she turned me down right at the brink of us having sex. My assumptions were confirmed when, later that night, I snooped through her cellphone, and realized she'd been sexting someone else for months. We were going nowhere fast. Her heart was for someone else, or, better yet, her booty was calling for him. *Was I hurting?* The tears running down the bathroom sink could have answered that. *When would I ever learn that long-distance relationships were not for me?* With Brittany, it was a lesson that there was no love lost—and no love found.

I had to admit, though, I'm the type of person who would follow everyplace my heart desires, no matter what the cost or how long the distance. I wanted to be loved. If I got hurt in the process, it was a risk I was willing to accept. Even though things didn't go according to plan, I was appreciative of Brittany's presence in my life because she was always there when I needed a friend. In addition to that, she paid for many of my expenses, including my flight from the O'Hare Airport to Jacksonville.

In late summer, the Sunshine State greeted me with its high humidity. Gallons of sweat pierced through my glands the moment I stepped off the plane. I would have been looking forward to another college basketball season, but my eligibility had run out. My ambition had changed, and I was looking forward, instead, to graduating from Edward Waters College with my bachelor's degree in computer information systems. I foresaw being part of the graduating class of 2009. I just had to prove to myself that I could do it.

My story had been written. I bounced around five different schools in five consecutive years. I played basketball for five dissimilar programs or leagues in 1,825 days. Anyone with knowledge of college basketball would understand that this was not normal for an athlete. Still, I stood unashamed. At the end of my college basketball career, whatever lessons I gained as a player, or as a student, would be shared with future generations. More importantly, I would learn from my mistakes and not repeat them.

As far as competiveness gained from collegiate basketball, EWC had left me with terrific memories. With one more year to complete my degree, I asked myself: *How will I survive without being the centre of attention at a basketball game? What will I do with all that extra time? No basketball?* It was the first time in eight years that I wouldn't be spending all my time on the court.

As usual, the international students were allowed to return to campus a few days before the beginning of classes. Since security guards were limited, the male students were placed in a secured dormitory where a selected number of guards patrolled the premise 24 hours a day—well, at least until the college officially reopened. This much security might seem excessive, but EWC's campus was literally in the heart of the Jacksonville ghetto. Thugs wearing saggy pants and abandoned homes painted with graffiti could have easily been mistaken for students and school property.

During the first few days back on campus, a resident lived up to the unscrupulous reputation of his community by going on a robbery spree with deadly weapons. Most of the victims who reported the incident were my schoolmates, and they were incredibly shaken up as they told their stories of being held at gunpoint. I, too, feared to walk the streets of Duval County. In fact, many students had threatened to abandon EWC and I think some actually did.

When the authorities became aware of the criminal activities taking place within their communities, especially at the oldest historically black college in Florida, an increase in security guards and police patrols chased away the stick up kids. The terror felt by the students and their parents eventually passed.

The first semester got underway in early August, which was an earlier start than most colleges across the nation. As always, registration started with an overcrowding of students gathered at their respective locations. At all the other schools I've attended, registration was typically done via the internet in a timely manner. EWC was slower than the '80s when it came to making technological advancements to decrease the amount of workload on staff. In other words, everything was still done on paper, and records were stored in files as hard paper copies in the administrative buildings. It took about one business week to register the entire student body. The first week was generally regarded as chaotic and frustrating for everyone involved. Students who applied months ago for financial aid were facing delays; seniors weren't able to register for the classes they needed to graduate; and, classrooms were too small to accept any more applicants. And then I came face to face with my own big problem.

On a Monday morning, after spending two hours in line, I approached the residential director. "Arnold Henry, Honours Village," I requested with hopes of retrieving the same bedroom that I reserved at the end of the spring semester, before leaving for Saint Lucia. Obviously, I would receive a new roommate since Travis had graduated.

"I'm sorry but all the rooms are full at the Honours Village," she said, beating her eyelashes at me.

I laughed. "What you mean?"

She wasn't laughing back. "I'm sorry."

"Sorry? Before I left for the summer, I reserved my room."

"Like we've been telling all the other students, Mr. Grant is no longer with us."

My eyebrows felt like they had connected while I took a few intense breaths.

"But I signed the reservation forms with Mr. Grant. Last semester, I made sure I signed it before the due date."

"Unfortunately, we lost all of Mr. Grant's paperwork when he left," she said, rolling her eyes.

My eyes quickly landed on my folded arms. I took a few more deep breaths before saying something I profoundly regretted immediately after it came out of my mouth.

"So, what about the rooms at Tiger Landing? Are the rooms there full, too?"

Living in the poor conditions of Tiger Landing was never my preferred choice and perhaps not a possibility I wanted. The infrastructure reminded me of a maximum-security prison. I wouldn't be able to focus on my studies if I had to constantly watch my back. To ensure that I never had to live in these horrific, outdated dorms, one of my priorities was to maintain a Grade Point Average (GPA) higher than the required 3.0. I had enough A's on my report card to accommodate for that. Still, my room was lost due to the irresponsibility of their staff.

In answer to my question, the residential director responded: "Full. There are no more rooms available at all."

"Wow, this is crazy," I said, my lips shivering as I left the classroom with cold feelings streaming all over my body. My mind was so spaced out that I couldn't remember getting to the bottom of a staircase. My reality became clear as I stumbled over a steel chair painted black. I sat down to absorb the fact that I had nowhere to live. *How can an institution be so careless? Where do they expect me to live? I have no family living in Jacksonville. I'm only a student. I have no money. I can barely work in America. Where can I stay?*

The leaves scattered on the pavement were a blur. Then, all of sudden, two rippled pairs of basketball sneakers barred my vision. Sam and Demetrice had appeared before me, and I only took noticed of their identity after hearing their voices. "Whatta gwan star?" Demetrice would always say to me at first sight, mocking the slang of Jamaican Patois. It was my first time reconnecting with these two, who were not only my former African-American teammates but friends who I considered my brothers on campus.

"Dawg, dem people just tell me dat I have no room," I said with a soft tone, bracing myself on the chair after shamelessly drying my eyes.

"Bruh, same thing they told us," said Sam, throwing his dreadlocks over his shoulder.

Demetrice sat next to me as if to show his sympathy. He knew that I was overseas and away from home.

"We can all get an apartment and split the rent three ways," he suggested enthusiastically.

It took a minute for me to respond.

"Like, you mean, to pay for an apartment? Like, to live off-campus? Just the three of us?" I asked each question with eagerness; only to realize that coming up with rent money would be out of my reach.

"Yeah, dawg," Demetrice said.

"Dawg, how I'm going to pay for school, books, food, and rent? I am an international student. I cannot work in America."

Rent money. Oh my God, rent money, the words were like echoes running through my mind. I gathered myself on the chair, footing for grip under my sneaker, as if I was about to sprint a race. Demetrice and Sam looked at me puzzled.

"Oh, Coach, I have to go see Coach Mosley," I said. Excusing myself from my buddies in poor fashion, I speed walked toward Kings Road in search for my favourite American basketball coach.

"I'll holler at y'all later," I shouted back at my friends.

REBIRTH

On my way to Coach Mosley's office, I remembered one of the greatest sentences that a coach had ever said to me, "I wish you had an extra year to play with us."

Whenever I thought of Coach Mosley, I remembered him saying that during a conversation that took place the week after we returned from the national basketball tournament in Missouri. His words made me rethink my potential as a player. If I had used all four of my eligibile years to play in only one men's basketball program, by now, I might have been documenting my experiences playing in the National Basketball Association (NBA). Maybe. Nonetheless, I've learned to live for the present and not the past. I've learned to work for a better future from the lessons of my past. If I was to dream again, I realized that dreams don't come true when you're asleep.

On arrival at the gym, I walked into Coach Mosley's office unannounced. He always had this calm demeanour about him, as if no one or nothing could break his cool. I wasn't sure if I would consider his attire cool—a polo shirt tucked into short shorts, ankle socks, and running shoes. The clothes weren't cool to my teammates who occasionally made references and jokes about the way Coach dressed.

"Oh hey, Arnold, good to see you back. Did you have a good summer?" he asked. Coach was busy, as usual, with paperwork.

"It was OK," I answered brusquely to avoid recounting the bad summer memories. Besides, there was a bigger issue at hand. "Coach, I have no room," I commiserated. "Plus, what about my scholarship? How I'm going to pay the school?"

Normally, I would have taken a seat when I visited Coach Mosley at his office. This time, I stood in anticipation of his answers. "Arnold, since you are no longer on the basketball team, the best I can do for you is," he paused, and then continued after his eyes fell back on the papers on his desk, "I can give you a partial amount of grant-in-aid. We do not have enough scholarship money left. I had to share it with the guys who are actually on this year's basketball team."

"OK, Coach, I understand." At that point, I desperately thought, *anything would do for now.*

"You should ask Coach Gallon to help with the rest."

"Oh, right." I quickly pictured myself throwing a shot put and a discus. "That's a good idea, Coach Mosley."

"I will start processing the paperwork and forward it to the accounting office."

"Thank you. I really appreciate it, Coach. I will make sure I graduate next year."

"You mentioned about having no room."

"Yeah, Coach, there are no rooms available on campus."

"Some of the other guys are encountering the same problem, Sam and Demetrice," Coach Mosley said. "But I will ask the other coaches if he has somewhere for you to stay. In the meantime, I highly suggest that you start looking for a possible apartment to rent."

I sighed. "I don't know about that, Coach."

Chapter 16

I Need a Home

I believe that others are introduced into our lives for reasons we cannot find until we seek.

"Kimberly, I doh have anywhere to sleep tomorrow night," I said over a cellphone call on the very last night of my temporary on-campus accommodation.

"What you mean you do not have anywhere to stay? Aren't you staying at the school?" she asked.

"I'm at the school right now, but the student dat is assigned for this room is taking it over in the morning."

Truthfully, I wasn't expecting Kimberly to provide me with the means of lodgings. We barely knew each other. I met her at a reggae party during the spring semester. If anything, we were better known for a night of dry humping each other at the party. I remembered Kimberly being impressed with me for leaving my country to pursue an education in America. She seemed to care.

"Your coaches couldn't help you find a room?" Kimberly asked.

"No," I answered after clearing my throat, "there are no more rooms available at the school. That's what dey tell me."

"That's so messed up. As an international student, aren't the staff supposed to ensure you have somewhere to stay?"

"I don't know. This is what's happening to me at the moment," I sighed.

After a long pause, Kimberly said, "Let me call some people and I'll get back to you."

"Thanks so much, Kimberly. I really appreciate your efforts."

I laid on my back, stared at the rotating fan on the ceiling, and reflected on the past few days with soaked eye sockets. I questioned myself. *Why does my life have to be so complicated? How am I supposed to survive? Is this all happening because my athletic status was removed?* This was a prime example of my days ahead, the repercussions of being just a normal student, or so I thought. The vibration of my cellphone triggered concern.

"Kimberly?"

"I spoke to my mom. She might have somewhere for you to stay." I felt anticipation overtaking the wrinkles on my forehead as I waited for confirmation. "She lives really close to your school, a 10-minute drive, maybe 20 to 30 minutes by bus."

At that point, I didn't care if she lived an hour away from my school. I just needed somewhere to sleep, a shelter, a home, and someone to care. Kimberly continued, "She wants to meet you first, though, so I gave her your phone number. If she doesn't call you tonight, expect a call early tomorrow morning."

"I really appreciate that, Kimberly. Thank you, thank you, and thank you." That night, I prayed to God, Jesus and the Virgin Mary before I laid my head to rest.

"Wake the fuck up, college boy!" I gasped for air, almost choking on my own saliva as my eyes slowly opened to the barrel of a chrome gun. My heart almost stopped.

"What's going on?" I shouted from the top of the bunk bed, slowly backing up to the edge of the bed. Two men with unfamiliar voices, wearing ski masks and armed with pistols were demanding my money, jewellery, sneakers, anything I owned.

"I don't have anything!" I cried out. "I don't have nothing for you!"

"Don't lie to me, college boy!" said the guy in charge, while cranking his gun. His accomplice began searching my luggage. *No one will ever rob me again,* I nervously thought to myself. I panicked, pelting my pillow at the face of the gunman, and then swiftly jumped in his direction on the ground like a heat-seeking missile. The gun went off.

"Oh my God! Oh my God! It's only a dream! It's only a dream," I yelled, clutching the left side of my chest. I quickly readjusted my sitting position to the edge of the bed. I was short of breath and my forehead felt like I had hit it against a brick wall. What a nightmare. *I gotta get out of here,* I thought, *the rightful owner of this bed will be here anytime from now.* I unplugged my cellphone from the wall charger. *It is almost 11 in the morning and no one has called me. What's going on?*

"Kimberly, have you heard from your mom?"

"She hasn't called you yet?"

"No," I sighed.

"OK, let me call you back."

In the meantime, I attempted to pack my bag. Seconds later, an incoming call from Kimberly had me holding my breath.

"Arnold, my mom wants to meet you at Burger King, within the next hour."

I exhaled. "Which one?"

"I believe it is the one on East Union Street."

"I will be there."

"Sorry about that, Arnold. My mom was having some issues with my older sister, but she will explain everything to you."

"OK, not a problem. Like I said, I appreciate everything you are doing for me."

I wasted no time. I hopped on public transit, and, in no less than 15 minutes, I was seated at Burger King. For every patron who walked into the fast-food restaurant, I smiled with the hope of hearing my name. When I was least expecting it, a lady with a southern accent called my name. "Arnold?"

"Deborah?" I said as I stood up to shake hands with a woman who looked like she was in her mid-50s. There was a lot of resemblance between Kimberly and her mother, especially in the face. They had the same brown skin complexion, with the same cheekbones and nose.

"Whoa, you're tall!" she said while grabbing a seat across from where we were standing. I joined her. From the moment she stepped foot in the restaurant, I ensured that my smile was as bright as the earrings in my ears. I've heard many times that my smile is comforting, so I wanted to portray that image since I was a complete stranger to her. I'd already covered my cornrows with one of my fitted baseball caps to look more presentable.

"So, Kimberly told me your situation. Sorry, I did not call you sooner. I had a big argument with my older daughter, Valerie, who thought that it was not a good idea to bring strangers into my home."

The tone in her voice made me feel like we were already acquainted with one another. She seemed like a good-hearted mother. *No wonder Kimberly seemed like a decent young lady.*

I looked into her eyes, trying my best to hide any look of disappointment on my face. "I truly understand. I didn't mean to cause you any grief—"

She interrupted me. "But I know if I had children in a foreign country and they did not have somewhere to stay, I would like for a parent to do the same for my daughters."

My smile extended beyond my ears, but I was a bit confused. "So, Valerie doesn't want me to stay with you? She lives with you?"

"No, she has her own house," Deborah said. "She is not talking to me anymore because I decided to let you live with me. But it is OK. God is good and I know He would do the same."

I wanted to kiss Deborah on the cheeks. Although I was saddened to hear it was partially my fault that the relationship between her and her eldest daughter had come to an end, I was relieved to have found a home with such a God-fearing woman.

"I will have your room ready tonight. So, you can come by at, let's say, seven o'clock. That works for you?"

"Yes! Yes, of course. Sounds great to me."

"Is there anything you do not eat?"

"I'll eat anything. I like lots of bread, though."

"Here's my address and my phone number. Call me if you need directions. See you later."

"Thank you so much, Deborah. I just want to let you know that I am so grateful for this."

With the assistance of Sam and Demetrice, I was able to get a helping hand with my luggage and a lift to Deborah's two-storey, light blue home. I was in awe upon arrival, as I was never expecting to find such a beautiful home in East Jacksonville.

"Yeah, boi, you living large now," Demetrice joked. "And you do not have to pay her rent, too? That's sick."

"Yeah, dawg. I call it a blessing from God."

Before I knocked on the front door, Sam yelled, "Look out for your boi. Let me know if she has an extra room for me."

I laughed and waved goodbye. "See you at the school tomorrow."

Chapter 17

Student – ~~Athlete~~

After coming in through the front door, I was given a tour of Deborah's three-bedroom house. The interior was spacious, neat, and inviting, with rugged carpet and modern furniture. I even had my own bathroom. A plate of soul food, which consisted of fried chicken, macaroni and cheese, mashed potatoes, and collard greens, was already prepared for me when I arrived. I swallowed the entire plate like I hadn't eaten in three days. *This was definitely a blessing from God.* I woke up in a bed with clean sheets and a warm blanket. I slept peacefully and felt content. *Why shouldn't I be?* The rules of the house were simple: all Deborah asked of me was to treat her house like my home. And I'd reminded myself to be on my best behaviour.

I was on a one-year road to graduation, and it was my first day of school. Academically, my intention was to finish the fall and spring semesters with straight A's to boost my GPA. During the previous school year at EWC, I'd completed 26 hours with a GPA of 3.115. For the fall semester, I had applied to take five courses: computer concepts; project management and practice; number theory; college reading; and, introduction to biblical studies. And for the spring semester: intro to business; managing information systems; systems analysis and design; African-American history; and, one elective. Taking these courses would mean that at the end of the school year, I would have completed a total of 135 hours, including all of my transferable hours from the other colleges and universities.

Of all my courses, college reading stood out the most because I was captivated with our in-class reading assignment. Truth be told, I'd never really been a fan of reading books. Up to that point in my life, the only interest I had ever taken in reading a book in its entirety was *The Wonderful Wizard of Oz* when I was 10 years old. For some reason, during my college reading course, I'd found a new interest in storytelling, thanks to Harper Lee and her brilliant novel, *To Kill a Mockingbird*. I was so impressed with Lee's writing style that I'd begun to write a short chapter about my life. Then, I decided to share it with my teacher. After she read it, she shared some important elements of writing for me to focus on. Her advice: write to persuade, write to entertain, and write to inform. I still take her instruction into consideration whenever I write.

Athletically, it was my duty to be prepared for any opportunities that may arise in my future. I was surprised that I hadn't heard any basketball news from Mike Brown. I was hoping that he would find me a professional basketball team to join by the end of the school year. I also intended to make the best out of my last year at college.

"Good morning, Deborah," I greeted my landlady as I stepped on the last flight of stairs. To my surprise, Deborah was injecting something into her arm. I thought I still had sleep in my eyes. I blinked twice. "Deborah?"

"Oh, good morning, Arnold. Don't worry about me. No, I'm not shooting heroin," she said in a joking manner, "I'm a diabetic."

I tried to play it off. "Not that I thought you were." Since I had a few minutes before I had to catch the bus, I joined her on the couch as she continued to speak.

"I've been suffering with this busted toe. It is really painful," she said, pointing at her big toe. The distress in her voice estimated the pain coming from her toe. That explained Deborah's slow, awkward movements and the limp in her walk. I guess diabetes and wounds are a treacherous combination.

"That really sucks. I wish there was something I can do. If you ever need help around the house, please let me know," I responded with a sympathetic tone.

"Oh, Arnold, thank you. You're so sweet."

I approached the front door. "Well, I have to go to school now."

"What time will you be back?"

"Probably after eight in the evening. I might stay to practice with my old basketball team," I replied, standing in the doorway.

"Oh yeah, Kimberly did mentioned that you play for your school's basketball team."

"Yeah, I did. Since I've played four years of college basketball, by rules, I'm not eligible to participate anymore."

"Must be hard for you. Anyway, I'll let you get on your way. I'll see you tonight before I leave for work."

"Oh, what time do your work?" I asked out of curiosity.

"I work the graveyard shift. I start at 11 p.m. I'm an LPN."

"A what?"

"A licensed practical nurse."

"Nice. OK, see you tonight."

"Be careful."

I smiled. "I will." That exact moment reminded me of how my mother showed concern for my safety and well-being. At that moment, I realized that a woman doesn't necessarily have to give birth to a child to be considered the child's mother; it comes naturally to those who know how to give love and devotion without expecting anything in return.

It was easy to notice the reasons for Deborah's warning signs as I headed through the door. Little did she know, I was brought up on similar turfs in the rough streets of Marchand in Saint Lucia, where drugs and violence were the status quo. I just ignored all illegal activity as I travelled to and from the college.

After a long day of classes, I made it a priority to visit Coach Gallon. He had the power to solve the other half of the equation to my financial worries. For an elderly, grey-haired man, Coach Gallon was one of the most energetic and funniest people I knew. It was time to discuss my future in track and field with him. I thought it was ironic how the sport I gave up for basketball was coming back into my life. Don't get it twisted, though; this was no attempt to make a comeback, but, rather, a means of paying off the balance of my tuition and meal plan for my fifth and final year at college. I walked into his office without a scheduled appointment. "Coach Gallon, long time no see. You spoke with Coach Mosley?"

"Yeah, oh yeah," he said, retracing his thoughts. Coach Gallon was always a loud, outspoken individual with a slight stutter in his speech. "So, track-and-field season starts in the spring semester," he said. "Will you be able to throw the hammer, discus, javelin, and shot putt?"

I opened my eyes widely. "I'm not too familiar with the hammer and javelin, but, Coach, if you teach me, I will definitely throw it for the school."

"Good, then we have a deal. I will take care of your paperwork. We will be starting practice soon. I will keep you informed."

Just like that, all my concerns with money were gone. In addition, I retained my on-campus job as a mathematics tutor, and the monthly income from tutoring was just enough to cover my everyday expenses and essentials such as cellphone bills and bus fees.

Like the old times in my secondary school years, I had to juggle academics and sports. It felt like my teenage years were coming back to haunt me. Basically, I went to class throughout the day, practised with Coach Gallon for one to two hours, and then joined Coach Mosley for another three hours of basketball workouts. Track may have been paying the bills for now, but my heart belonged to basketball. My biggest challenge was being able to keep myself in top shape without playing in the upcoming basketball season. Still, I trained as if I was trying to make the team.

Being in the presence of the new recruits for the school's basketball team made me feel naked, as if I didn't belong. *How am I supposed to keep myself motivated when nothing is guaranteed? They say anything is possible, nothing is impossible, and I'm possible, but what happens when your dreams are marred by failure? Are we supposed to keep on believing through the fate of possibilities?* Last season, I was a champion. This season, I wasn't even on the team, but that didn't mean I would settle. A true champion will always strive to become a champion again. I am a dreamer, and I would rather take the risk than to be a failure by way of never having taken the risk.

Nothing was promised to me, but I still kept on dreaming. Why shouldn't I? Basketball had given me five years in the land of opportunity to create my own destiny, and countless times I had failed to capitalize on this. Some might say, in the end, I would have a bachelor's degree in computer information systems, and end up with a good-paying job, but that wasn't in my Plan A, B or C. Basketball was my joy, the happiness within my soul, the key to my goals. I wanted to play forever. That is why I persevered through my failures.

Despite being naive about my current situation, I reminded myself that success is dependent, not only on the believer, but also on those who execute daily routines to be part of bigger successes. Every little progress is still progress.

It was soon to be the start of a new year. Back when I first picked up a basketball, my psyche had led me to believe that I would have become a professional athlete by now. *I knew it was a wise decision to finish my degree, but where were the offers for a pro basketball contract? Was it because I wasn't a good enough player? Instead of focusing on finishing school, should I be knocking on other doors looking for opportunity?* These were questions I asked myself on a daily basis. Nonetheless, it was my duty to hang on to my dreams, at least until I didn't have the strength to hang on any longer.

With the absence of a basketball season, I was able to improve on my on-campus social life. I was able to attend numerous school functions, and I was often seen at the clubs on weekends. Before my school year ended, I was also hoping to become part of a brotherhood. After some words of encouragement and support from Sam, I decided to join him to pledge for one of our college's organization. Sam was highly interested in Phi Beta Sigma, a fraternity that was founded at Howard University of Washington, D.C., on Jan. 9, 1914, by three African-American men. Luckily for him, I was interested in the same frat because my old roommate, Travis, was a Sigma and had shared with me the many perks that came with going Greek. Some guys were more interested in the beautiful women and parties that come about as a result of joining a frat, but the professional network was what intrigued me.

The pledging process started on a school night, when Sam, three other mates and I had to dress in all black from head to toe and meet up at Big Brother's house at 9:14 p.m.—a time that was related to the year of the fraternity's founding. Due to American laws and the privacy of the brotherhood, I will refrain from saying what happened behind closed doors. Let's just say, these frat boys are tougher than they look. However, I couldn't say the same for me. I wasn't able to handle the pressure, and I quit after the first week.

Chapter 18

Family Reunion in Florida

On Tuesday, Jan. 20, 2009, the people of the United States of America witnessed the inauguration of the first four-year term of President Barack Obama, the first African-American president. History was being made. While President Obama was just a diminutive member of the U.S. Senate and campaigning for president, I was fortunate to attend one of his rallies on Nov. 3, 2008, at the Jacksonville Veterans Memorial Arena, located a few minutes from Deborah's house. During Obama's speech, he sounded so articulate, confident, and professional that it seemed like he had already won the election. His supporters had shown up in very large numbers. That day, after I witnessed grown men and women crying, I labelled him the Rock Star of American Politics. If I had to look up to someone who represented the hope of dreams coming true, it had to be President Obama. He was a true inspiration to me. This came as no surprise to me, especially considering that the titles of his two first books, *Dreams from My Father* and *The Audacity of Hope: Thoughts on Reclaiming the American Dream*, contain the words dreams and hopes, as well as the phrase American Dream.

And that's not all I took from Obama and his run for presidency. Drawing from the Democratic Party's slogan during the 2008 U.S. presidential campaign, "Change We Can Believe In," I realized change was truly necessary. *Yes, I can.* I was on a home stretch to graduation. I needed to be more open-minded and have a different outlook toward the real world. I was preparing for Plan D, which was to get the most out of my college degree, in case there was no basketball career in my future. To prepare myself, I signed up for an eight-week course with CSX, a company that had partnered with my school to promote a leadership program for African-Americans. At the end of the course, we would have a final presentation that represented all the material we'd learned. The most valuable trainee would be awarded a summer internship that had the potential to turn into a full-time job with the company. Whenever there's a challenge, I take pride in competing to come out on top. Unfortunately, I was not in good standing with the instructor, mainly because my attendance and participation were lacking, as I had been absent due to conflicting schedules with track-and-field meets. To make up for lost time and to show my professional dedication, I cut my hair only a few days after my 24th birthday. After six years of growing my hair out, I was now clean-cut. Furthermore, it really helped me to adapt to a more professional look. Ever since Allen Iverson, who will always be remembered as the cornrowed, tattooed NBA great, cut his hair, the hairstyle was slowly going out of fashion in the basketball world. Most of the basketball players I knew on a personal level had followed suit. I was on a pursuit to maturity.

During the opening month of the New Year, I'd decided to attend a basketball game to support my former teammates and coaches, and my school's team. Although I was now a spectator, I mainly attended because I needed a brief reminder of the games atmosphere: the screaming fans, the blowing of whistles, the squeaking of basketball shoes, the buzzers—the whole nine yards. I believe it was a way of trying to keep myself motivated and focused on my goals.

Five months had passed since I jotted my signature on that agreement, and I still hadn't heard once from my supposed manager, or agent—whatever he called himself. I decided to reach out to him. "Hello, Mike, how's everything going? Any news for me?" I asked him in early January, shortly after watching a basketball game at my school's home court.

"I think I might have something for you in China," he said. *That's strange. And you didn't find the time to call to advise me?*

"Oh yeah? So, when you will know for sure?" I said.

"I have to get in touch with a few people. I will keep you in the loop when I have more information."

"Please do. I will be finished with school by the end of April. It will be cool if I could play right away."

Patience is a virtue, or so the saying goes, so I started to practise being patient.

On the flip side, my brother Marvin's 2008-09 freshman basketball season came to a conclusion on March 10, following a 92-82 defeat by Highland Community College of Illinois during the district championship—a game that would have advanced his team to the National Junior College Athletic Association (NJCAA) Division I National Tournament. Marvin finished the season with an average of eight points, six rebounds and one block per game. His overall team record ended with 28 wins and five losses. The advancements of online video streaming technologies allowed me opportunities to witness some of Marvin's live home games. Year by year, he showed improvements. I was adamant that we would both be playing professional basketball someday. I continued to be his mentor.

While my relationship with Deborah felt as if we had developed a strong family bond, Valerie was still keeping her distance. She hadn't spoken to her mother since the day I moved in. To this day, I'm still unable to write a physical description of Valerie. Deborah was not bothered by the selfishness of her daughter, but what hurt her most was the fact Valerie was keeping the grandchildren from seeing their grandmother. I didn't know Valerie, yet I despised the way she treated her mother. Even when Deborah had gone for an operation on her busted up toe, Valerie did not visit during her mother's recovery. One of the sweetest things that someone ever said to me was what Deborah told me on her sickbed. Despite her pain and suffering, she said, "I may have lost a daughter, but I gained a son." My heart was touched. My Mummy had some competition with Deborah. The words coming out of Deborah's mouth were genuine. However, she never had to say it, because her natural motherly instincts were obvious through her actions. Truly, her actions spoke louder than words, and they were evident by how comfortable I felt in her home. She played the role of a substitute mother very well. When I was sick and needed and catering, Deborah was easy to approach; after all, she was a nurse.

One week before graduation, there came an opportunity to introduce my biological mother to my adoptive mother. There was no better reason for my mother to plan her first vacation to America than to see her first child graduate from college. I noticed my mother looking around from a distance outside the Jacksonville airport. The car came to a halt near the passenger pickup area. I honked and then smiled at her as she squinted her eyes peering at the windshield. "Hey, Mario, you that's there," she yelled, taking her loud mother voice everywhere she goes. "You can drive now?" she asked with an outburst of laughter, sputtering saliva like a water gun.

I left Deborah inside the vehicle, seated in the passenger seat, and ran around the car to initiate an overdue embrace with my mother. It seemed as if she had been losing more and more weight. I was not sure if the weight loss represented struggles or good health, but I figured it must be slowly helping to eliminate the stress on her recovering leg. From time to time, though, she still complained of occasional pains.

"Mummy, I'm so happy that you made it safely. So good to see you here."

"Good to see you too, my boy. But tell me, when did you start driving?" she asked.

"I'll tell you all about it. But first, meet Deborah." I gave Deborah the cue to exist the car. "Mummy, remember Deborah?"

"Yes, I've heard so much about you," my mother said. "Thank you so much for everything you've done for my boy. How can I ever repay you?"

Deborah brushed my mother's comment away and reached for a hug. "You don't owe me anything. I would have wanted the same for my children."

I was content as the two exchanged hugs.

It was about a 20-minute drive from the airport to Deborah's house. As I merged onto I-95 south, I finally answered my mother's question. I looked at her from the rear-view mirror. "I wanted to surprise you, Mummy."

I noticed her white teeth. "Well, it was about time you got your licence," she said.

I laughed, and thought that my oldest brother, Kervyn, would be proud that I finally got my licence, too, since he was my original driving instructor.

"This is Deborah's car. She taught me how to drive on these big, busy streets of America. For about two weeks, every night, she took me to an isolated parking lot and taught me everything I needed to know. I failed my first practical driving test, but Deborah told me to try again."

For the remainder of the car ride, Deborah and my mother connected through introductory conversation, and, for the most part, they continued to talk about me. Deborah generally had very nice things to say about me, and my mother was all smiles hearing about my best behaviours.

My mother's reactions to the foreign environment had me reminiscing about my first time in America. I found it amusing when she recognized businesses from the TV commercials. Back at the house that same evening, after Deborah provided us with a plate of food and a cup of tea, I did some catching up with my mother.

I walked into the guest room unexpectedly. "Mario, Deborah, she is a nice lady, eh? I'm so happy to see that you are doing well here," Mummy said.

"Yeah, I was lucky to meet her. She has taken good care of me."

My mother changed subjects after we sat on the edge of the bed. "So, Mario, I wanted to talk to you about Marva." I didn't say a word, as I already knew what was coming. "You're still not talking to your sister? That's your one and only sister."

I briefly choked for words. "But Mummy, she stole my things like I was a stranger."

"I know, Mario, but you have to learn to forgive your sister." My mother paused. "Please do not mention this to anyone, but Marva is not doing good at all."

I looked away. "What happened to her?"

"I ended up having to talk to her. She broke down crying, saying that she has been using drugs."

I kept staring at the floors, holding back tears. "What? Are you serious? Who's de guy selling drugs to a teenage girl?" I asked with a soft tone after clearing my throat.

"Some man that hangs around the place where Lucius have his fishing boat. Mario, I was so mad. I wanted to find that man and kill him for what he did to my daughter. A young schoolgirl like that you giving drugs. That's why I hated when Marva use to go visit with her father. All these desperate, ragamuffins that does be there, too."

I carefully shook my head so that the tears wouldn't escape my eye sockets. "So, Marva, how is she doing now?"

"Well, she and Shervy are no longer together. I pray to God every night, thanking him for that. And with the little bit of money I have, I pay for her to seek professional help. She is almost done with her program."

"Oh, OK," I said.

"So, Mario, please talk to your sister. That's the only one you have," my mother reminded me again.

"OK, Mummy."

I kissed my mother and said goodnight. I walked into my room with an overwhelming feeling of stupidity, disgracefulness, and distress. *How can I hold a grudge toward my own flesh and blood for so long? I was hurt by her actions last summer. But did she really mean to do me any wrong?* I placed these thoughts on the back burner because I needed some time to reconsider many of my decisions.

The following day, I had one more surprise up my sleeve for my mother. While Deborah had taken my mother out shopping for the entire day, I was doing some running around, preparing to deliver something that would guarantee joy for everyone involved. Deborah was already in on the secret and had given me the cue through text message for when they were back at the house. It was time.

I knocked on the front door.

"Maria, can you please get the door?" I overheard Deborah asking my mother.

"Shhh," I whispered, placing my index finger on my lips. I walked into the house, holding a camcorder to capture the moment. My mother's eyes followed my movements inside the house.

"Why you have a camera uh, Mario?" she asked, looking into the lens.

"Yo," I yelled, ignoring my mother's question. "Yo," I shouted once more, hinting for my surprise to come in. My mother got suspicious, so she looked around as she heard giggling and footsteps coming from outside.

"Yo!" I yelled one more time.

What happened next was priceless. As my mother's jaw hit the floor, her eyes bulged almost to the brink of popping out. She held the back of her head as if it had been hit by a rock and fled away from the camera, calling on God in our Kwéyòl language. "Bondyé! Bondyé! Bondyé!"

My mother's cries drowned out Deborah's laughter. Once my mother was able to compose herself, she rushed to the front door to finally exchange hugs with Marvin. This sight can never be erased from my memories. My mother almost had to climb up a stool to reach Marvin's six-foot-10 frame.

Tristy Smith was part of the surprise, too. She was Marvin's girlfriend and had established a good relationship with our mother when she lived in Saint Lucia. Tristy stood only five-foot-three, but she was tall enough to have caught my brother's eye.

Earlier that day, I picked Marvin up at the airport and Tristy at the train station. It was my first time meeting with Tristy in person. I'd heard so much about Marvin's love life when they first became high school sweethearts in Saint Lucia. It was clear that Tristy was responsible for my brother's happiness. With Tristy now living in Bermuda, Marvin was having a tough time coping with the long-distance relationship. I was certain that the love they displayed for each other would allow their relationship to survive the distance. I could easily foresee her as my sister-in-law.

Although I never had that many close relations to appreciate as my immediate kinfolk, it started looking a lot like a family reunion in Jacksonville, Florida. For the first time since 2006, my mother was able to touch and see her two basketball-playing sons at the same time. She was so happy that she wanted someone to capture her smiles on camera. As our picture was being taken, my mother busted out a joke, asking, "You sure you can see my face between these two giants?"

My mother's smile in the portrait that I still have today shows a very proud moment. With Deborah's hospitality, I started to believe that the word *family* was best defined as an action—not a noun. My family was here, and I was definitely ready to walk the stage at my graduation.

Chapter 19

Class of 2009

"My boy, here is your graduation present. That is all I have to give," my mother said on the morning of my graduation. She handed me an envelope that contained a $50 bill and a Hallmark card congratulating me on my graduation from college and on my years of success.

"Mummy, it is OK," I said while we stood face to face in my bedroom. I noticed the hurt in her eyes, as if she wished she could have provided me with something more valuable. But little did she know, my mother being at my graduation ceremony was the best present ever. I lived for moments to make my mother proud.

I placed my hand on her shoulders. "I like the card, Mummy. You can keep the money. I do not need it."

"Mario, you sure?" she asked, with a pouty tone.

"Yes, Mummy, I am sure. You can keep it."

Before I exited my bedroom, she made a few adjustments to my cap and gown. "I'm proud of you, Mario."

I smiled. "Thank you, Mummy."

I kissed her goodbye as I exited the house for the preparation of the ceremony. "See you soon."

A few minutes later, I arrived at the Adams-Jenkins Community Sports & Music Complex, the gymnasium where I played my home basketball games and the venue for my graduation ceremony. My graduation was held on Saturday, May 2. *I made it. I did it,* was all I could think as we took our seats. The gym had been transformed into a theatre-like setting with a stage and chairs. The graduates sat at the front of the stage, and the parents and invited guests were seated in the rear. Our guest speaker was Judge Glenda Hatchett, from the television show *Judge Hatchett.* It was such an impactful ceremony as I listened to her inspirational speech. I remembered when Judge Hatchett instructed us, the class of 2009, to get up on our feet and applaud the people who were responsible for us being there that day. From the instant we were advised to do so, I did not hesitate to find my mother, Marvin and Tristy, and Deborah and Kimberly in the audience. They all waved back at me with proud looks on their faces. Sam and Demetrice had even come out for my big day. Judge Hatchett then made a valid point. She said, "They prayed for you when you did not have the sense to pray for yourself. They prayed for you." At the same time, I recalled the days when my mother said to me, "My boy, I said a prayer and I lit a candle for you."

Occasionally, I wondered where I would be without my mother's prayers. Maybe I would be dead or in jail like the majority of the typical young black men who grew up in poverty. I knew that God had answered many of my mother's prayers throughout the years because it seemed like the Holy Spirit had lifted me each time I felt like giving up on college. Then again, I always tried to be deaf to negative intentions and blind to regrets. I believed, for sure, that there was a higher power that had been watching over me, as if I had my own guardian angel, from birth.

For me, the day I walked across the stage represented a new chapter of my life, a start to new beginnings. I never felt as confident as the moment the announcer called my name: "Arnold Mario Haig Henry, bachelor of science, computer information systems."

My ears picked up the proudness in my mother's voice as she chanted, "That's my boy! That's my boy!"

Later that day, my mother made fried fish, cheese-stuffed baked potatoes, and coleslaw. Deborah was finally able to taste why I called my mother the best cook in the world. Then, out of the blue, while we were all at the dinner table indulging in a mouth-watering meal, Deborah mentioned to my mother, "I know your son's favourite food."

This opened the door for my mother to tell one of my most embarrassing stories. For my mother, it never gets old. "Oh, you talking about bread?" I rolled my eyes because I knew what was coming next. Marvin had already started laughing. "I have a joke to tell you," mother cried out. "So, when Mario, I mean, Arnold, was visiting with his grandmother, I mean, his step-grandmother in Saint Lucia, the boy was crying and he refuse to sleep. So his step-grandmother asked him, why you crying and not sleeping?" My mother paused, mocking me, "I want bread."

Deborah laughed so hard that she nearly choked on a piece of fish, and I'm sure that everyone could see redness in my cheeks. My mother continued, "Every night, the boy must eat bread. Up to now ih!"

Deborah added to the joke. "I always made sure there was bread in the cupboard."

The discussions and laughter had died out after all our bellies were full. My mother broke the silence, suggesting to me, "So, Mario, why don't you write a book?"

Shocked, I looked her in the eye as the thought of writing a book about my life had already crossed my mind. I even had a few paragraphs to back it up. With all eyes on me, I asked, "Me? Write a book?"

"Yes. You've come a long way. I'm sure someone would like to read about your experiences."

I smiled. "Um, that sounds like a good idea. We will see."

I was so inspired by my mother's encouragements that I excused myself from the table, ran upstairs, switched on my laptop, and proceeded to write until my eyes became weary.

The following day, my Hotmail inbox notified me of a new email from Marva. I breathed in and out before clicking on it. Much to my surprise, it was a fairly long letter addressed to Marvin and me.

From: Marva Henry
To: Mario Henry; Marvin Henry
Subject: Hey Marvin and Mario
Date: Sunday, May 3, 2009 08:23:22

Hey, I miss you'll so much. I wish I was around my big brothers. I miss you much. I wish things were different but I know you'll had to follow your dreams. Well I know mommy told you'll about my situation. I'm sorry, but I'm in treatment now hoping to get better soon. Since you'll been gone everything has been different. Honestly my life changed completely, for the worst. Mario, I never apologized to you from the incident that happened and now I feel like my life is missing something. I really miss you, Marvin, and I miss daddy so I filled up these spaces with drugs and alcohol. It made me feel good most of the time but I got addicted to it and never thought that would happen. I know I really hurt and disappointed mommy and I'm so sorry that things happened that way. I can't wait for you'll to come back home and play the role as big brothers in my life, because I need that. Mommy is always there for me but I just feel that a part of me is missing and it is you guys.

Mario, I love you with all my heart and I'm ardently sorry. I hope you can forgive me and accept me back into your life because no matter what I will always be your one and only little sister. Maybe the next time you come down we can get together. Now I have come to realize that you only wanted right for me because you saw me as your little sister and I shouldn't have a boyfriend as yet to be washing and cooking for him. I understand you now and I took you wrong at the time. Anyway I'm getting older. I will be 18 soon, but I know in your eyes I will always be little. I understand.

REBIRTH

Marvin, I miss you so much, I feel deep down in my heart I was very close to you and now I feel so distant from you. I wish things were how they were when we were younger. I felt so happy and I hope for these times to come back one day, we can be home again like a nice family. I keep thinking of that and most times say to myself I am dreaming but I'm still hoping.

Mommy tries so hard with me and gives me everything. I keep thinking she doesn't deserve this from me. Look how successful you two turned out to be. Why couldn't I be Mommy's only girl to make her proud too? Well to me it is not too late because I know I can be a better person, daughter, and sister to you guys. Jus give me one more chance.

Anyway, I hope you two understand me and forgive me and just give me encouragement, love and support because I really need you guys at this point in time in my life. Bye for now. I hope you reply.

I love you, from your little sis.

Every word I read caused a sting in my eyes until, finally, the tears dropped on my laptop's keyboard. I was shaking as if it was freezing cold. My guilty conscience made me feel as if I should reply immediately, but I needed some time to gather my thoughts first.

A week later, the house was back to being occupied by only Deborah and I, and my days had gotten so quiet that it seemed as if I had rented my own apartment. My mother had returned to Saint Lucia, and Marvin and Tristy had gone back to their everyday lives. Their presence was missed instantly by the lack of echoes in the hallways.

Now that I had time to myself, I decided to respond to Marva's email.

From: Arnold Henry
To: Marva Henry
Subject: Re: Hey Marvin and Mario

I had to do a lot of thinking before responding to your email. Last summer what you did to me was unbelievable. I still cannot believe that my own flesh and blood can do this to me. Even when I got my stuff back I still did not believe it. I seriously did not want anything to do with you and I just never wanted to hear from you ever again.

But I realized that was not the way to approach the situation. I just wanted an apology from you and finally you decided to apologize. You really hurt me. But I accept your apology. You will have to show me that you are serious about this and you are making progression in your life with all that drugs vibes. Until then, I will be very cautious with you because I do not know yet if I can trust you. I am just being honest. I know what drugs can do to someone and it does not come and go just because you in rehab. It will have to take a lot of commitment from you. You have a lot of work to do. How can you even think drugs can help you with any situation that you were going through? Do you think that drugs help me or Marvin get a basketball scholarship? Did you think drugs helped me graduated from college? The obvious answer is, No! Drugs are never the answer.

You need to figure out what you going to do with the rest of your life after you become drug free. You need to stop using those drugs, or else you going to end up wasting your precious life. You need to turn to God because he is the only way. You need to go to church and ask God to come in your heart. You need to do something with your life, Marva. No one is going to figure out that for you. When I was in Saint Lucia, I had goals and dreams. You need to have the same.

I love you and I am happy that you are trying to become a better person. You have a lot of thinking and changing to do. Remember it is not going to be easy. You need to work at it. But keep the faith in God and never give up.

A misunderstanding is temporary; family is forever. I felt so comforted after I clicked the send button. From that moment on, I decided to put the past behind us and give my sister another chance. Soon after, I received a text message from my mother, which indicated her happiness at the news that I had reconciled with my sister.

Chapter 20

Promoted to Admiral

I still hadn't heard a word from my so-called manager/agent. With basketball opportunities out of my range, I was now contemplating between two other options: pursuing a master's degree or finding a job. I figured it was smart to at least get a job to earn some money for the summer. And, in the meantime, continue to play recreational basketball. I started to believe that in the world of competitive sports, basketball had already given me my greatest years. Perhaps my years played at the collegiate level were the peak of my basketball career. Possibly, I was at my prime during my senior year. I was dreaming a dream, and maybe, I should consider another profession. However, I wasn't ready to give up on my dreams.

One of the best things about receiving a sports scholarship was that, upon graduation, I had no student loans and no debt. All of my future paycheques would go directly into my Bank of America savings account. I just needed to find an occupation that would allow me to save up for my dreams.

I emailed my resumé as application to numerous job postings in Jacksonville. Day by day, I was beginning to realize that basketball might not be in my future. At the same time, finding a job was proving about as difficult as finding a pro basketball contract—until I received a phone call from Coach Mosley. "Hey Arnold, how are you doing?"

"Coach, I'm just trying to find a job," I replied, hoping he would sense the frustration in my tone.

"How about trying out for a professional basketball team?"

"Yeah, Coach. I really wanted to but I do not see that happening any time soon. I don't have money. I feel like I have no way of getting there, wherever *there* is," I replied, sighing.

"Well, Arnold, I have good news for you. They're starting a professional basketball team here in Jacksonville. You should go to the tryouts. It is only $70. The home games will be held at our own gym on campus."

"What? No way! OK, thanks Coach, I'm on it."

After finding out more information about the tryouts, I was hoping to seize the opportunity by making sure I was prepared. Since the school's gym was closed for the summer, I became a member of the YMCA, where I continued my strengthening and conditioning training. I was also able to play basketball with local competitive players. And when it was too late to catch the bus to the gym, I ran laps around the neighbourhood for at least an hour or two. By the time the tryout came around, I knew I was ready.

As always, whenever it came down to anything to do with my future in basketball, I always put on my best performance. Players from Jacksonville and surrounding areas showed up in large numbers to be part of something great. On arrival, we were introduced to James Easton, the African-American head coach who was just as excited as we were about professional basketball coming to the city of Jacksonville. Of all the players who showed up, only 12 were needed to fill the roster. I figured I had home-court advantage, and I was determined to outshine everyone in my path. On the bus ride to the house, I was confident I gave it my all.

"How did it go?" Deborah asked me as I entered through the front door. She was seated at her usual spot on the couch, elevating her feet like her doctors suggested after the operation on her toe.

"It was OK," I replied with an exhausted breath. "I think I did good. I hope I did good."

"So, that means you made the team," Deborah assumed.

"I have no idea. The coach will call me tomorrow. And then I will know."

"I hope you made the cut. I saw how hard you worked and I know how much it means to you."

Déjà vu, I thought. That brief episode I'd experience with Deborah reminded me of scenes from my past in Saint Lucia, where I'd came home from a basketball game to a suffering mother who was my biggest supporter.

After a shower, I laid on my bed. Immediately, I was trapped in my thoughts. *I think this is it. This could be a start of something good.* I truly believed that I had a great tryout because I focused on portraying my ability with defensive stops—something coaches always want in their players. However, I also tried to stress how good I am at teamwork. I attempted to reveal to the coaches my full potential and the benefits of having me on the team. *If I make the team, I will be able to capitalize on better opportunities. Maybe I could even make it into the NBA Development League. Maybe I could play in one of those European leagues. Or maybe, just maybe, I will end up achieving my ultimate dream of suiting up in an actual NBA uniform.*

The sound of my cellphone ringing pulled my attention away from my thoughts. *Hmmm, unfamiliar number.* I wondered who it could be, and decided to answer it even though I didn't recognize the number.

"Arnold?"

"Speaking. Wait a minute, is this," I took a deep breath, "Coach Easton? I thought I would have heard from you tomorrow."

"Yes, Arnold. Myself and the other coaching staff were able to pick out a few players. We are moving in a fast pace, because we already have a home game coming up next week."

"Oh, OK, Coach," I said, waiting to hear the more relevant news.

"Anyway, we've made a final decision and have selected the best players to be part of the Jacksonville Admirals. We would like for you to join us if you're up for it," Coach Easton said.

"Of course, Coach! Thank you very much for the opportunity. Yes! Yes! I'm in for sure!" I was so thrilled that Deborah probably overheard my excitement from downstairs. When I got off the phone, I personally delivered the good news to her. "Deborah, I made it."

"Oh, Arnold, I am so happy for you."

Since the opening of the season was fast approaching, practice was scheduled for the following day. Upon entering the gym, I was introduced to the members of the team, which included my teammates, the coaching staff, trainers, managers, and owners. At first glance, it was evident that the coaching staff had selected an athletic team with a fair amount of size. I quickly noticed I was not the only former player from Edward Waters College. The previous year's starting guard, who graduated with me, had also made the cut.

Practice commenced on time with everyone being punctual, stretched out, and ready to go. We had a kind of instant team chemistry that made it feel like we had been playing together since high school. Everyone acted like it was a privilege to be playing pro basketball, and, for that, we were all encouraging and supportive during our drills. From the jump, it was an intense session, and we realized that we needed to be team-ready for the first game of the season. I knew that a spot in the starting five was up for grabs, so I pushed myself as hard as I could. By the end of our first day, we were all pleased with our accomplishments. That night, I was so content to be part of a professional basketball team that I decided to write about it in my diary. I hadn't expressed my feelings in written form in more than two years.

Dear Diary,

Today, I am living the dream; my dream. I am considered a professional basketball player. I am the happiest man alive. I am part of the Jacksonville Admirals, a professional basketball team affiliated with the United States Basketball Association (USBA). We will be facing against other teams based in Georgia, Alabama, Tennessee, South Carolina, North Carolina, and Virginia.

I am so happy to be part of that new league that is forming in America. And even though we are not getting a salary like NBA players, it is nice to know that I will be getting paid to play. My teammates, our fans, and coaches seem to be excited, too. Today, we had practice and I can already see a championship-winning team amongst ourselves. I can't wait for tipoff to see everything unfold.

Apparently, I'd spoken, or rather, written, too soon. It was only a day later when every member of the Jacksonville Admirals was called in for an emergency team meeting. I arrived at the gym expecting to get geared up with my practice-ready teammates; instead, I joined everyone seated on the sidelines, waiting for our coaches to arrive.

"You know what's going on?" asked one teammate.

"I have no idea," answered a teammate to my left.

"Today is payday. We about to get a fat cheque," said the clown of the group.

A team meeting out of the blue? I put my head down, thinking to myself, *please, God, please do not let anything bad happen. I really need this team.*

A few minutes later, my thoughts were interrupted by Coach Easton's greeting.

"Thank you for coming here on very short notice," he said. As I looked around, I read the anxiety on the faces of everyone around me, even the rest of the coaching staff wanted in on the news. "I know your cheques were supposed to come in today, but we haven't received them. And I know some of you who came in from miles away were depending on the money." The sounds of annoyance were slowly building up. I was a bit confused.

"So, do you have any idea as to when we will get paid?" asked one player.

"We're still waiting to hear back from some people," Coach Easton replied. "Well, coach, thanks for the opportunity. I have been in similar situations like this. I have children to feed and I cannot waste my time here, practising and playing basketball for free." My eyes opened wide with shock and my mouth dropped after hearing the words of my fellow teammate, and silence took over the gym as he walked away. I turned to hear Coach Easton's next words.

"I understand everyone has their responsibilities," Coach Easton calmly continued. "I haven't even gotten my cheque either. We are waiting to hear back from the league's management. Apparently, the other teams haven't gotten their cheques either." It seemed like some of the more experienced players were fed up after hearing the same lame excuses. Two other players got up and exited the building like it was nobody's business.

"I cannot do it, coach," they all said before approaching the door.

By the end of Coach Easton's speech, I was the only player still seated in the same position. I continuously shook my head in disbelief. *Why me, Lord? Why the game I love so much is causing me so much heartache?*

A few days later, word on the street was that the USBA league folded due to financial struggles. I felt crushed. *What would come next in my beloved world of basketball? Was it time to simply let it go?*

Chapter 21

An Idea

So, Mario, why don't you write a book? My mother's words stuck in my mind on one deep and muggy summer day in Florida. A professional basketball league had just folded right before my eyes. A dream I could feel in the palms of my hands slipped through the tips of my fingers suddenly, turning into a horrendous, cruel awakening. I was feeling like a child who just had his favourite toy snatched away. *Was this confirmation that not all dreams can come true?* To make matters worse, I was unable to find a job in my field of study. Furthermore, I was given only an extra year on my F-1 student visa to remain and work in America before I would have to go through the difficulty of applying for a work visa. Optional Practical Training (OPT) was the term used to describe this process. One of the advantages of qualifying and undergoing OPT is that, after completing a 12-month training period, if my employer is satisfied with my performance, the employer could offer me a full-time position and apply to sponsor me. Otherwise, I would be without a visa and need to return to Saint Lucia; I was not ready to go back, especially during such tough economic times.

In addition to applying for advertised jobs, I also uploaded my resumé using the most popular employment websites, including careerbuilder.com and monster.com, in the hopes of being recruited for a position. Instead of opening my email's inbox to a capacity of job offerings, I was the recipient of the harsh realism of the depression—a new world that I was introduced to immediately after graduation. I recall stepping into locations that hosted job fairs alongside more than 10,000 new graduates, all of whom added to the increasing unemployment rates. All I got out of the job fairs were handfuls of useless pamphlets.

"You have to be patient," Deborah told me on a daily basis, seeing that I was becoming more depressed. She remained my support throughout being jobless. Without her, I probably would have been homeless, begging every passerby for a meal, just to survive in America. There is no doubt in my mind that God has disguised his angels as living humans and Deborah was proof.

With every situation I faced, I drew a valuable life lesson for myself as I wrote in my diary. *Whenever you get to the bottom of a hill, never forget what it took for you to get to the top, for whatever it was, you made it happen. If you are experiencing some downtimes in your life, understand that you are the same person who was at the top. The courage it took for you to get there will be 10 times better, because no one picks themselves up from struggles without learning a valuable lesson. Wherever you choose to go, be happy with the paths you take. Happiness is rich.*

I then realized that I needed to capitalize on all this free time on my hands. I was not going to allow the hardships of the economy to shape for me a future of pain and suffering. I needed to take control and construct a path that led to success.

I asked myself, *write a book?* It felt as if writing about my life would take the same number of years as it did to live it. The truth was that most people who have walked into my life have mentioned thoughts about putting their own life stories on paper, but they could never face it. Moral of the story, never put your words where your mouth is, rather, put your words, your ideas, your stories, on paper, and into action.

Write a book? This thought was replaying in the corner of my mind to the point that it started to form reality. *Stop being a lazy brat,* I told myself. I rose from my bed in search of all my journals that I'd kept since I was 10 years old. I figured, in order to recollect some of life's earlier events, I would have to relive these moments by reading my own words.

My advice to the world: no one can tell your story like you can, so tell it yourself; no one can write your story like you, so write it yourself. I turned on my computer, launched Microsoft® Word, and started to write my life away. Two minutes later, after completing only one paragraph, I shut down my laptop to fix myself for bed. Writer's block had me feeling like a baby who can't speak a word of English. I felt like the notion of me writing a book had been a horrible idea.

Chapter 22

Putting an Ex to My Past

We all have firsts in our lives, experiences with memories that linger no matter how many years have passed. For example, I am sure you can remember the first person who really took your breath away, that first awkward French kiss, and the ultimate first—the day when you lost your virginity. Unfortunately, I was too young to even guess the exact age I was the first time I had sex. I've sometimes wondered how my two-inch infanthood could have pleased some of the teenagers who had sexual encounters with me. *Or, did I? Was I even able to get a stiff? How did they get it in? Did I ejaculate?* For all I know, I was too young to understand the events that took place, but I think that my first sexual encounters happened between the ages of five and 10. Maybe I was younger, but I'm not entirely sure.

There had to be an explanation for my overactive sex drive and interest in having multiple sex partners. Writing was my personal psychologist, and it allowed me to study my fucking mental state and my behaviours toward sex. As an adult today, looking back at the context of my behaviour, I believe that the early introduction of sexual activity in my life played a strong role in my hyperactive sex drive. Then again, it could also be the genetic and hormonal makeup of a young boy's mind. Sex before marriage had forced itself on top of me, but I was not complaining. Not even the most active cougar had lived enough years to have gained more experience than me.

Although I was a very horny teenager throughout my secondary school years, I was not always active. I blamed my horniness on an unintended abstinence from sexual intercourse, at least without a partner. My friends used to tease me, saying that Palmela and Handela were the only girls I could fuck. My friends were right. And the best time to get a tight grip on Palmela and Handela were during those late-night shows that aired on Cinemax and HBO.

At that stage in my life, I had zero game when it came to scoring with girls, especially when it came to an intense infatuation for someone I thought was unattainable. My lack of game was probably exacerbated by my use of the Top 10 worst pickup lines ever used by a man. Acne and self-confidence issues were among the other factors negatively impacting my dating life. However, nothing lasts forever—ironically, those same words best describe my past relationships.

REBIRTH

By the time I was approaching the age for R-rated movies, I had gained confidence—and pubic hair. Women were somehow finding me attractive, but I felt like it had to do more with my ambitiousness. As a young adult, I understood that I was not fully fledged, but I wanted to attempt grown men things on my own. Since I had no father to teach me these lessons, I was motivated to learn them myself. For all I knew, women needed and wanted to be pleased by a man. And I intended to keep them coming back for more. I like to describe myself as a master in the art of lovemaking, and I had a specialty: the ability to vibrate my tongue, which was guaranteed to create a waterfall between a woman's legs. I was enjoying the lifestyle in all sorts of positions and locations, while exploring the limits to my fantasies. I have to admit, though, there were places I'd gotten down and dirty where God, or rather, the Catholic priest, never would have approved. I just hope I am forgiven for my sexual sins.

At 17, I topped my early bucket list by having sex with a female police officer on the lower bunk bed of the upstairs barracks of the Marchand Police Station. Did I say I fucked her inside the police station? The way I was up inside of her during the wee hours of the morning, it sounded like civilian brutality on a police officer. She had no rights to remain silent. I wondered if the prisoners were awakened by her moans as I stroked her with my baton. After our first night, she tried to handcuff me and throw me in for life.

I wasn't very far into checking off items on my to-do list, when I started to get involved in serious relationships. Whenever I made a commitment, my partners always asked me that same question, "How many girls have you been with?"

How many girls have I been with? I, too, have wondered and was never able to come up with a number. But here's something I've figured out—no matter how many years go by, the number of women I've been with will always be greater than my age. *Who knows?* I never kept track of the number. It was probably disgraceful to some but for me it was an addiction. Sex had been essential to my everyday living. I'm surprised that I didn't end up becoming a porn star.

It wasn't always about sex. I wanted to be loved—and to love without limitations. When I proposed to Alice on Feb. 14, 2006, I knew for a fact that I was ready to settle down with one woman for the rest of my existence. I was tired of chasing women. I started to believe in the possibilities of finding my soulmate. I could see myself walking into the sunset, carrying my child with one arm and holding on to my wife with the other hand. To make a relationship work, I needed to make some drastic changes to develop a team-building philosophy. I needed to understand that it took two people actively involved to build and navigate a strong relationship, to conquer and remain on the same paths throughout rough seas. I needed to understand if I wasn't on the same page with my partner, it becomes difficult to stay afloat in any weather. In a relationship, making compromises means you'll both be led on the same journey.

In my first book, I failed to mention how, a few weeks before I got down on one knee and asked Alice to marry me, she, too, was disloyal. On that day of heartbreak, she was gone for hours and didn't return to her dorm room until close to midnight. She later told me that she had been at her ex-boyfriend's house and had kissed him. Still, I did not hold it against her and proceeded to think that she was the one.

Frankly, down the road, I realized I was only fooling myself because I was stacking upon my insecurities. In fact, it was hard for me to move on with Alice in our long-distance relationship. My suspicion had led me to the finding of flirtatious emails in her inbox, which did not help any chance for our reconciliation in the future.

My trust in relationships was gone, so fake love became the weapon I used to get whatever I needed out of a woman. There were no actions and feelings when I said *I love you.*

After Alice, I dated a tennis player named Ina Durcakova, of the Czech Republic. We were both student-athletes at the University of North Florida (UNF). As always, the relationship started great, but Ina failed to mention that she had slept with Gallo, a basketball teammate at that time. I had to find out by eavesdropping on conversations in the locker room. My instincts proved correct that there was a lot more hidden behind Ina's innocent demeanour. I was not the type of guy to pursue a girl who had bounced around the basketball team.

Following Ina, there was Allie, another girlfriend I mentioned in my first book. My insecurities for her began in the early stages of our relationship. I'd suspected there was another guy involved. With Allie, I took another chance at a long- distance relationship, although the distance this time was shorter. My intuition was right. During a visit to see Allie, she admitted having sexual relations with a basketball player from the Vermont Frost Heaves. A few months later, she had an abortion, a tragedy that causcd me to raise my eyebrows. *Did the condom we used break? What happens when I'm back on campus at UNF? Was she still in contact with that pro basketball player? Was the baby mine? If so, why did she have to kill my baby?* If Allie ever decided to write a story about our relationship, she would describe all the times that I used her or took advantage of her kindness, as well as my infidelities. When I'm wrong, I will own up to it and admit I'm wrong. I was wrong for loving her, while, at the same time, having sex with every woman who opened her legs for me. She gave me all of her and I was too young, blind, and stupid to realize that was all I needed.

All the women I've ever slept with ought to consider this a confession: If I were to say that I never cheated on any of my other girlfriends, I would be lying. No further questions, please. I would not give anyone else the satisfaction of revealing where, when, and with whom. Two wrongs don't make a right. And in case one of my exes decides to read my story, I don't intend on reopening old wounds.

Often, I ask myself, *how can I ever trust my partner?* I've been in situations where the universe has supplied me with answers. Nyree Figueroa, who I'd met in Burlington, Vermont, through White Mike, was a prime example. Like me, Nyree was born and raised in Saint Lucia. She was actually the first female Saint Lucian I met in Vermont, back in December, 2004. There was an immediate mutual attraction from first sight.

The timing was off for both of us. Nyree came into my life when I was accused of a crime, and I walked into her married life—reasons that never prevented our urges for each other. I kept on questioning myself. *How can one get married and still be intrigued by infidelity? Nevertheless, who am I to judge?* I guess I wouldn't know until I was in a similar situation. For all I knew, we were both wrong.

One lonely winter night, Nyree decided to transition our online chat into an up-close and personal conversation; she needed the real thing, not cybersex. She picked me up at White Mike's house, which, you may recall, was my temporary home during my investigation at the University of Vermont. It was about 11 p.m. on a Sunday night and we were driving around in the cold in her SUV, trying to find an isolated location to park. I gazed at the twinkles in her brown eyes. Our heads converged like magnets. I closed my eyes. As our lips were about to touch, I noticed that Nyree was staring down at the steering wheel. She got shy after noticing the headlights from the oncoming traffic. She had better plans, though. "Let's go back to my place," she suggested.

"What? You kidding, right? Isn't your husband there?" I asked with wide eyes.

"Yeah, but he should be sleeping by now."

"Sure, let's do it," I said, thinking to myself, *anything to get between her legs.*

After a short drive, Nyree pulled inside her attached garage, leaving me behind until she indicated the coast was clear from the inside of the house. We crept through the darkness like thieves in the night to a guest bedroom on the second level. "Stay here," she whispered. "My husband leaves for work at five in the morning. I will come get you when he leaves."

I replied with an ounce of anxiety, "Uh, OK."

Throughout the night, insomnia overtook me, and my sweat had pooled and soaked through the bedsheets. About three hours later, I was startled by footsteps and the sound of a nearby door opening. The silhouette came into sight; I immediately covered my body, from head to toe, with the comforter. I held my breath as if I was a dead man in a coffin. The vigorousness and loudness of my heartbeat could have easily been heard in the hallway.

I am so dead. I am a dead man, my thoughts shrieked. I'd even decided to say a prayer. *Lord, if you can help me get out of this situation, I will not have sex again until I get married.*

"Arnold, he just left."

"Oh my fucking God, Nyree, you scared the shit outta me," I said, quickly standing to my feet while catching my breath. "Is he gone, gone?"

"Yes, he is. See for yourself."

Peeping through the nearby window's curtains, I noticed the sight of a man getting into a vehicle, confirming her answer. Seconds later, Nyree and I were no longer searching for consummation as our sexual milestone was fulfilled in the master bedroom. I had expected the experience to be hours of great, wild morning sex because my manhood was as hard as a bowling ball aiming for a strike. I was hoping she was wetter than a bucket, overflowing at the brim. Needless to say, after all the sinfulness, it was a match made in hell. The sex was such a waste of my time; for an older woman, she was as good as a virgin. Judging by her dead reactions, I felt like we were practising CPR. She killed my childhood fantasies of older women.

Throughout my years, I've realized that there is a thin line between a woman and a man. Whatever a man can do, women are capable of doing the same. What are manly things anymore? When it came down to unfaithfulness, today's society gives us many examples of women balancing out the scale of infidelity with men. So, if a woman was to call a man a dog for his cheating habits, today, a man can simply reply, *Who you calling dog, bitch?*

Why do women cheat? A better question is, why did some of the women I was involved with choose to feature me in their love affairs? What was I doing right that their men could not? I was only a college boy with a basketball dream.

During my last year at EWC, I had an opportunity to get into a relationship with a freshman by the name of Briana, an African-

American athlete involved in our school's track-and-field team. We dated for a few months. When my mother came to Jacksonville, I introduced Briana to both my mother and Deborah. Disagreements had caused Briana and I to go our separate ways. I never imagined Briana would marry her ex-boyfriend only months after we broke up. Less than half a year had gone by, and I found out about Briana from Coach Gallon, one day when I was working out at the school gym. I'd rebounded many balls during the course of my college basketball career, but this was the first time I found myself at risk of being the rebound guy. However, she must have been one confused girl, because we were still having sexual encounters after she exchanged vows. I assumed he was just not hitting it right.

Come to think of it, there was always someone in my life who was a friend with benefits. *What kind of lifestyle was I living? Why couldn't I just be happy with one person? One after another, when would it stop? Was I scared of something?* There always seemed to be an instant replacement to each girlfriend. Looking back, I think I was afraid of being lonely. Was it because I was a Mummy's boy and always needed to feel loved by a girl? Or, was it because I was still living a little boy's life and needed a woman to take care of me? Whatever it was, I had to grow out of it.

When one heart closes, another's heart opens—which brings me to Donna. I don't know how to refer to her, but we had something real. One thing was always certain: I always got what was never mine.

The first time I met Donna was at Square One's Martini Mondays, a nightclub in Jacksonville's San Marco area. The nightclub had a grown-up sexy scene with a live DJ playing top 40, hip hop, and R&B hits. I was wasted on discounted martinis, and flirting and dancing with two women when I noticed Ms. Silicon Chest across the dance floor. We connected faster than true lovers at first sight. From the get-go, my relationship with Donna was complicated. She was engaged to someone else, further contributing to my lack of trust and commitment with women. For the most part, it was strictly a physical relationship. Donna would creep away from home at night so that we could quench our sexual desires. Our relationship was best summarized through the lyrics of the song I wrote for her, simply titled *Complicated*.

Complicated

Why we had to make things complicated?
Get rid of your man, then take my hand.
Why we had to make things complicated?
If you like me better, give him back his ring.

Damn, girl, I see you looking so I'm looking back,
Picture-perfect lens made our eyes contact.
From the back of my mind, I knew you were shy,
So I approached you for a change.
One penny for a dime.
Baby girl and I had this instant connection,
No roaming fees, never had a conversation.
We were vibing, grinding on the dance floor, for sure,
Making love in the club like we've met before.
But things got strange when I noticed a ring,
A big rock on your finger,
I don't want to be a homewrecker.
I say, do you got a man?
You said, yes, I do. But I ain't happy with him,
So, please understand.

Why we had to make things complicated?
Let's make it better, then take my hand.
Why we had to make things complicated?
If you like me better, give him back his ring.

It took a lot of guts for me to write this hook,
So when you hear this song, please don't get me wrong.
I'm tryna get on that ass like baby phat jeans,
I'm tryna resist, but you're such a tease.
And I'm trying to please, but you're still with him,
All these complications, really fucking with me.
Remember when I ate you up so good in the kitchen?
You tasted so delicious, I had to get some seconds.
All these seconds, minutes, hours,
You spending with that nigga,
Really fucking with my emotions,
Feelings deeper than the ocean.
When I see you, it's like magic,

REBIRTH

When you leave me, it's tragic,
You and I, we are classics,
Burning flames, just like matches.
Remember when I told you Imma meet you halfway?
Well sooner or later, Imma fade away.

Why we had to make things complicated?
Let's make it better, then take my hand.
Why we had to make things complicated?
If you like me better, give him back his ring.

Chapter 23

Memorial Day, 2007

Life. *Why do our hearts beat if at any time they can stop? Why do we welcome people into our lives, knowing they hardly ever say goodbye? Are we destined to find our soulmates in one lifetime? Who are we to govern our futures? How many times do we have to pray to seek answers from God? Why do we fight to have it all, if, at the end, it becomes nothing for all?* Every decision that we make can change the course of our lives. Like a daredevil, our futures are all determined by the chances we take.

I've always appreciated the meaning behind America's annual traditional holidays, but two specific holidays—one Thanksgiving and one Memorial Day—gave different meanings to my life. In 1843, President Abraham Lincoln stipulated the fourth Thursday of November as Thanksgiving, a day to glorify and give thanks to our Lord. On Thanksgiving in 2006, I was thankful for a new relationship. On Memorial Day, which takes place the last Monday of May to remember the men and women who died while serving in the United States Armed Forces, in 2008, I was the recipient of a message that shattered my heart. Let me explain.

"Dawg, you've ever been to Chicago?" I asked my teammate and roommate, EJ, as we carried our luggage to the airport's security line.

"No, sir, my first time," he replied.

Coach Matt Kilcullen and the rest of the coaching staff were at the front of the pack, leading my UNF basketball team to the security checkpoint at the Jacksonville airport. While the coaches wore business suits, the players were all dressed up in our navy blue Nike warm-up suits. We were about to catch a flight to face the Northwestern University Wildcats of the Big Ten Conference.

"EJ! EJ!" I shouted. Did you see that?" An outburst of excitement tapped at his shoulders as I discreetly tried to get his attention.

"What? What?" he asked, as we slowly made our way to the front of the line.

I stood in front of EJ's six-foot-eight frame to block his vision. "No, don't look now," I said softly, pointing halfway through the line. "You see that girl over there, she keeps on looking at me, dawg."

"Wow, she looks good," he said.

I blushed, thinking, *yes, she is looking damn well good.*

"But I think she is looking at me, though," EJ joked.

I rolled my eyes. "Back off! She's mine!"

I kept my eyes on her until we were cleared security. When I least expected it, she looked back again, flashing a clean, pearly white smile. Since we had a few minutes to kill before boarding time, I wanted to at least say hi to her. I quickly put my sneakers back on and grabbed my luggage.

"Dammit, where did she go?" I asked, desperately searching in both directions.

"Calm down, there she is," EJ said while pointing. I wiped the sweat off my forehead, and there she was with her long, dark hair falling delicately on her back. Her skinny jeans fit snug, projecting a fine butt. She came to a standstill. *Maybe she was waiting to be approached by someone, maybe her boyfriend. Nah, she's just looking up flight information on the monitor.*

The idea of approaching her seemed easy enough in the back of my mind. However, putting these actions into reality was a psychological challenge. I was standing only a few steps away from her, but the distance might as well have been a mile—I felt as if I was walking on a treadmill, going nowhere fast. EJ had a smug look on his face, as if he was saying, there she is player, and you're scared to talk to her?

I took longer strides through the busy crowds, leaving EJ and the team behind. I chugged saliva down my throat and exhaled a wind of confidence. "Hi, excuse me," I said, tapping the beautiful, young lady on her shoulders. She turned around, and I could have sworn the next few seconds were in slow motion. She brushed her hair behind her ear, revealing a sparkly diamond earring. Her glossy smile shone brighter.

"Oh, hello there," she said with a welcoming tone. Usually, I'd assume, girls as gorgeous as her are arrogant and unapproachable. But her welcoming demeanour proved me wrong.

"You OK," she asked, snapping me out of my trance. I was awestruck by her flawless beauty.

"Ye, yeah, yes," I stuttered, choking before I could recite a catchy pickup line to make her beam. But my nervousness was already putting a smile to her face.

"So," I paused, trying to find the words. "Where you going?"

"Utah, to see my family for the holiday."

"So, um, you live here in Jacksonville?"

"Oh no, I'll be back in Florida, but I'm residing in Gainesville for now," she replied. "You? Seems like you play basketball for the University of North Florida."

"Yes! Yes!" I replied with enthusiasm. "How you know that? You've seen me play before?"

"It says it right there," she said, pointing to the logo on my chest. We both giggled.

"We have a game in Chicago on Saturday. Yes, I play for UNF basketball team. And yeah, I have an off-campus apartment here in Jacksonville."

"I hear an accent. Where are you from?" she asked with curiosity written on her forehead, barely revealing any wrinkles.

"If I tell you, you wouldn't know," I said.

"Come on, try me."

"OK, Saint Lucia."

"OK, you got me," she laughed. I chuckled along with her.

"It is a small island in the Caribbean. The most beautiful island ever."

She pouted. "Then, you're not going home to see your family for Thanksgiving?"

"Back home, we don't celebrate it in November. Besides, I am used to my family not being around. Coach said we'll have turkey dinner when we get to Chicago."

An announcement about her flight's first boarding call distracted her.

"That's me," she said, shrugging her shoulders.

"So, um," I looked away, "ca-can we keep in touch? I mean, you don't have to if you don't want to. I just feel like it will be good. You know, like I can say hi from time to time—"

"No," she replied.

I cleared my throat. "Well, it's cool. That's cool. It was really nice knowing you. I mean, it would have been good to keep in touch. I just wanted to be friends. Nothing serious, you know, like—"

"But I can take your number and maybe I will call you."

I blushed. "Maybe, huh?"

I quickly jotted down my Florida phone number on a piece of paper. "Hope I hear from you."

She continued, teasing, "Maybe."

With every step she took, her strides sounded with a click on the floor, reminding me of a model on a fashion show runway. Her hips alternated confidently and glamorously.

"You got her number?" EJ asked as we set foot onto the aerobridge.

"Yes, of course I got her number," I said, boosting my ego.

"What's her name," he asked.

I looked away. "OK, she didn't give it to me. But she took mine. I think she is going to call. I hope she calls. I don't even know her name."

Aboard the aircraft, I gazed at the screen of my cellphone several times before the captain finally instructed passengers to turn them off. There were no new text messages or missed calls from any unknown numbers. I thought to myself, *maybe she follows that three-day rule, where girls take a few days to contact guys they've just met.*

Usually, when I'm away for a basketball game, my focus is solely on the game plan leading up to game day. However, this woman had me strategizing ways to win her love. On arrival to Chicago, I desperately switched on my cellphone to discover a high-quality photo sent via picture messaging. She wrote, "Rebecca but friends call me Becca. What's your name?"

I was literally drooling over the image because she was even more beautiful in the photo. *She has to be some type of model or something,* I thought to myself. After responding to Becca with my first name, we continued texting back and forth, building the urge to meet again. And when my tireless thumbs were irritated from all the texting, we switched to phone calls. During our phone conversations, we both agreed that destiny has its way of connecting compatible hearts. We were convinced that this wasn't just a coincidental meeting at an airport.

We became friends on Myspace.com, where I instantly made Becca's top friends list. I was able to find much intriguing information while creeping through her profile page and photos. She was a model and had graduated from the University of Florida in December, 2005, with a bachelor's degree in health sciences. She was the total package—gorgeous and smart.

I was impressed with how Becca found joy in the simplest of life's offerings. She had a humble demeanour with the image of a supermodel. I also learned that she's obsessed with writing poetry.

Myspace Details

Here for: Networking, Friends
Hometown: Oregon
Body type: 171 cm/Slim/Slender
Ethnicity: Other
Zodiac Sign: Taurus
Children: Someday
Occupation: Grad Student/Sales/Model

Interests

General: Snowboarding, biking, hiking, fishing, running, skydiving, working out, modelling, spending time with my close friends and family, watching football.

Music: Jay-Z, 50 Cent, Fabulous, Eminem, Bob Marley, Tupac, Alicia Keys.

Books: Love, love, love, to read … everything! I must admit, I'm a sucker for Nicholas Sparks' books and a very guilty/quick airplane read would be Candace Bushnell … I also love books that deal with near-death experiences. Very intriguing to me!

Heroes: My Daddy, who is no longer with us.

Who I'd like to meet: "A great man, is one that can be a survivor, as opposed to somebody who is born into something and made a few right business decisions and has accomplished, what, money?" All people are Giants … They have the Potential to see beyond the hills, past the skies … and into forever. Just over there … beyond a road … beyond the horizon … I am waiting for caring, loyal and most of all true people. True to themselves and true to others. Remember, whenever you feel scared, there is always an Opportunity.

After a disappointing one-point loss to the Northwestern University Wildcats in Chicago, I found myself back in Jacksonville. Becca was running through my mind more than the suicides drills I had to run at practice. We were only a one-hour drive from one another, but our conflicting schedules kept us apart. Becca was busy with continuing her education in the nursing field and her modelling gigs, while I was busy with school and basketball. However, we tried our best to keep in touch by phone, text, and email. All we wanted now was to gaze into each other's eyes—a dream that seemed impossible.

After 10 minutes of giving Becca directions from the passenger seat, she pulled up in the parking lot of the Jacksonville Landing, located on the west end of downtown. "Where you directing me to, Arnold?" she asked, dithering while getting out of her car. I got out and I jogged over to the driver's seat, opened the door, and spread my arms wide.

"Trust me," I said. She did—without question.

We stood holding hands at the edge of a large pool, a few metres from the St. Johns River bank. In the distance, across from the neon blue Main Street steel lift bridge, is a series of skyscrapers. The moon reflected off the calm river waters. Becca leaned against the pool railing. "You expect me to dive in there?" she asked, gazing at the chilly, early December waters.

"Of course not, babe."

"So, um, what's next? You wouldn't bring me here to look at a pool full of water and coins. Oh, you want me to throw a coin in and make a wish?"

I laughed. "Just wait," I replied.

Then I looked at my watch and counted down the seconds to midnight. "Five, four, three, two, one—"

In sync, Becca jumped back with fear, nuzzling under my arms, as three pumps of the fountain pushed 64,000 litres of water in the sky per minute. "It is OK," I said, pointing out the series of colours generated by the neon lights inside the pool. "Take a look. It's just a water fountain."

"Wow, that is amazing," she said, finally overcoming her shock.

I felt content as I gazed into her eyes, where I could see the reflection of the fountain. I tucked her in closer under my right arm. As we embraced in the moment, I thought of new beginnings—not only with my basketball career, but a once-upon-a-time fairy tale with a happily-ever-after ending.

"They call it Friendship Fountain," I said. "You might think I'm crazy, but whenever I come here, it reminds me that I'm my best friend and I'm my worst enemy."

She caught my stare. "What you mean, Arnold?"

"Oh, it just means every decision I've made is the reality of every decision I make … whether it is good, or bad, I'm the only one accountable for it."

"Sort of like controlling your own destiny?"

"Yeah, sort of."

"You know, I've seen you before," Becca said, staring back at the fountain deep in thought.

"You have?" I asked, looking down at her.

"Yes, Arnold, I have. I've seen you before. You are the man of my dreams." Her eyes were telling the truth. I felt my heart hint to me, *is this love?*

"Oh, yes," I agreed. "It almost feels like I'm dreaming right now. Like I don't ever want to be woken up again."

Becca had agreed to drive to Jacksonville to spend a weekend with me. On the evening she called to say she was coming, I thought we would have a memorable evening at the Friendship Fountain—a long walk filled with quality conversation. This was one dream that felt so incredibly real. I wanted it to last forever.

Unfortunately, I was awakened by the sound of my alarm clock and, even worse, a devastating text message from Becca. It read, "Arnold, we need to talk."

"Becca, is everything all right?" I asked after speed-dialling her.

Her voice sounded brittle. "We cannot keep in touch anymore."

"What?" I screamed, forcibly eliminating the sleep out of my eyes.

"Wait, it is not you. It is me," she stressed. "I haven't been completely honest with you. This morning, my boyfriend."

"Your who?" There was a long pause. "Becca, what are you talking about. You got a dude?"

She responded under her breath. "Sorry, I meant to say, my husband. Yes, I am married."

"What? Why you didn't tell me?" I asked.

"Arnold, I am really sorry. I'm not happy in this marriage, and I just wanted to meet someone like you. But this morning, he found one of your Myspace messages you sent to me. And I am sorry. I cannot keep in touch with you anymore."

"Becca, wait, don't go. I deserve an explanation. You cannot just tell me this and expect me to never contact you again. Please talk to me."

"Arnold, I am sorry, I have to go. Please do not hate me. Maybe we will meet again in the future. If we're meant to be, then destiny will allow us to meet."

"Becca!" I screamed again, only to hear dead air on the other end. I called her phone a few times, well, for a few days, actually, but she never answered or replied to my messages. As I scrutinized her Myspace page, I noticed I was no longer in her top friends list. I had been completely erased out of her life in a matter of seconds. The only things she left me with were questions. *Why did she pursue me? What were her intentions with me? Why did she hide her marriage from me? How could something so wrong have felt so right?*

I had to go through my usual breakup routine—sleepless nights, heartaches, and being unable to eat—until I was able to refocus on basketball and school. A few weeks later, I was able to move on to establish a serious relationship with Allie, from Vermont, but you already know how that turned out.

Following my breakup with Allie, I thought life was moving along. But on Jan. 28, 2008, more than a year since I had any type of communication with Becca, I found myself missing Becca dearly. I wasn't able to control my urges. I wanted to hear from her. I wanted Becca to answer my "What if?" questions. *What if Becca got a divorce? What if she was never married? What if I had never sent her that Myspace message?*

Because I had erased Becca's phone number from my phone's contacts, I sent her a message on Myspace. I sought to rekindle our friendship, with the hopes that my message would cause no further harm. Minutes later, I was alerted with a notification of a new message from Becca. I was so excited, I even remember praising and thanking God. When I opened the message, my smile flipped upside-down. My mouth dropped as I read the message. My eyes stung and tears slowly descended down my cheeks. My body shivered, my stomach turned, and my fingertips and toes went numb.

Hello Arnold,

By your message, I assume that you were really good friends with Becca. I am sorry to be the bearer of bad news. Becca is no longer with us. She passed away on May 28, 2007 in a car accident. I am Becca's sister and I took over this Myspace page after Becca's death. We are all still devastated that she is gone too soon. She lived a wonderful life.

At first thought, I assumed it was Becca's husband playing a sick joke. So, I did some research to find out more information on Becca's death. I came across an online article that said: Rebecca A. Davis was killed on Memorial Day, May 28, 2007. She was only 26. She was driving southbound on I-15, near Provo, when she lost control of her vehicle and hit the centre median. The vehicle rolled over into the northbound lane. She was ejected from the vehicle.

That morning, while sitting alone in my room, I bawled my eyes out until I gained the strength to live with the fact that I will never see her again.

Rest in peace, Becca.

Chapter 24

Oh Canada!

Whether good or bad, there are always lessons to be learned from the people who walk in and out of your life. Have you ever heard of meeting all the right people at the wrong time? I find that life has its ways of introducing me to the unexpected.

By mid-summer, 2009, I was fortunate to have found a job at Florida State College at Jacksonville—assisting a professor in designing software to keep track of inventories in the college's laboratory. Unfortunately, it was only an eight-week program, and I would be jobless again by late July. With the money I had earned, I came to the conclusion that I needed to explore new environments, cultures, and relationships. With the budget I had in place, and a passport that only permitted me to travel to a few Commonwealth countries, a visit to Canada was at the top of my list. However, my real motive for wanting to visit Canada was the fact I had just reconnected with Julissa, an old-time friend who was now living in Toronto, Ontario.

Julissa and I had been friends on social media from the time I was introduced to virtual bonding. We've kept in touch through all the popular eras of networking sites, including Yahoo Messenger, hi5, Tagged, Myspace, and Facebook. However, MSN Messenger was our best means of communicating. Julissa and I would video chat until the wee hours of the morning. She often persuaded me to show off my six-pack abs, but she was quite the shy, innocent one in front of the webcam. She would never strike a pose for me, which left me wondering if she had Photoshopped her pictures. When we were tired of being on our laptops, we communicated through long-distance phone calls, vibrating the sound waves of the fusion of her distinct accent. She also had a Caribbean background, claiming she was from Saint Vincent and the Grenadines, located about 77 kilometres south of Saint Lucia.

My flight was booked and I was eager to go to Toronto. Julissa's expression blossomed into one of excitement the minute I shared the good news of my trip with her. I was also happy for the escape. Boredom had taken over my entire summer. Two weeks away from Jacksonville was exactly what I needed.

"I'm going to take a trip to Canada," I told Deborah after booking my flight with WestJet. Just like any other loving mother would do,

Deborah, who was sitting on the couch elevating her feet, expressed a few concerns.

"Where are you going to be staying? How long will you be there? Do you know anyone there?"

I joined her at the opposite end of the couch. "I have a cousin living up there, so I will be good for accommodations," I replied. "Her name is Shantal, and, just like in New York City, I should know a lot of Saint Lucians there."

Deborah was a smart lady. She figured out what I was up to, most likely by the glow of my smile. The late-night calls with the Canadian area code listed on her home phone bill were one clue about the new girl in my life. "You're going to see her, aren't you?" Deborah teased.

Blushing, I responded, "Who?"

"The girl you talk to in your room. Every night, I can hear you from upstairs."

Feeling slightly embarrassed, I replied softly, "Yes, I'm going to see her. Julissa. I met her online."

"Well, just be careful and don't leave any babies back in Canada," she joked.

I smiled. "Yes, of course not."

This was the second time Deborah gave me a ride to the airport because of a girl I had met online. The first time was when she dropped me off in a similar scenario. That time, I had flown to Vermont to meet with a young lady I met on AOL.

On July 29, 2009, as planned, Julissa, this time the real McCoy, picked me up at the airport. She was just as captivating in person as she was on camera. At first sight, I expected a magical moment, where she would run into my open arms, I would pick her up in a tight embrace spinning in circles, maybe even lock lips. But all I got was a hello and a haphazard hug. It was tough to take my eyes off her, though. Her leggings emphasized the best of her curvy physique, which made it nearly impossible for me to stop staring at her behind as she led the way to her car.

The first few moments of the drive to my cousin Shantal's house were spent listening to the lyrics of Drake's latest tracks, with some intermittent conversation. I noticed Julissa looking at me from the corner of her eyes with a scrutinizing stare. When I caught her peeking, she simply giggled.

"What?" she asked with a soft, cute tone.

"Nothing," I replied, shaking my head. The awkwardness had generated tension between us. Suddenly, I started to regret my decision to visit because I felt like Julissa wasn't showing me the same interest as she did over the internet.

"Is everything OK," I asked as she swerved onto Lawrence Avenue.

"Yeah," she replied, cutting her answers short. I thought, *maybe she needs more time to get used to me.*

Upon arrival to my temporary accommodations, I introduced Julissa to my cousin, whom I hadn't seen since my visits to Soufrière, in the Saint Lucian countryside, where she and Lucius's mother lived. Shantal wasn't able to stay long because she was only there to drop off the keys to her one-bedroom basement suite before rushing back at work. "You can use my room," Shantal said before leaving. "I will sleep at my boyfriend's house."

Julissa and I were now alone, and the awkwardness continued. We both sat at the end of the bed, facing the walls. "So, here I am," I said. She smiled. I reached for her left hand, gently caressing her brown skin. She pulled it away, making me feel like a stranger.

"Julissa, is everything OK? Thought you wanted me to be here for you." I began to sweet talk, saying genuine words from my heart. "I'm really feeling you and I am so attracted to you." I engaged with her hand again as we met face to face. We locked eyes, eventually accepting the forces that brought us nose to nose. I shut my eyelids, puckered my lips in a quest for a glossy kiss. Julissa intentionally grazed my lips, and then quickly stood up.

"It is getting hot in here," she said, fanning her face with her hand. I slowly approached her, planning to wrap my arms around her.

"Is there something you're not telling me?" I asked, stroking her black, shoulder-length, natural plaits.

"I can't do this," she said, turning her back toward me.

"Julissa, please, what's going on? I came all this way to see you. Why you're being like that?"

She walked away. "I think it will be a good idea if I leave now."

"OK, whatever," I said frustratingly as she left through the front door.

I sat down on the edge of the bed, fighting back tears, feeling lost. *Why should I ever trust another woman? How can someone be so cruel? Julissa could have easily told me that she was not interested in me. Why did she lead me on, all the way to a different country? All these late-night, long-distance phone calls, all the video chatting, and all this time wasted.* In addition to all that venting to myself, I remembered that my return flight wasn't for another three weeks. A few days later, after pressing for answers, Julissa finally admitted that there had always been another guy in her life—and things were just complicated. *Was I sad? Did I shed some tears?* Yes, the waterworks came down heavily. But I wasn't crying because it was over; I cried because it happened. Sometimes, it's as if I was born for my heart to be broken. Whatever we had was over and done. I was not about to let one disappointment lead to another, and I wasn't going to allow false hope to ruin my happiness.

Besides, with it being summer, I had arrived in Toronto during the best time of the year—at least the majority of Saint Lucians would agree. It was the week of Caribana—the biggest annual street festival reflecting Caribbean heritage and traditions of the islands, including Saint Lucia, Trinidad and Tobago, Barbados, Grenada, Guyana, and Jamaica, etc. The togetherness of Caribana was also a great way to meet people and reconnect with some former schoolmates, teammates, and old friends.

Since it was my first time in Toronto, I decided to link up with Chevy, a former classmate at Entrepot Secondary School. After graduation, Chevy moved to Canada, and I hadn't seen him since. Nothing had changed with my old pal, including his troublesome ways. I was reminded of the three-inch scar on my right forearm he gave me during a biology lab class. We were divided into groups to conduct an experiment that involved using a Bunsen burner, water, and chemicals. However, after the lab was completed, Chevy wanted us to keep experimenting. "Arnold, tell me if dat hot?" he asked me, pressing the end of the hot burner on my skin.

"Ouch," I screamed. "Chevy, wha' da fuck!" I shouted, covering the excruciating burning sensation with my hand. "Am gonna fuckin' kill you." It became a game of cat and mouse, as we rounded the lab's wooden tables and stools. My rage and loud cries brought out the fear in Chevy's eyes. To block my path, he shoved some stools in my direction.

"Arnold, chill," he cried out.

"You're a dead man," I shouted, hurdling over the stools. Chevy left the lab, sprinting toward the principal's office, and hid behind Madame Cadette, our vice-principal.

"Stop him! Stop him!" he shouted.

Back then, I really wanted to kill him. Now, we were able to laugh about it. In spite of this one incident, we remained good friends. Chevy now had dreadlocks running down his back and he still had a strong belief in black power, or rather, Afrocentrism. I used to think of him as Malcolm X reincarnated.

Chevy introduced me to many places in Toronto. The Caribbean diversity and dense population reminded me of New York City. I called Toronto the NYC of Canada. With the time I had left, I planned to make the trip worthwhile. Through Chevy's social connections, I was able to build new relationships with a number of Torontonians. I also connected with a few Saint Lucians who had made names for themselves in Canada, including Gilson Lubin, a comedian best known for his work with MTV.

The day I met Gilson, he shared all of the struggles he faced as a comedian. I learned that failures could become victories. For me, hearing someone else's challenges is one of the most rewarding things to experience. I am able to find even the slightest inspiration in every story. Have you ever dreamt another dream while dreaming? Even the dreams in your dreams can come true. To feel inspired to dream another dream, it is beneficial to surround yourself with fellow dream-setters.

During Caribana, Chevy came up with a marvellous idea for showcasing the talents of Saint Lucia. His show gave the audience a taste of Soca, calypso, hip hop, and comedy. It was an honour to witness such patriotism being displayed in a foreign country. I showed my pride by standing at the sidelines, waving my blue, yellow, black, and white flag for all to see.

The highlight of my trip actually came when I participated in the Caribana street parade, commonly known as the Grand Parade of Bands. On Aug. 1, 2009, I was half-naked, dressed in a purple costume, and masquerading in a Carnival band called the Toronto Revellers. Julissa and I had planned to enjoy this event together as a couple. Nonetheless, I wasn't allowing the loneliness to get to me. At the starting point, I chugged a bottle of vodka and orange juice. By the end of the parade, my camcorder and camera held the only memory of my stories. The footage and photos showed nothing but good times. Maybe I had nothing to regret about my visit to Canada after all.

Myself, Deborah, Kimberly and Mummy

Myself, Coach Mosley and Mummy

Third Quarter

Satisfy

Chapter 25

Instant Messenger

I looked at my life and wondered, what's next? I said it like I was preparing to overcome another stumbling block. *Is that all you got? Wouldn't life be so much easier if we could predict our futures? Have you ever been so depressed that you thought life was not worth living? Have you ever felt like you were destined to be something greater than your present state?*

I was a single, jobless 24-year-old *boy*. At that moment, the only accomplishment I was really proud of was graduating with a bachelor's degree, especially after my lengthy and hectic college basketball career. *But how useful was my college degree if it only looked good on paper?* The same logic seemed to have applied to my basketball scholarships. *How great of a player was I, if it depended on having a signed document?* Autumn was approaching, and I was still dependent on Deborah for shelter and food. She was one of the best things that ever happened to me. Without her, I would have felt the impact of the recession. To keep sane and motivated, I had to write, write, and write.

Dear Diary,

I was on my first page. Thought I'd written my last sentence. I got lost for words while stumbling upon my own past tense. So I held my ground to move forward to the next chapter. And got woken from a dream as reality presented my new character.

A blank white sheet of paper initiated eye contact with me like we were destined to be lovers. However, I couldn't cheat on life. 'Cause life, I really love her. At times, I question, how can I love life when that bitch played me for a fool, said it was gonna be easy on the first day I met her? Yeah, life's a bitch—an HBC, in fact. 'Cause whenever I manned up, pulled up my pants, and nearly broke up with her, she walked around like she's the head bitch in charge.

I wanted to end it all. One jump away to breakaway, I bet she would not catch my fall. A couple of more pills would seal the deal. There'd be no chance for CPR.

I was so close to seeing what's next after life. Probably paradise, cause I would have just escaped from hell. I got saved from what was written and I continued to write because I had tales to tell. For what is right 'cause I had nothing left. Not a penny to my name. Feeling like a homeless man, hungry for my next plate.

And still I write to overcome my wrongs. A word already written is history in my autobiography, and, moving forward, I can only learn by my faults. And still I write—not for myself but for who knows who?

Our life's course can change in an instant, often when you least expect it. People deliver new messages like couriers dropping off packages at busy offices. Traditionally, humans have five senses. Instant messaging can limit us from reaching our full physiological capacity for perception. Video chatting establishes sight and hearing, which helps us perceive compatibility. A simple conversation can evolve into a relationship. How far two lovers can go depends on the mindset of each individual, as well as their motives. Nonetheless, I believe fate had a plan for me.

On Nov. 8, 2009, it all started with a "hi" on MSN Messenger, followed by:

Arnold: Are you home alone?

Cho: I am always home alone.

Arnold: Aww, you don't feel lonely?

Cho: Not really. I am content. Not that I don't like to be with someone. Of course I do, but I am very picky. Have to be with the right one. If I can find that special someone, then I am happy, too.

Arnold: Yeah, I feel you. What's your type?

Cho: My type? Happy, not moody, honest, ambitious, clean-cut, kind, generous, loving, respect of himself and others.

Arnold: Are you done? Lol

Cho: No lol. Down to earth, have nice, fresh breath and clean teeth, and go to church with me. If I can have that, then he will be the luckiest man on Earth.

Arnold: OK cool. I can dig that.

Cho: Honestly, I don't need a man to take care of me financially, but I do need the emotional support that we all do.

Arnold: That's what's up.

Cho: So, who did you take off from Facebook to add me as a friend? I know you said that you reached the friends limit.

Arnold: Some guy I don't know.

Cho: Of course it is a guy. I feel so privilege now.

Arnold: LOL.

Cho: I didn't know what LOL was before. I thought it was lots of love. I think I like my version more. Lol, I don't think anyone knows it. Now you do. Are you just chilling out today?

Arnold: I'm just going to write. I got a lot of writing to do.

Cho: Music?

Arnold: No, I'm writing a book. Have you added my author page on Facebook?

Cho: No, not yet, but nice. Will be inspiration to lots of young people out there. Positive thinker, I like that. What is NCAA?

Arnold: National Collegiate Athletics Association. NCAA Division I is the highest level of collegiate sports in the U.S.A.

Cho: Impressive.

Arnold: Anyways, I would love to stay and chat but I have to finish Chapter 15 before tomorrow. I'm about to sign off from everything because it can be disturbing.

Cho: OK. Have fun writing. Love to read all about it along the way and the end product. Talk soon.

Arnold: Thanks, babe. Goodbye.

It was the beginning of a new, I'm-never-going-to-learn, long-distance relationship. I was back on the internet searching for all the wrong kinds of love in Canada. I'd met Cho Kim Wang online earlier in the year. For some reason, we'd lost connection on Facebook. Eventually, she'd typed herself back into my life. I was intrigued that an Asian woman was interested in me.

The following day, I caught Cho online. It was 6:20 p.m. when we started video chatting.

Arnold: How are you?

Cho: I am great. Back at work today. Work tomorrow, then the office is closed on Wednesday for Remembrance Day in Canada.

Arnold: That's cool.

Cho: You have nice teeth.

Arnold: Thanks. Are you a dentist?

Cho: I am a dental hygienist. If you are here, I can clean your teeth lol. Do I look 43?

Arnold: No, beautiful. How tall are you?

Cho: I am only 5'2". I am very small.

Arnold: Wow. I'll be a giant next to you. You think you can handle all of that?

Cho: Then, I will feel safe beside you. No one dare to come closer to me with you around. You can be my personal bodyguard.

Arnold: Lol OK.

Cho: Did you manage to finish that chapter yesterday?

Arnold: No lol. I got a lot of work done, though.

Cho: At least you accomplished something. Do you have an idea when you want to finish your book? You could come here and write.
Arnold: You think that's gonna help?
Cho: Maybe.
Arnold: Why's that?
Cho: I can take you up the mountain. I just thought the fresh air will do you good. Better for thinking. Unless you have other things in mind lol.
Arnold: Lol.
Cho: Lots of love? LOL. I think new environment will do you good. And the mountain air is always refreshing.
Arnold: And new race ;)
Cho: Sure, absolutely. I'll treat you well. You still have a few chapters to go. Think about it.
Arnold: Well, I have a lot of writing to do.
Cho: I'll have you longer then LOL. How's the job prospect in the U.S.?
Arnold: Horrible. No work.
Cho: Maybe better here. In computers?
Arnold: Yeah. How far you live from Toronto?
Cho: 3.5 hours flying time.
Arnold: Oh damn. That's far.
Cho: I am up above Montana.
Arnold: So your ex is nowhere in sight?
Cho: No.
Arnold: OK, good. Now I feel safe to come there.
Cho: You don't have to worry about the ex. Even if he lives in the same city. Once it is done, it is done with me. No turning back. And I am not cheating so why should I care? He had his chance and he blew it. I was so good to him.
Arnold: You're not cheating. What you mean?
Cho: I don't cheat. When I am with someone I don't care how far he is. I don't sleep with others.
Arnold: That's good. Are you freaky? lol
Cho: Well I am very passionate in bed. But I don't know about freaky.
Arnold: I like that. Well, I am very freaky. I love to please, too. I'll do anything to your body. Anything!
Cho: Pleasing is not freaky.
Arnold: So you know what freaky is then? lol. Do you have a wedding ring on?
Cho: Just my fashion ring.
Arnold: Hmm ... OK.

Cho: It is not a wedding band. Although it has diamonds. Sometimes I wear on the other hand so men won't ask me if I am single.
Arnold: Oh lol.
Cho: And I don't like to be asked by my patients.
Arnold: So where is your ex-husband?
Cho: He is in another city as well.
Arnold: How far?
Cho: 2 hours flying time. And my son is with him.
Arnold: Oh OK cool. I just don't want your ex interfering with me lol.
Cho: Funny. No ex.
Arnold: OK lol. So, is it hard to find a job in Calgary?
Cho: Not really. Are you contemplating on coming here?
Arnold: Maybe.
Cho: I know that in Canada, especially in Calgary, job prospects are more favourable than in the U.S. Calgary is a booming city. Oil and gas. Rich province.
Arnold: Oh, that's cool.
Cho: What do you do on Sundays? You go to church?
Arnold: Yeah. You?
Cho: Sunday, I start my day with 7:30 mass. I go to church early. After that, I can do whatever I want. But mostly I do laundry on Sundays and take a drive to Banff if the road is good. I am not a party girl.
Arnold: OK that's cool. So no guys give you TLC?
Cho: Tender loving care? No, I go for professional massages.
Arnold: Aww.
Cho: The only man in my life right now is my son.
Arnold: And me? Lol.
Cho: Yes, of course. My son don't live with me so every year, my ex and I alternate year with my kids. So, this year, he is with his dad. But since my daughter is away, he doesn't want me to be alone for the holiday.
Arnold: Oh OK.
Cho: So my son is coming here after Christmas to be with me for a week. He'll be spending Christmas with his dad but New Year's with me. We are going to the hockey game when he is here. And maybe dogsledding up in the mountain.
Arnold: That's cool.
Cho: You look confused.
Arnold: Yeah, dogsledding? You do that.
Cho: Yes, on snow lol.
Arnold: You're like an outdoor person. Seems like you like the wild and nature.

Cho: Yes, I love it. I feel free when I am out there with nature.
Arnold: Where did you go? Phone?
Cho: Yeah, my university. Think they called for donations and gossip. Sorry, I won't pick up the phone anymore. Where were we?
Arnold: You were teasing me lol.
Cho: LOL you want?
Arnold: Hell yeah. You shy?
Cho: Modest. I think we were talking about how boring I am.
Arnold: I think you were seducing me.
Cho: Do I need to? I don't need to seduce you to get you hot.
Arnold: Do you like to be on top or bottom?
Cho: Doesn't matter. Top, bottom, side. I am very flexible.
Arnold: Hmm. Do you love romance?
Cho: Of course. Romantic fool to the core. I love tenderness. Do people still believe in that? The loving and the tenderness. Life is too busy and people do lose sight of the good thing. Everything is a rush.
Arnold: I do. You so sweet.
Cho: Yeah. Instead of going out, I much rather stay home by the fireplace and snuggle to my loved one. Perhaps, massage each other's feet or just lay still. Even just to hear the beating of his heart.
Arnold: Awwwww. The guy that left you was a fool.
Cho: Well he likes the fast life. I was here waiting for him and faithful to him while he was in Toronto out partying every weekend and some weekdays. But he is not my concern anymore. To be honest with you, my life only evolves around my children and whoever the love that is in my life. My career, too.
Arnold: Kool.
Cho: I talk too much.
Arnold: It's OK babe. I enjoy talking with you.
Cho: I am old-fashioned when I am at home. I am very independent outside of the house.
Arnold: OK, I see that. You doing your thing.
Cho: I like to think that I should not be dependent on the man but the two of us taking care of one another.
Arnold: True.
Cho: My ex-husband told me that he wanted me to be independent because he was worried about if anything ever happened to him that I can survive on my own and take care of our children. It was a good lesson for me to learn. And when I left him, I went back to university. It was a struggle but I did it on my own.
Arnold: So, are you stable now?

Cho: Of course. Now, I am financially independent. You do not want to know how much I make. I have everything I ever dream of. But to have someone to share it with is awesome too.

Arnold: Aww, that's awesome. I am proud of you. I'm trying to get like you.

Cho: Just be patient and believe in yourself.

Arnold: Yeah, I'm being patient. My time is near. I'm working hard. I'm very ambitious.

Cho: I'm planning to get this house paid off in nine years. When I left my ex-husband, I had nothing, not even a job. And he had his master's. Tough times don't last but tough people do.

Arnold: Yeah.

Cho: Sorry, I bored you.

Arnold: Oh no babe. You make me happy.

Cho: I like to give you some insight into my life and perhaps it will give you some inspirations. Believe that there is light at the end of the tunnel.

Arnold: I would love that.

Cho: Let's just hope it is not an oncoming train.

Arnold: Lol.

Cho: Thought I'd lighten up the conversation.

Arnold: It is already 11:33 p.m.

Cho: Have you eaten yet? You better get to bed.

Arnold: No. I needed to go but I didn't want to leave you.

Cho: We'll talk again tomorrow.

Arnold: OK, cool. As much as I want to stay, my belly is crying for food.

Cho: OK. If you are here, you can eat with me. I can cook. You better cook since you are living on your own.

Arnold: Oh no, I don't live on my own. I'm here with my aunt, Deborah.

Cho: Spoil lol. Your aunt cooks for you?

Arnold: Sometimes, but she left for work. She's an LPN.

Cho: Nice. She works at night?

Arnold: Yup.

Cho: But you should go and eat. I don't want a grown man starving to death lol.

Arnold: Lol. OK, baby. Muah.

Cho: See you. Not goodbye. Just see you soon.

Arnold: OK, see you later ☺.

Cho: Kiss and hugs.

Chapter 26

Another Long-Distance Relationship

What exactly defines our love for each other? Is there a time limit for when two hearts meet? How can one's love be replaced by hate? I ask myself these questions on a daily basis to allow me to seek out the answers in all manner of possibilities. This might just be the beauty of life. We just never know what to expect when connections are made.

On Nov. 20, 2009, I found my heart trapped in yet another long-distance relationship. Or, was it real love? Despite having limitations on how we could interact, Cho and I were becoming an everyday event. With how fast strings were being attached over wireless internet, it seemed like we were quickly finding cyber love. I caught Cho online after a day shift at my seasonal Thanksgiving job at HoneyBaked Ham.

Cho: How was work?
Arnold: It was so long. I worked 12 hours today. My feet are killing me.
Cho: What do you do?
Arnold: Oh, it is just a job for the holidays. I just sell ham.
Cho: If you were here, I would run a hot bath for you and give you a massage with rubbing oil.
Arnold: Aw, you're so sweet. I would love that.
Cho: I'll love you like you have never been loved. I think love is the most wonderful thing when it is productive love. Unfortunately, most people have dysfunctional love. People stay in a relationship for the wrong reasons. When I see dysfunctional love, I get scared. I much rather be alone.
Arnold: OK. I understand. You got a lot of love.
Cho: I am sorry if I said something wrong.
Arnold: Oh no. You didn't.
Cho: You are welcome to input your feelings, too. This is how we can get to know each other.

Twelve days of constant instant messaging was only building the urge to see one another. The emoticons of MSN Messenger were insufficient to illustrate my dirty intentions. Falling in love was already on Cho's agenda. If we were playing a game of hide and seek, her love would be easy to find. While she did most of the typing, I found myself wondering what she found so thought-provoking about me. I was so out of her league; or rather, I played the rookie, while she took on the role of the veteran. She bragged about being an established, mature career woman who works in the dental industry and makes a six-figure income. And even though she had a son and a daughter with her first husband, she lived alone in a three-bedroom, three-bathroom house with a double-car garage. Cho claimed that she had everything she needed, except for a lover with whom to share life's milestones.

Meanwhile, in a land hundreds of miles away from Cho, I was strategizing how to juggle multiple women. I had no sympathy for a monogamous partnership. There was an X marking the spot to my heart and whoever desired to dig would not discover any treasure, but, rather, confusion buried inside pain and suffering. Deception was hiding deep within my soul. I just wasn't ready and I was ashamed to face the truth, so I continued with my womanizing ways as a form of survival. I tried to keep my actions a secret. Unfortunately, old habits die hard. I disregarded the fact that someday all of this would catch up to me, or I would catch up to it.

Cho knew little about my lifestyle or my past, yet she acted like I was the man for her. I carried so much baggage that it was becoming too heavy to carry and needed dumping. It contained all of the women who met my desires in the Sunshine State and in every country stamped on my passport. These women understood that commitment was our nemesis, and they understood the roles in our relationship. Pursuing Cho would mean I'd have to give all that up. Another piece of baggage came in the form of Melainie, a woman from South Carolina who had a hard time keeping our private lives private. Melainie and I had had two sexual encounters during her visits to Florida, but she treated me like we had plans to get married. While our long-distance relationship continued, Cho was becoming suspicious and insecure about my Facebook activity. "Just dropping by to show you some love," Melainie had posted on my Facebook wall a few days before Christmas in 2009. What I thought was a harmless comment was a stab to Cho's heart, and I saw, for the first time, how feisty an Asian woman could become.

Arnold: Why you keep on asking me questions about my friend?
Cho: What friend?
Arnold: Melainie.
Cho: If you want, I am not going to say anything anymore. I am sorry to bother you so much.
Arnold: I'm just saying that you worry for no reason. She knows that I'm in love with you. She knows that she cannot have me no more. We are still friends and that is all.

Cho: That doesn't mean she doesn't still try. Especially if you still talk to her.

Arnold: She is not trying. I will talk to her! I don't want to break off our friendship because she has been a great person to me. When no one was there, she was all I had. She is a friend for the last time.

Cho: She won. She can have you.

Arnold: She won what?

Cho: There is something going on. You deleted that Facebook message.

Arnold: I deleted it because I didn't want you getting upset for no damn reason.

Cho: I don't want to know anymore. You can have whoever you want. It is very painful for me to see your wall to wall with her. You guys actually publicly displayed your love for one another on the Facebook wall for everyone to see. And I am here trying to keep our lives private.

Arnold: There is nothing going on between Melainie and I.

Cho: I have to go.

Arnold: Bye!

Cho: My heart is tight.

Arnold: You're so weird.

Cho: I cannot breathe.

Arnold: Go run away.

Cho: You took me off your Facebook.

Arnold: You need to stop trying to create false problems.

Cho: I'm just feeling cold all of the sudden.

Arnold: You are overexaggerating for no reason. You need to stop it. I'm in love with you and only you. I don't want no one else. I'm happy with you. I won't go back to anyone else.

Cho: Well if you just told me the reason why instead of getting defensive about it then it would be OK.

Arnold: You are my only option.

Cho: You said if I have any question, just ask my man and I did.

Arnold: But it is not the first time you asking me about it when I've already told you that she is a friend now.

Cho: I love you.

Arnold: No one can make me change my feelings for you.

Cho: I am in love with you.

Arnold: You are my No. 1 because you are my champion.

Cho: I love you and no one else. I guess I am just feeling a little sad without you. I should be used to being alone.

Arnold: You alone? If you alone then I don't exist.

Cho: I guess I am never alone as long as I have you and your love. I love you so much. I did not anticipate falling in love with you. Now, here I am helplessly and hopelessly in love with you.
Arnold: I am here and I ain't going no where.
Cho: I have so much plans for us and yet I am scared. I don't know how to date, you know.
Arnold: Well, I am here and we can do it together. I can show you how to do anything that you can't. Even sex lol. I will be there for you no matter what.
Cho: Just be loving to me, honest with me. I would love you above all. I would die for you. This is the reason why I don't like to fall in love. Being a devoted and passionate person is my weakness but also my strength. Sometimes it can fall into the wrong hand and I am doom.
Arnold: You will be so happy when we finally get together. You are worrying too much now.
Cho: I will love you like no one ever loved you before. I know things will be better once you are here.
Arnold: Yes, baby.
Cho: I am sorry for everything.
Arnold: It is OK, baby.
Cho: Don't put me back on your Facebook, OK? I don't want Facebook to be the reason that we fight all the time. I could write on your wall and let people know that you are mine but I did not. I am a very shy and private person. You don't know women's mind like I do.
Arnold: Yes, I know about women's mind, too.
Cho: Women are mean creatures. Why do women sleep with married men? To humiliate the wife.
Arnold: Lol.
Cho: People know I am on your Facebook that is why some of them wrote some nasty comments because they know I will be seeing it.
Arnold: I don't think people know you on my Facebook lol. Unless they see you. Are you a jealous person? Yes or no?
Cho: That is the unknown that I am afraid of.
Arnold: I think you are!
Cho: Yes, but not to the point I am going to humiliate myself.
Arnold: If you are a jealous person, then we will have problems.

Famous last words, I think they'd say. Day by day, whether it was positive or negative, I was starting to get a glimpse of what to expect as I moved forward in a relationship with Cho. Rather than just rediscovering dating, it seemed like she was looking to jump into another marriage. She saw a husband in me before she got to know the person I was. On the other hand, I was more attracted by the stable environment that she built in Canada, especially when she bragged about her financial freedom. She would say, "I don't need a man to take care of me. I can take care of myself. I make my own money. I just want someone I can share it with."

At first, I thought all that money talk was Cho's charming way of capturing a man's attention. But I later found out, she would think nothing of wiring me hundreds of dollars. Quite frankly, her money was more convincing than the maturity of our affection for each other. We claimed we were in love before we even held each other's hands. On Dec. 31, 2009, our online conversation reiterated my migration to Calgary. I was ready to face the next phase of my life.

Cho: Baby, you make me the happiest woman alive. I will always appreciate you.
Arnold: And I will continue to do so for life.
Cho: And I am, too. Love you for eternity. I am so looking forward to spending the rest of this journey with you.
Arnold: I will make you so happy. You are going to hate that you didn't find me earlier in your life.
Cho: If it is fate, we will find each other eventually. Perhaps then, you were not ready for me. That is why God has given you to me now. We have to live and learn how to appreciate love. That is why we have to go through so many bad relationships to appreciate the better one.
Arnold: True.
Cho: I never give up on love. I don't take love for granted. You are here with me now and I am going to spend every moment loving you for the rest of my live. Better late than never, right?
Arnold: Yes, baby.
Cho: You will be the best husband alive.
Arnold: We are destined.
Cho: Six days and you will be here. I am anxious. I feel like a kid in a candy store.
Arnold: Lol.
Cho: Everyday I come to work, I would say 10 days, nine days, and yesterday, I said one week. People must think I am nuts or something.
Arnold: Lol.
Cho: I am very easy to please. I don't ask for much. Just love and respect.
Arnold: OK.

REBIRTH

Cho: I love you and I know you will bring me joy. But it is important that you feel the love from me and that I bring you joy, too. I believe in us, baby.

Arnold: Baby, we will be fine.

Cho: Everyday I am falling in love with you over and over again. I will forever be in love with you. This will be the longest six days of my life.

Chapter 27

Goodbye, America

Before departing for Canada, I had one last opportunity to say my goodbyes to the women of my yesterdays. I was being discreet with them about the reason for my move. And I don't meant to sound vain, but I believe they're still waiting for me to return to Jacksonville.

A long connecting flight had become even longer after I claimed my luggage at the Calgary International Airport. "Saint Lucia, huh? What brings you to Canada?" asked an immigration officer, while he flipped through the pages in my passport. I cleared my throat, placing my two pieces of luggage on the ground. "Um, I came to see a friend."

"Who is your friend? A girl, a man?"

"A lady," I replied softly.

"How long do you know her for? Where did you meet her?" he asked. There were no signs of amusement as he awaited my reply. I stood motionless, hoping he wouldn't spot the nervous sweat dripping down my face.

"I met her in Saint Lucia in May. She was on vacation." He alternated his stare between my eyes and on my American student visa, pinning his thumb on the page to prevent it from flipping. "You have an address and cellphone number for your friend?"

"Yes, of course. Here it is."

He then pointed across the floor. "Can you please wait for me in this room?"

"Sure," I said. I was escorted into a nearby room that made me feel like I was sitting inside a courtroom waiting for my sentence from a judge. Fifteen minutes had gone by, and I could feel wrinkles forming on my forehead. Through the windows, I could see that the other passengers on my flight were long gone. I was locked up in the isolated room with a man who could have passed for Osama bin Laden. Five months ago, I didn't remember having so much trouble when I entered Canada through Toronto. *What is going on? Why is this taking so long? Maybe I shouldn't have carried so many clothes. Maybe I shouldn't have lied.*

Travelling to Canada to visit a friend? As a non-resident of North America, I was once told to never, ever tell an immigration office that I was crossing a border to see a lover. Otherwise, I would be returning to where I came from as fast as I got there—which, in my case, would mean I'd be sent back to Saint Lucia. My student visa would no longer allow me to cross the U.S. border. In addition, I was too embarrassed to mention that I was there to visit someone I met through Facebook.

I felt shaken up in the isolated room, but it gave me time to think about the choices I've made in life. I flew to Canada with no intentions of returning to the Sunshine State. I had finally been offered a full-time job as an educational advisor at a community college in Florida. The job would have started at the beginning of the 2010 spring semester. I would be giving that up, too. I kept thinking about how quickly I had fallen for Cho. It was even clearer that, within a few more minutes, I was about to disembark from the two months of virtual reality, to arrive at a real sense of Cho's love.

Deborah, too, had known of my intentions. "Take care of yourself, my son. Don't forget to save up some vex money. And if she causes you any trouble, I will make my way up to Canada to kick some butt," she jokingly said to me the day I left.

I laughed at her jokes. "You will always have a home here in Jacksonville. Don't forget that," she added.

As soon as Deborah was no longer in sight at the airport, I felt the same as when I said goodbye to my mother in 2003—letting go in pursuit of becoming a man.

Maybe the roadblock by the immigration officer was a sign that Cho and I weren't meant to be. Was this true love? Earlier on my flight, I had a dose of what real love should entail, or so I thought. Jodi was my seating buddy on our connecting flight from Dallas, Texas. She shared a movie with me, and also shared her amazing Facebook love story. Jodi was an older Caucasian lady, returning to Calgary after reconnecting with her long-time friend, Bob—a man she hadn't seen since she was a teenager. Jodi and Bob caught up over Facebook. I found it fascinating how two old friends lived their lives separately for so many years, but were able to find one another and build a life together. During that plane ride, Jodi's contentment, expressed through her smile, painted a masterpiece. The twinkle in her eyes portrayed the love she felt for Bob. Their story was the spot-on example of the most popular breakup words, *if we are meant to be, then we will reunite again in the future.* Their Facebook shows that they are now married.

"Arnold Henry?"

"Yeah, yes, sir." I jumped out of my seat. I was guided back to the immigration officer's station. He was still looking through my Saint Lucian passport, but his facial expression was one of amusement.

"Why did you have to lie?" he asked. I replied with a silent smirk. "I spoke to Cho. You're free to go." He stamped my passport with the admittance date, Jan. 6, 2010.

"I am?" I cleared my throat, scrutinizing the stamp. "I mean, thanks, thank you."

"It is OK to meet people on Facebook," he joked, shaking his head. Instantly, he regained seriousness, jotting a date with his pen. "You have to leave the country on Jan. 31. Understood?"

"Yes, sir. Of course," I replied.

The weight was lifted from my shoulders. *I really have to check my underwear for shit stains.* My thoughts were abruptly interrupted when I looked up and saw Cho standing there in the flesh. There were no more keyboards between us, no more monitors, and no more internet connections. Only a few more steps, and we would be walking together on the same paths. As Cho approached me with a shy stare, I inhaled to the start of a new life. The warm coat wrapped over her tiny body gave me a quick idea of what to expect in terms of weather. Cho stood to my chest, with her long, black hair almost touching her buttocks. Seeing her in real life made our age difference more apparent. She was twice my age; however, for someone almost in her mid-40s, Cho sure looked good. She wouldn't reveal details of her dental work, though. "What did the immigration officer say?" she asked furiously as I reached below my normal hugging radar.

"Well, he said that I have to leave the country at the end of the month. He stamped my passport with the expiry date."

She sounded annoyed. "You shouldn't be messing around with these immigration officers. He was going to send you back on the plane. You're lucky he called me and I told him the truth," she snapped at me as we walked in the chilly winds to a nearby parking lot. *She gets mad easily,* I noted to myself.

The warmth from the black Honda Civic gave insight that I had to get used to the white frozen rain falling from the sky. The 30-minute drive from the airport in northeast Calgary to her house in the southwest had given us time for the tension to ease, and for us to accept the fact that we were now united as one. Although I had an expiration date stamped on my passport, I really didn't know how long I would be staying in Canada.

Chapter 28

Now I'm Loving Life?

Cho was a living inspiration when it came to being ambitious, goal-driven, and not allowing the past to determine the todays. She was born in Kim Chau, in southern Vietnam, on Dec. 2, 1966. During that time, there was an ongoing war that forced Cho and her family out of their homes and businesses due to the invasion of North Vietnam. To escape from these harsh conditions under the new Communist regime, Cho and her family had to make long, risky trips on overloaded boats to refugee camps. I was told that not everyone made it out of the country alive. At an early age, Canada became her new country, where she got married and had two children with a Canadian. After her divorce from him, she put herself through university and dental hygiene school.

With the limited time that was given to me to stay in Canada, Cho and I had no option but to skip our first date and cut right to the chase. The lust we had for each other was uncontrollable. On my first night in her king-sized bed, we went straight for third base, engaging in a night of physical and emotional connection. We slept into the following day. Breakfast was served in bed, and I grasped that Cho was happy to cater to and romance her man. She instantly made me feel welcome, like I had just returned home to my lover after a long absence.

I rose from the bed, ready to explore my new surroundings. Cho was right when she said that a drive around the city showed that Calgary was a developing city filled with opportunities. Having a visitor visa meant I'd have to continue living the same bum life as I did in Florida, where I was dependent on others for my own survival. It was stressful being a foreigner in a new place again. Early on, Cho made me feel at ease about my dependency on her. She had told me that she had enough money to feed her family, while still being able to take care of herself. It almost felt like I was being persuaded into this better lifestyle for her contentment. Cho had taken over Deborah's catering role, leaving me feeling like less of a man. I couldn't help that I was new to a country where I was unable to legally work.

As far as my happiness, Cho knew that I was still hanging on to my dreams to become a professional basketball player. She showed support by paying my gym membership at the YMCA, where I would spend my week training while she was at work. She understood if I were to get a contract in Europe, I would leave her behind to pursue my lifelong dream.

My workouts started at five in the morning. By noon, I was back at the house, kind of like a hired house-sitter. Cho called the house from her work phone many times throughout the day to check up on me. With no friends or family in the area, my days had become long and boring. Cho had a high admiration for photography, and the fully furnished house was neatly decorated with a lot of portraits on the walls. The other bedrooms were still filled with memorabilia from her son, who was living with his father in Winnipeg, and her daughter, who was studying in Australia. I could sense the seclusion Cho must have felt prior to my arrival. She was a lonely soul detached from her loved ones.

Cho had some great qualities. She had a passion for going on spontaneous adventures. As the new man in her life, I was always up for the ride. During my first few days in Calgary, Cho introduced me to Alberta's breathtaking scenery. We visited Elbow Falls, Banff, and Lake Louise. I also experienced my first National Hockey League (NHL) game with her.

When it came to domestic life, Cho had expensive taste in the kitchen, and she was an incredibly talented cook. She cooked all of my favourite dishes at my request. She could dig up anything in the pantry to fix me a plate. I swear she could make a full-course meal with only two ingredients. She was such a good cook that she deserved to have her own TV show on the Food Network. In the absence of worldly distractions, we were a happy couple, and she made me feel like a king on a throne.

I was appreciative of everything, but, quite frankly, I didn't feeling good about myself living like a freeloader. I felt like a child must feel after being adopted from a poverty situation in Africa and plunked into a modernized, rich home. *Was I truly in love with Cho? Or, was I in love with what she had to offer?* From my outsides, the layers of my skin were gratified with security and warmth. The man I was determined to become was sealed within my innermost being, yearning to be released in a burst of manhood. The dissatisfaction with my situation surfaced once I realized I wasn't wearing the pants in the relationship. She invested 100 per cent of her heart to me, but I only dedicated a fraction of mine to her. She didn't notice this discrepancy.

As boredom overwhelmed me, I felt like pulling out my eyelashes or striking my head against a brick wall. There was only so much writing and working out that I could do before I'd go completely insane. I felt trapped. There were days—make that, weeks—when my mind shouted at me to reconsider my immigration decision. *Was I ready to commit my life to someone I barely knew?* But then again, reality struck me with a smarter question: *Do you have any better options?* My life was rapidly spiralling into a completely new lifestyle. It was my first time living with a female partner. I wasn't sure if I was ready to change my habits, especially my bad habits.

The activities on my Facebook page were an ongoing problem. Any issues that arose from insecurities left me having to abide by Cho's laws. Female friends were no longer allowed to call me babe or hun. After Cho read the manuscript for my first book, I had to remove all my ex-girlfriends from my contact lists, I wasn't permitted to reply to other women's comments, and I wasn't allowed to like images of women. If I couldn't provide a clear description of my female friends, Cho would secretly send them Facebook messages, which they would ignore before advising me that my girlfriend was a crazy bitch. Although I never added Cho as a Facebook friend again, I was not allowed to keep my page private or to block her. The list went on. If she didn't get her way, I would be subjected to non-stop nagging. I would rather have self-destructed by swallowing a grenade, than to be the recipient of Cho's irritating and wearisome nagging. Sometimes, she would suspend my cellphone service. Instead of admitting to my old flirtatious habits with other women, I would deny her allegations to protect my image. I guess I had to learn the lesson that with a relationship comes compromise.

Deep within my soul, I knew Cho didn't share the physical characteristics of the type of partner I used to imagine for myself. My ideal woman would be tall, gorgeous, intelligent, and street smart. I would love her so much that our bond would be stronger than love on steroids. She would be the mother of my children and the only one in my eyes. We would be so happy that we would serve as inspiration to other couples. Married life would come later, after we took time to discover the world. As I envisioned my future with Cho, I asked myself, *how could this be real when our love for each other never had a chance to grow?*

To make matters worse, I missed having basketball in my life, and that contributed to my dissatisfaction. Although a Canadian invented basketball, it came second to hockey in every community. I wasn't sure what I expected from a country that has such a long winter. As a basketball player, I found it depressing to walk into the YMCA and find kids knocking a puck with a hockey stick on the facility's only basketball court. I shook my head in disgust. In order for me to fulfil my visions, I had to branch out. It seemed a near impossible venture to pursue, because I had no more ties to the land where basketball was played on every street corner.

America was no longer in my books. Returning to Saint Lucia would have been like relapsing into my past, as if I had never left my hometown. Gaining status in Canada was my new objective. In fact, it was my best and only option. Cho made it very clear that she wanted me to be like putty in her hands, or like a lapdog on a leash. She was willing to do anything for me to encourage me to stay.

Before it got to the point where I was at risk with the Canadian government, Cho and I sought professional guidance from an immigration attorney. After an hour-long consultation, Cho had to pay $1,000 in fees. *Damn, why didn't I become a lawyer?* The lawyer advised us that it would be best if he applied to extend my visitor status on the grounds that Cho and I were madly in love. We went forth with the application for extension. Although it was a two-month process, my visitor status was no longer in jeopardy since the paperwork was submitted before the expiration date stamped on my passport. If my application got approved, I would be granted a maximum of a six-month extension—just enough time to make some big decisions.

Chapter 29

Making It Official

In the past, gazing through windows,
My skies were surrounded by thick white clouds,
My environment was deserted, isolated from everyday crowds.
It felt like no one cared, and nothing seemed cleared.
As leaves touched the grounds, its branches suddenly became,
Naked; Empty; Lonely; Worthless.
My life had disappeared …

Presently, today, my day, your day, our day,
I can fight all my fears.
For March 28, I see a better future,
A world bright, filled with joyfulness.

Staring at your eyes, I envision happiness,
A friend, a wife, a lover.
It's the beginning till the end, our very first chapter.
Dis' engagement will stay strong, shall never be broken,
For our hearts were meant, for a magical reason.

Your actions speak for themselves,
There's no need for you to say,
I Love You.
You've engraved my heart for life,
An everlasting tattoo.

No more cold nights, forever loving this spring season,
As our love grows stronger and blossoms.
The sense of warmth, from my queen,
Has stepped into my kingdom.

I'll be your knight in shining armour,
We will overcome thy pain and rain.
I'll give you everything you deserve and more.
Sweeping you off your feet,
Conquering the highest mountain.

No more lonely nights,

For you, no more looking for Mr. Right.
For my eyes only see you,
And yet, everyday still feels like love at first sight.

The sunrays bring out your beauty,
The sunset shows your shining light,
The moon reflects your love.
You are my brightest star of my darkest nights.

Suddenly, my life reappears,
Clear blue skies,
And, like the leaves of the spring trees, shows rebirth.
My feelings inside portrayed,
Hope; Love; Wanted; Appreciated.

For it's all because of you,
My Wife,
I am now loving Life.

Have you ever felt like a guest at your own event? My big day was not what I imagined it to be as a teenager. For me, the sound of weddings bells should induce a tingling in my stomach, with love so deep that I needed it to breathe. I wanted to be able to define the word *love*. I pictured a church in Saint Lucia filled with my family and friends; nothing too big—it just needed to be meaningful to everyone in attendance, especially to my mother and me.

"Mummy, I will be getting married in March," I sadly said to my mother on the day when Cho finalized our arrangements with the marriage commissioner.

"My boy, you getting married, and I'm not even going to be there," she replied with a hurtful manner.

"Yeah," I paused, choking for sympathetic words. "Well, you know we had to get it done. We not risking anyting with immigration."

"As long as you happy and you know what you're doing, my boy. Your mother will always love you."

On March 28, 2010, I stood on the banks of the Bow Falls, located on the Bow River near Banff. Despite the cold, the scenery was captivating, with the partially icy waterfalls streaming down the frigid river. Our ceremony was overlooked by the town's largest mountain. A few inches of snow were still melting away in certain areas. And apart from my bride, the sun shying away behind the partly scattered clouds was the only familiarities in my wedding circle.

REBIRTH

I was dressed in a black suit with a white dress shirt and black dress shoes that Cho bought for me at the Mr. Big and Tall store. Cho, being a woman of all traits, took on the title of wedding planner. She planned the entire day and paid all the expenses. The only thing I contributed was my presence as the groom. All of the guests were Cho's friends, including my best man, who was Cho's co-worker's husband. I don't mean to imply that Cho was robbing the cradle, but all of her friends looked like grandparents and I felt like the baby at the centre of a baptism. Since the Town of Banff is inside a national park, passersby were often seen capturing our moment. I waited for the arrival of my bride at the make-believe altar. We would have chosen a real church but couldn't because it was Cho's second marriage.

A few moments later, a car driven by Cho's friend, Kristine, pulled up. Kristine had travelled all the way from Vancouver Island to be Cho's maid of honour. *A Groovy Kind of Love,* by Phil Collins, a song selected by Cho, suddenly came blasting through a stereo's speakers.

> *When I'm feeling blue, all I have to do*
> *Is take a look at you, then I'm not so blue*
> *When you're close to me, I can feel your heart beat*
> *I can hear you breathing in my ear*

Oh my God, this is real. There is no turning back now, I continuously thought to myself as the song tried to snap me back to reality. Cho and Kristine walked toward where I stood alongside my *best man* and the marriage commissioner. I made a tight fist, cracking my knuckles, periodically bending my knees to loosen the tension. Cho wore a long, pink sleeveless dress that covered her silver high heels. She carried a bouquet of white and red roses, she had arranged herself. She stared at me with a shivering smile as the chilly Alberta wind reminded us it was early spring. I mirrored a smiled at her to signal a sense of reassurance that I was ready to commit to her on this day. As the song came to an end, she stood by my side facing the marriage commissioner.

The wedding was peaceful. When we declared our marriage vows, Cho recited a two-page letter that brought her to tears as she read the words she had written. The tears kept flowing down her face as I in turned to read my poem. Shortly after, we exchanged our rings. As I placed the diamond ring at the tip of her finger, the marriage commissioner said, "In ancient times, it was believed that the vein in the fourth finger of your left hand led directly to your heart. So by encircling this finger, your heart is forever touched by the one who loves you. Let these rings represent your promise to each other. Let them be a reminder of this moment, your love, and your commitment to each other. May they always be touching your hearts."

When instructed to kiss the bride, I gracefully placed my arms around her waist as she wrapped hers around my neck. And as I picked her up off the ground, we locked lips. A round of applause was heard in the background.

I often thought, *if I'm supposedly madly in love with her, how come there were no goosebumps?* My heart beat normally and there was no numbness in my chest. For Cho, this was her second shot at love and marriage. It almost felt surreal to me, as if she had given herself a time limit for finding a second husband. *How could she possibly think that this was real love? Weren't we doing this backwards? Aren't we moving too fast?* She must have known that I was more concerned with establishing a legal status in Canada so that I could continue to pursue a life with her. Four months of knowing each other, plus three months of living together, plus two months of online chatting. When I added it all up, I realized that we had tied the knot faster than preschoolers.

Chapter 30

A Married Life

Newlyweds usually devote some time to venturing off on a honeymoon, where they celebrate their marriage in an intimate, secluded paradise setting. But that wasn't the case for us because I was advised to remain in Canada to undergo the application for my permanent residence. This sponsorship process could take more than three years to get approved by immigration. I always imagined enjoying a two-week vacation with my new wife in Africa or South America. It would just be the two of us in our own little world, lost in each other's soul, caught up in hours and hours of hot, wet, passionate lovemaking. The sex would be raw and so deep that we'd be bound to make a baby.

Unfortunately, babies likely wouldn't be a part of our future. Before I'd decided to move to Canada, Cho revealed to me on MSN Messenger that she was no longer able to have children. It was a day after Christmas when I brought up the topic.

Arnold: Would you have another child?
Cho: Absolutely.
Arnold: That's a risk though at your age.
Cho: That we'll have to talk about. It's complicated. I can have a child but someone has to carry it. Like a surrogate.
Arnold: OK. I seen a movie like that.
Cho: You know, I always wanted another child but my ex did not.
Arnold: So, you can't get pregnant?
Cho: I can't.
Arnold: Hmm, OK.
Cho: 2006, I had a major surgery. I had a tumour growth on my uterus. So they had to remove it. I still have the ovaries to produce eggs but I can't carry the baby inside me.
Arnold: I understand.
Cho: Are you disappointed?
Arnold: Because you cannot have a child?
Cho: Because I cannot carry your child.
Arnold: It is all good. Can we make someone else carry our child then? I just want one.
Cho: We could find someone to carry our child for us. With my egg and your sperm.

Arnold: That's possible with your eggs?
Cho: Yes. My sister volunteered once for me.
Arnold: How old is she?
Cho: 39. Maybe I'll ask my daughter to do it.
Arnold: Your daughter? You're tripping lol.
Cho: You know how beautiful our baby will be?
Arnold: Yes, of course. Half Asian and half black, like Tiger Woods lol.
Cho: Let's do it when you get here.

Four weeks after our wedding, a scheduled appointment had my wife and I seated at a doctor's office in a Calgary fertility clinic. It was her idea to seek consultation on the process we would have to undergo in order to reproduce. As we waited for the arrival of the doctor, my heels constantly clicked on the floors. I was thinking, *Amarion will be making his debut in this world. I will finally have my own son to love, to protect, and to be in his life from Day 1 until the end of my time.* Having a stable family has always been important to me. I wanted to bring my child into a cultivated world, an environment that was much better than my upbringings.

For some reason, I've always felt that my first-born would be a boy, someone to continue my legacy. I would name him Amarion Henry, a.k.a. Amarie. I would be the only man he would ever call Daddy. Everyone would love Amarion. He would have a strong faith in God, I would encourage him to excel as a student, and I would be there to experience all of his firsts. If he stumbles, I would motivate him to push forward, and, more importantly, I would be there to guide him through all the good and bad times in his life. I would be the best father ever to my son because I know how it feels to be neglected and unloved by the father named on my birth certificate. Happy Father's Day to me.

If I could help bring one child into this world, I would be the happiest man alive. Becoming a father would help me to know what it feels like to have a father. I can truly say it would be a blessing. But, as always, our dreams can take awhile to come true. To achieve our goals, we typically have to go through a few setbacks first.

I've never smiled so much while waiting to enter a doctor's office. But after all the anticipation and a 15-minute meeting with Dr. Richard, my heart shrunk as small as a newborn's fist. He was using unfamiliar terms such as in vitro fertilization (IVF), a process that joins a woman's egg and a man's sperm from outside the body using reproductive technologies to form an embryo. Since Cho would not be able to carry the baby, gestational surrogacy was our only option. Surrogacy meant that the embryo would be implanted into—and carried by—a surrogate mother. Receiving that information all at once felt like an atomic bomb had exploded in my head. Essentially, as Cho was approaching 44 years of age, we had slightly more than a 10 per cent chance of achieving pregnancy. In addition, miscarriages and birth defects were among the other factors. Not to mention, the cost. We were looking at spending tens of thousands of dollars for a procedure that might not be successful.

The tears welled at the corner of my eyes, reflecting my disappointment, as Cho and I stepped out of the doctor's office. Despite the severity of the numbers, Cho was favouring our odds at reproducing. To her, the money wasn't an issue. She knew how important it was for me to have a child of my own, and she was willing to risk it. But I was more sensible about our chances. My hope of becoming a father had to be put on hold at least until I gained permanent residency and was able to work in Canada.

I was legally married, but I wasn't feeling very committed to the relationship, or to Cho. The way I was going about my life was with a single-status state of mind. My vows did not come from my heart. A few weeks after my wedding, I posted pictures on Facebook to notify friends and family of my marriage. Some close friends were surprised; some were happy and congratulated me on my marriage. Then, I received private messages riddled with sexist and ageist remarks.

"Wow, you got married? You could have done much better than her," one self-centred asshole wrote.

"How old is she? Definitely looks much older than you!"

"Chinese, really? I'm disappointed in you," someone else wrote.

I was hurt by these comments, and decided to unfriend or block anyone who said something mean. Eventually, I removed all of the posts related to our wedding, keeping my married status a secret. I couldn't handle any more unwanted attention. With that, came consequences. I made matters worse when I told Cho about all the negative remarks people had made on Facebook. This made Cho feel insecure, and she constantly reminded me that she felt old, fat, and ugly. I blamed myself because I was supposed to be protecting the heart that she had handed to me.

As the days went by, the wedding drama continued. When Cho's daughter, Kris, found out about our marriage, their mother-daughter relationship soured. Kris was almost my age and had disapproved of me for reasons I never understood. She sent a very disturbing Facebook message to her mother calling her a bitch and saying she was desperate for men. The tears streaming down Cho's face and the shivering of her lips signified the hurt she felt, as her only daughter disowned her. "Everything will be OK," I said, trying my best to heal the wounds.

Why did Kris see me as a monster? I was just happy that she lived Down Under.

"Happy wife, happy life," Cho always said. However, I know I wasn't living up to her expectations. I could only be the husband Cho wanted me to be on occasion, and sometimes I could do it for days. Although I felt like I had started to get the gist of living with a woman full time, Cho would sometimes come home from a day's work to find an untidy house, piles of unplowed snow on the driveway in front of the garage, or unwashed dishes in the sink. I'm not trying to justify my irresponsible behaviours, but when Cho was angry, the way she spoke to me was belittling and offensive.

One evening, Cho decided to ignite my fuse at a time when I felt most depressed about being unemployed. "You couldn't clean up your damn mess? I have to wash your fucking dishes for you every time, Arnold?" she shouted from the kitchen while I was in the master bedroom, writing my book. I intentionally ignored her cries in order to keep my raging beast caged. "Arnold," she nagged, "you sit at home all day. You couldn't shovel the fucking snow in the driveway and wash your dishes!" Again, I just ignored her, keeping my eyes on my computer screen. She continued.

She had disturbed my peace of mind, like an annoying mosquito buzzing in my ear while trying to get a good night's sleep. "Fuck it!" I shouted. I went ballistic and jumped off the bed like a hungry lion that had escaped from the jungle. "Leave me the fuck alone," I shouted, grabbing anything I could get my hands on, and smashing it at full force toward the kitchen floor. Cho stood silently in the midst of my outburst, showing no emotion.

Five minutes later, the kitchen and living room areas looked like they had been hit by a tornado. I hated myself, seeing the sadness in Cho's eyes as she picked up the remnants of my rage. Plates were shattered, portraits from the walls were broken, and holes were punched in the drywall. It was so bad that I had to remove shards of glass from the bottoms of my feet.

Every time we fought, the after-effects painted a clearer picture of our incompatibility. Married life was sucking. I was not impressed with the monster that she brought out in me. *Aren't we supposed to bring out the best in each other?* I was having childhood flashbacks. *What is wrong with me?* Many of our disagreements could have been avoided if we understood each other a little better. Communication is definitely a key to a healthy relationship, and there was a barrier between ours.

REBIRTH

I relied on time, excuses, and apologies to fix my mistakes. Cho would only be mad for a couple of hours, but she never forgot. I also used sex as a way of making up for my faults. I never expected a 40-year-old to have such an intense sex drive. Judging from my experiences, I came to the assumption that the older women get, the more they want it. *Or, does it depend on the passion in the relationship? Maybe some people are born nymphomaniacs.* Cho acted as if she needed it every day. I had to pick it up, or keep it up. *Could this be why she's attracted to younger men? Was I the cub to this cougar?* To be honest, I felt more like a sex toy that was used upon request. I understood that I was amazing in bed; however, I was being worn out by its repetitiveness. If I wasn't able to fulfil her sexual desires, I would suffer the repercussion of her mood swings the following days.

I had a lot of thinking to do. I was not a man. When a boy is ready to become a real man, he will make that transition on his own. Time makes us realize that life isn't always about fun and games. There are a lot of responsibilities. When a boy finds a real woman, he'll have to be the right man for her, or he will lose her. Then again, when he loses her, he'll be forced to realize it is time to be a real man.

I was definitely not dedicated to this marriage.

Chapter 31

I Wish I Knew Him

May 6, 2010, was a slow Thursday evening when a devastating message made my heart sink to my feet. It was 8:47 p.m. My BlackBerry notified me of a new Facebook message from Dr. Tobias. Each word I read hit me with a suffocating blow. Coldness wrapped its arms around me as I absorbed the message. And, for the first time, I found it difficult to shed tears. I was emotionally confused. The message read, "Our father isn't doing good. He won't be with us much longer."

Thoughts started to circulate in my head as I searched for a private location in the house. I wanted to be left alone. "Cho, my father is sick," I said, locking myself in the bathroom.

"You're OK?" she asked. I ignored her question so that I could get in touch with Segun.

"What? Are you serious? Where is he? Can I talk to him?" I asked. My fingers were shaking as I typed.

"We're treating him at home with some drips. He still isn't speaking, but it seems he can hear a bit because he sometimes responds by turning his head when someone calls him. I will let you know how it goes."

"OK, cool. Please keep me up to date. Thanks lots."

My thoughts were scattered everywhere, as if I had just suffered a 12-gauge bullet to the head. *No! This isn't happening right now!* I wanted to cry, but my conscience acted like a levee, holding back my tears. *Why should I cry? He was never really in my life. Still, I was not ready for him to go. There was so much I wanted to say to him. I needed him to hear me say what I think of him. I needed to speak to him one last time. I needed him to read my book. I wanted to know if he was proud of me. I needed to know him.*

I banged the back of my head on the bathroom's wooden sliding door because I needed to feel some pain. Shutting my eyelids tightly, dry cries were the only way I could express my emotions. For every new update I read, I felt like an upside-down fish, floating, motionless—dead inside.

On May 14, my oldest brother, Kervyn, sent me a Facebook message, "He ain't looking good at all. We trying to be hopeful but today I looked at him and to be honest I don't know if he will last another week or even the weekend. He is no longer able to move,

156

speak, or eat. He is on IV and we have to feed him through a feeding tube. He deteriorated really fast. Will keep you posted on any developments."

Cho was having a hard time coping with my mixed sentiments. For all she knew, I despised my father for his absence in my life. She had already read most of my first book before it was published. I, too, couldn't understand my reasons for caring whether he lived or died. But a part of me wanted to know more about the man who planted the seed.

"I want to go to Saint Lucia to see him," I said to Cho.

"Why? Why go down and risk your status in Canada. You heard what the lawyer said. You have to remain in Canada," she said.

"I know. I just need to go down. I need to see him before he leaves."

"You know, I can never understand you, Arnold. You write about your father not being in your life in your book, and you want to go down to see him?"

"Yes, I need to go down. I don't care about our past. I'm doing it for myself. I just need to go."

Cho had to dig into her bank accounts to raise the funds for a plane ticket. I disregarded any financial burdens because I desperately needed to see my biological father one last time. Maybe I also wanted to get away from Cho. Maybe it was my way of forgiving him. Maybe I would have a chance to speak to him before he passed away. Or, maybe, I needed to feel sorrow. Whatever it was, I had to fly to Saint Lucia as soon as possible before it was too late.

It was too late.

Death called upon my father the next day. A Facebook message from my other older brother, Chidi, confirmed it. He wrote to me, "Sad news. My father just died at 12:28 p.m."

I was alone in the basement of the house when I first heard the devastating news. *"Fuck! Fuck! Fuck!"* I repeated in my head. Cho was at work, so there was no one there to embrace me. Still, I wasn't feeling any type of empathy for anyone, or myself. I just gazed into the distance with the hope of being able to understand my indescribable emotions. *How could I feel anything when, to me, my father has been dead since before I was even conceived?* Still, I felt the need to Google and download a picture of him to upload as my new Facebook profile picture with the caption, "RIP Francis Tobias, a.k.a. Toby, a.k.a. Photobias, a.k.a. *my father*." I did it because I was proud of my father for his services as a cameraman and journalist. He was well known on the island for his work ethic, and he captured many years of memorable events in Saint Lucia. While others were expressing their sympathy, most of my friends said, "I didn't know he was your father."

Another question I had to ask myself: *Should I go to his funeral? Would it be a waste of my time? Would I feel comfortable standing next to his casket?* I still needed answers, so I decided to get on the next flight to Saint Lucia.

I wasn't too worried about jeopardizing my Canadian status because my application to extend my stay was approved for six extra months. For the next 14 days, I was planning to finally end 25 years of mourning the loss of my father since birth.

Due to time constraints with his unexpected death, I begged Cho to stay behind, as she had to attend work. Besides, with our age difference, I wasn't very comfortable with the idea of introducing her to my family and friends. My people are quick to criticize anyone of their kind for being with an older woman. It wouldn't have been Cho's first time to my country; she had visited a year earlier with her previous Saint Lucian boyfriend.

I was worried that my return home might be too soon after I missed that court date for the petty allegations against me in the summer of 2008. I made a couple of phone calls to friends in the police force and learned that the case had been dismissed due to the fact that the arresting officer, Corporal Vincent Peters, had been gunned down and murdered during a failed robbery attempt. In other words, my police record was clean. Additionally, I was concerned about becoming another victim of crime in my community.

Upon arrival in hot, humid Saint Lucia, Kervyn picked me up at the airport. While greeting him, I noticed my oldest brother didn't seem very remorseful about the loss of the man who had been in his life from the beginning. He was as calm as the seas along the coastline on a good day.

"So, you didn't bring down de wife?" he asked as we drove away. "I saw on Facebook that you got married."

"Yeah, I got married about two months ago. She couldn't come down cause she have to work." Our conversation from the south of the island to our final destination was mainly about the last two years, including my graduation, my married life, and my future with basketball.

To avoid staying in my insecure childhood community, I was relieved to be offered accommodation at Chidi's newly built residence. He lived with his pregnant wife and daughter. It was a good opportunity for us to get to know each other better. I wasn't as close to Chidi as I was with Kervyn and Segun. My other brother, Chima, never seemed to care to get to know me on a personal level. Even though it wasn't the mature thing to do, I reflected the same attitude toward him. With the few days I had with my brothers, I was hoping to gain some insight into my father through their eyes.

The funeral was scheduled for the coming Saturday. While I sat back and watched, my brothers were busy getting all the necessities prepared for the ceremony. I was riding in Kervyn's car when I first heard my father's death announcement on the radio station. My heart started to race as I waited for the part in the segment where the announcer mentions the names of his survivors. *Will the radio announcer mention my name? Is he going to say my father had only four sons?* If I was left off the list, I probably wouldn't have said anything because I knew that my brothers were the ones who handled the obituary. I just felt the need to know that my four older brothers actually recognized me as family. I listened with anticipation, but the announcer's information was generic. He mentioned that my father left behind his wife and sons—which, technically, included me.

Death brings families together, and my father's bereavement was no exception. I had a chance to meet and greet many new relatives, including a few of my aunts, uncles, and cousins that resided in other countries. For the very first time in my life, I stepped foot on the grounds of my father's home in Reduit, Gros Islet. He probably rolled over in his grave. I couldn't believe how close my father's home was to the main road—a road I had been on countless times. Come to think of it, I was nowhere close to finding his house when I ran away from home that one time. This awkward moment came to pass when I entered the property through the front door. Inside the house, I met my father's wife. Out of respect for her, I emphasized condolences for her loss. Then, I immediately went back outside and sat on the balcony to escape from further emotional discomfort. Usually, I can remember what a living room looks like after only seeing it for a few seconds, but all I remembered was Mrs. Tobias sitting on a chair in the darkness, asking my brother in Kwéyòl, "Is that Jean's son? Look at how tall he is." I was in total disbelief that she knew who I was, which made me wonder how she found out about me. I also wondered if my father's family was on the verge of dysfunction the day she found out about his affair with my mother. If I saw his widow again, I probably wouldn't recognize her.

As people used the balcony to enter through the front entrance, I stared longingly at their faces until people caught me. I only spoke when I was spoken to. I felt like a lost puppy in a crowd. I met my father's sister, who suggested that I visit her in Trinidad so that I could be introduced to the rest of my family. I accepted her offer, but I have yet to comply. One day, I will venture to my father's motherland when I feel the need to discover the other half of my background. It had never occurred to me that I was half Trinidadian until I heard my father's death announcement over the radio. All I knew was that I was born and raised Saint Lucia.

On Saturday, May 22, I was dressed in my suit, riding in the back seat of Chidi's SUV on the way to our father's funeral service at the Cathedral Basilica of the Immaculate Conception in Castries. As I stepped out of the vehicle, I quickly adjusted my tie and covered my eyes with my sunglasses, in preparation to enter the church. My intention was to feel relaxed and not bothered by the look of confusion on some people's faces when they saw me. Many of my former classmates, teammates, and neighbours turned up in large numbers to show their support and pay their respects to the man responsible for capturing some of their best moments on camera. The church and streets were overcrowded, which was not a surprise to me at all. I was ecstatic to see my mother in attendance.

Although I was not pleased at the absence of my name on the program's list of pallbearers, I was still honoured to be alongside my brothers carrying our father's casket to the church and to his grave. Although I was seated in the front row with the family and close friends, the brochure fed my suspicions that I should not have been present at my father's funeral. I felt unaccepted. To that, I say, thank you *bros* for making me feel like a piece of shit on the day I was trying to find peace with my sperm donor. Despite all the hints that I shouldn't have come, my time at the funeral wasn't about some recognition on a piece of paper. And we weren't at the best place for me to be complaining.

I had overcome my fears. The bitterness of my relationship with my father was no longer pounding on my chest. I got some perspective and brief insight into my father's life from newspapers, family and friends, and the reading of the eulogy at the service. Eleven never-before-seen photos of my father were included in the program. I kept a copy so that I'll be able to at least show my children a picture of their grandfather. This was especially important to me because I never knew what my mother's father looked like.

Francis Tobias was laid to rest at the cemetery near Vigie Beach in Castries. As the undertakers prepared to lower my father's body into his hole, I felt like all my questions had been answered. I found peace within myself. I accepted the fact that the past was inescapable and my father was gone forever. I would continue to be the father to myself.

REBIRTH

Being present at his funeral was part of an emotional healing process that allowed me to spread forgiveness. Seeing my father's face one last time helped me gain the strength to move forward. In that instant, I promised myself to *always* be in my children's lives.

Just before the casket was shut, I captured my first photo of my father on my camera. First, it was a portrait to show appreciation for all the footage and images he had captured of me throughout my sporting career in Saint Lucia. Secondly, I needed something that would allow me to try to envision the life he had lived.

Chapter 32

Gone But Not Forgotten

Intro
Francis Tobias was born in Trinidad on June 8, 1937.
He first came to Saint Lucia in the 1960s,
As part of a Catholic youth group.
After graduating from the University of West Indies,
Tobias moved here, where he and his wife worked,
And raised their family of sons.
Tobias was a photojournalist.

Verse One
Aquarius born, I swear my mom,
Was the only one at the hospital.
So, until this day, by her I stand.
Life without my father was never our plan.
There are so many things I never knew about him,
Like the year he was born—1937.
I'd never met his wife, never met his four sons,
And all this time, I never knew where he lived.
If it weren't for the news,
I would have never known his name.
Calling him dad would have been such a shame.
And I never knew he was born in Trinidad.
And I never knew if I ever made him proud.
I can erase the pain but my memory lives on.
I wish I knew him more but now he is gone.
Looking down his grave, tryna stay strong.
It's a pity he never gonna hear my song.

Chorus (repeat twice)
Standing behind this camera lens,
Tryna picture the type of life he lived.
This is how it feels to be the kid on the side,
Standing on the outside, looking in.
I wish I could bring my father back,
I wish we had time to kick it back.
He's gone too soon, I don't understand.
I guess I'll never get to know that man.

162

REBIRTH

Verse Two
Going through all my photo albums,
Ain't got one damn picture with you.
Reminiscing of all the times we had,
Never had one great moment with you.
I came in this world, you never said hi,
Even when you left, you never said bye.
Still wondering if it's all my fault.
I guess I was the child you never want.

Chorus (repeat twice)
Standing behind this camera lens,
Tryna picture the type of life he lived.
This is how it feels to be the kid on the side,
Standing on the outside, looking in.
I wish I could bring my father back,
I wish we had time to kick it back.
He's gone too soon, I don't understand.
I guess I'll never get to know that man.

Verse Three
You was never there for me,
But I made your funeral.
I never plan to stoop to your level.
Feeling awkward at the cathedral,
All eyes on me like I didn't belong.
The last time we spoke, I really needed you,
So in his mind, I still needed him.
But I kept my head high above the rough waters,
And swam to the shore and forgave him.

(Words taken from a TV interview)
"I don't think that people understood the person Toby was in terms of what he stood for, what he wanted to see done in sports. And Toby was the person who really didn't voice his opinion."
"He will be missed all over."
"Sports journalist Robertson Henry called him a father figure in broadcast."
"I do hope that we will find some meaningful way of honouring Toby. Not just everyone turn up at his funeral. What's important is, how do we honour Toby's legacy."

Chorus (repeat twice)
Standing behind this camera lens,
Tryna picture the type of life he lived.
This is how it feels to be the kid on the side,
Standing on the outside, looking in.
I wish I could bring my father back,
I wish we had time to kick it back.
He's gone too soon, I don't understand.
I guess I'll never get to know that man.

Outro
Damn, what can I say, I really,
I really wish I knew him,
But such is life, life goes on,
Damn.
Rest in peace …

Have you ever tried to figure out what's more important: sharing your true feelings with the world, knowing it could change someone else's life; or, keeping your feelings hidden deep within your soul, where you will never know if someone else can relate to your story?

Aug. 11, 2010, was the night I posted my music video dedicated to my deceased father, entitled *I Wish I Knew Him*, on Facebook. I was now back in Calgary. It took me about an hour to write these words on a day when I was feeling extremely depressed. I needed to expose my true feelings toward my sperm donor; I wanted people to hear my story. In one night, I had received more than 250 likes (sharing posts wasn't an option back then) from all sorts of people around the world. People were commenting and expressing similar views based on the contents of my lyrics; they related to my story and completely understood where I was coming from.

On the other hand, my words had a negative affect on my relationship with my brother Segun. To him, I had gone too far, and, for that, he removed me as a friend on Facebook. I was hurt. For a moment, I wished I hadn't said anything or written and recorded the song and posted it on Facebook. Why didn't Segun support my song? I was the one who had to deal with being an outsider my whole life. I'm the one who had to live my life knowing my father was here on Earth but never there for me. I tried my best to reach out to Segun with numerous apologies, but he didn't respond to any of my messages. Still, I reflect on that day with no regrets, and I meant every word in my lyrics. By making my non-existent experiences with my biological father public, I may have lost a brother, but a positive thing came of my actions, too.

Near the end of August, a few weeks later, I was seated in Zaine's living room in downtown Calgary. Thanks to Facebook, I had made a new Saint Lucian friend. Zaine, who was studying engineering at the University of Calgary, was having a social gathering at his high-rise apartment. He had invited mostly Saint Lucian friends for some good ol' lentils bouillon soup with oxtail—a famous Saint Lucian dish. The event reminded me of Jounen Kwéyòl, a festival that celebrates Creole culture. Zaine was the nephew of the prime minister of Saint Lucia, Dr. Kenny D. Anthony. We shared the same passion for our beautiful island. Being in Zaine's company, I felt less isolated in a city that was not known for its Caribbean diversity. Whenever I visited with my friends, I left Cho at home because no one was her age and I didn't feel like she was the partying type. She would say that I was ashamed of her. To be honest, I wanted to be far away from the marriage and party with single friends—whether or not that entailed hooking up with female friends.

I was enjoying a bowl of one of my favourite dishes when an incoming call from my mother caused me to excuse myself from the crowd. "Mario, what am I seeing on the computer?" she asked with a panicky tone.

"What you talking about, Mummy?"

"You have me in a video with my picture and your father."

"Oh, Mummy, don't worry about that. I just did a song expressing my true feelings."

"But Mario, why you never tell me these things? I never knew you had these feelings inside of you towards Toby. You know you can always talk to your Mummy. That song made me cry."

I was on the verge of shedding tears also. I didn't think that my lyrics would be so impactful. "I'm sorry Mummy."

"I still like and enjoyed the song. I just wish that you talk to me more. Remember, I will always love you."

When my mother told me that she liked my song, I felt a sense of relief. I couldn't afford to lose another family member. Little did she know, the book I was writing featured more intense contents. The song gave her a glimpse of what to expect, and I got an idea of what her reaction may be after she reads my book. I dried my tears before rejoining my friends.

All of a sudden, the vibration of my BlackBerry Messenger notified me of a new friend request. *Hmm, Heidi? Must be an old classmate from Saint Lucia.* I went ahead and confirmed the request, without really looking further at my new contact. I pocketed my cellphone to regain focus and continue mingling with my friends.

Buzz, buzz, buzz!

Ugh, who's ringing my cellphone now? I retrieved the device, searching for the culprit who'd invaded my good times with my friends. *Oh, Heidi again.*

I opened up the chat and glanced at the screen for a split second. "Hey Arnold, I think we are in the same boat." After the sentence registered with me, I did a double take.

"What? Same boat?" I replied out of curiosity.

"Being an outside child," she wrote.

"What … what you trying to say?"

"I'm impressed with your music video."

"Oh … oh … oh, thank you," I typed, ignoring her initial sentence. I figured she was one of the many who related to the song.

"By the way, my name is Heidi Alleyne."

"Nice to meet you, Heidi. My name is Arnold."

"Nice to finally meet you, too."

Huh? Nice to finally meet you, too? My eyebrows converged. "Are you trying to tell me something?" I asked.

"WELL, FRANCIS TOBIAS WAS MY BIOLOGICAL FATHER, TOO," Heidi texted in all caps. Reading that sentence transfixed me into a zone where I felt as if I was the only one seated in Zaine's apartment. *My father has another illegitimate child?* As I tried to type, my hands shook uncontrollably. I excused myself, and then proceeded to walk onto the balcony.

"Are you trying to tell me that you're my half-sister?"

"Yes, LOL," she replied. The tears that filled my eyes made it hard for me to see the screen of my smartphone. Still in disbelief, I dried my eyes and asked, "Seriously, you're really my sister?"

"Yes :)"

"How old are you?" I asked.

"34."

"Wow, you're nine years older than me … and all these years, I thought I only had one sister."

"Well, you have two now," she boasted. By then, my depression had been displaced with a smile that came straight from my heart. I felt like there was finally someone on Earth who understood my situation of being an outside child. Heidi was a newly found sibling with more life experience.

"So, where are you from, Heidi?"

"Barbados," she replied. "I guess my mother met him when he went to university here. She doesn't really talk about him."

"So, when was the last time you spoke to him?"

"I never did. In 2008, he was here in Barbados and left a number for me to call him. I never called."

"Oh, OK," I typed, as fresh tears rolled down my face. Luckily, Heidi wasn't able to see her little brother acting like such a big crybaby.

"So, you know you have four other brothers, right?" I asked.

"Well, I only heard about them after his death from articles I read on the internet."

"Wow, really?

"Yeah, but I didn't have a clue. To be honest, I didn't know he had a family, or, for that matter, lived in Saint Lucia. I thought he lived in Trinidad."

"I'm sure your brothers will be happy to know they now have a sister," I wrote, assuming the best.

"Are you close with any of them?" she wondered.

"Well, when I was 16 years old, Tobias's oldest son, Kervyn, heard about me from his wife, who had moved into my neighbourhood. Then, Kervyn came looking for me at my home on Christmas Day. We've kept in touch ever since … and that's how I met my other brothers, Segun, Chima, and Chidi," I answered. "I can introduce you to them if you like … they're all on Facebook."

"Not right now … not right now … I need some time. I will let you know when I'm ready," she wrote.

"OK, cool, just let me know, sis."

I felt like it was my duty to introduce Heidi to her other brothers—just as Kervyn had done for me. My older sister had been walking in my shoes all along, and here I was thinking that I was the only neglected child of Francis Tobias. Heidi definitely had it worse than me, as she was on a completely different island. I wondered how it was making her feel to know that she has no more hopes of ever seeing our father. But maybe she never hoped to see him. It hurt my heart to have to witness such abandonment.

How could my father be so mean to his own offspring? Why did he never man up to his responsibilities? Heidi was just an innocent child. Sigh! Still, today, the issue of absent parents is ongoing in our society, and it's my belief that the statistics aren't getting any better. I'm so sick and tired of hearing stories about parents not wanting anything to do with their own flesh and blood. It leaves a disgusting taste in my mouth and makes me feel like vomiting. I understand that parents can have relational issues, and, sometimes, it can be difficult to deal with some people; however, that should never be an excuse for any man or woman to run away from his or her child. Parents who are no longer involved in a healthy relationship should be able to compromise effectively to raise their children in two happy homes. But I digress.

When I saw a picture of Heidi, I could tell by first sight that she had my father's nose. On the day when she was ready to be introduced to her other brothers, I decided to post a message to Chidi and Kervyn on Facebook. Since Segun and I were no longer Facebook friends, I wasn't able to add him to the conversation. And Chima was the one brother who never seemed to care to keep in touch, so I didn't even know if he had a Facebook account.

I wrote: "Hey bro, I wanted to let you know that your father had another outside child. Her name is Heidi. She's 34 years old and living in Barbados. She had no way of reaching out to you until now. As an outside child myself, I understand how it is to have no contact, but, thanks to Kervyn, I was able to get to know more about my big brothers. I don't know about you, but family has always been very important to me since I don't have that much to brag about. Every time I meet a new member, I am always grateful and thank God for the new addition. I was so thrilled back when I was 16 years old to see Kervyn at my front door, on Christmas Day. That was the best Christmas ever. Then I met Chidi, Chima, and Segun. I was even happier to know that my brothers accepted me. And for that, I respected my brothers! I hope you take the opportunity to get to know Heidi, as I have. Thanks for your understanding."

I believe that they all took initiative to get to know Heidi. For me, I'd accepted her as an older sister from Day 1. By the way, I failed to mention earlier that my baby sister, Marva, and I finally hugged it out on my last trip to Saint Lucia. On my final night there, I'd spotted Marva at a bar with her new boyfriend, and I respectfully introduced myself to him after making peace with her. She seemed to be happier, and, despite her boyfriend being in his 40s, I'd only heard good things about them as a couple, unlike her previous relationships. As long as my baby sister was happy, I was happy.

It felt so good to know that I have two blood sisters.

Chapter 33

What About Basketball?

Marvin—or Aloysius Henry, as he's known in the basketball world—was starting a new season at the University of North Carolina at Greensboro (UNCG). He became the fourth Saint Lucian to be awarded a full men's basketball scholarship to play at the NCAA Division I level. I was happy for my brother's achievements. My brother's very last game at Three Rivers Community College ended with a disappointing overtime loss, 85-80, against Howard College—a victory that would have crowned my brother and his team as the NJCAA Division I men's basketball national champions. He was so close to becoming the first Saint Lucian national champion. His team ended the season with an overall record of 28 wins and seven losses. My brother had an average of 12 points, seven rebounds, and 1.2 blocks per game. If we were to compare our records at the end of our sophomore years, Marvin's stats and accomplishments were more outstanding than mine. I was happy for him. Whenever my brother achieved success, I felt like I did, too.

At the other end of the spectrum, I was slowly being reminded of the difficulties to obtaining a professional basketball contract. I would have settled for any opportunities that came knocking at my door. At the very least, I was yearning to get my feet back on the court. I had to wait on my upcoming spousal sponsorship in Canada before I could pursue advancing my basketball career. Let's be real, I couldn't have accepted any international offers, even if I'd wanted to. I wasn't willing to travel to Europe for a season and risk losing my entry to Canada. In fact, I patiently waited until I became a permanent resident to leave and re-enter the country as I pleased. I wanted Calgary to be my home because of the many job opportunities in the city. It felt safe.

In the meantime, to retain my visitor's status, Cho realized she was able to complete an online application on the Government of Canada's website, a process with a renewal fee of only $75, as opposed to being cheated out of $1,000 by going through a lawyer.

To ensure that I kept on top of my game, I would spend my days at the gym, working on my weaknesses and strengths. I focused on conditioning, weightlifting, and basketball skills development. Since hockey was more popular in Calgary, I found myself desperately seeking competitive basketball. The gatherings on the court helped me to connect with new friends. Although I was the new kids on the block,

I was approached by players trying to convince me to join their teams in the city's men's league. My basketball skills felt welcomed in the city.

I've come across three types of dreamers: those who pursue their dreams by going through tremendous amounts of hard work until they fulfil their dreams (and, even then, they're hungry to achieve more); those who just dream of success but never take any steps to get there for fear of failure; and, those who live to see their dreams come true but aren't able to live up to the expectations to continue living their dreams.

On a daily basis, I've introduced myself to many of these types of dreamers, but I will never forget Tarek. He was a Calgarian who I met at the YMCA. From the first day I met him, he was thirsty to be part of a college basketball team. So, I taught him everything I knew. I picked him up at 5 a.m. to train with him in preparation for the open tryouts for the University of Calgary's men's basketball team. Tarek was just finishing high school and was not as talented as the average star player, but he had the patience and the willpower to learn. He was extremely coachable, too. I remembered telling him, "You have to put in the work every day. Taking any days off is giving someone else the opportunity to take your spot."

After months of training, Tarek failed to make the squad. It was a disappointing day for both of us, but Tarek knew it was not the end. He continued putting in the effort to become a better player and then decided to pursue another opportunity at St. Mary's University, which was sanctioned by the Alberta Colleges Athletic Conference (ACAC). We rejoiced on the day when he was successful in making the team at St. Mary's.

Tarek thought making the team was the end of his journey, but he quickly learned that his work was only just beginning. Then, before the commencement of his season, he quit. He blamed ongoing issues with his bad knees, but I blamed his weak mentality and his lack of interest in the game. I was awfully dissatisfied with his decision to leave the team. After I had invested so much of my time in him, he had the audacity to quit without consulting with me. I looked at him as my student, and he made me feel like a failure. I guess I didn't prepare him enough to hang on to his dreams. He was one of those dreamers who aren't able to live up to the expectations to continue living the dream. If I had allowed my injuries to control my fate, I probably would have been a spectator to someone else's dreams coming true.

Despite being unable to travel outside of the country to pursue my dream of playing professional basketball, I was still reaching out to possibilities elsewhere. I wasn't going to point my fingers at quitters if

REBIRTH

I couldn't live up to my own statements on dreamers. After Googling organizations in Europe, I composed and sent numerous emails and attached my basketball resumé, which included a YouTube link to a video of my college basketball highlights, to team owners, agents, and coaching staff. Since I hadn't played within a systematized basketball league for more than two years, most of the responses I received included invitations for me to fly to upcoming open tryouts. Again, travelling outside of Canada wasn't a risk I was willing to take. If I did anything to jeopardize with my visa in Canada, I most certainly would have ended up back in Saint Lucia. Although it felt like I was at the end of my rope, I had tied a safety knot and was still hanging on to my dreams as tight as I could.

In late-September, I would not let myself be defeated. To stay motivated, I participated in as many gigs as possible. Every ounce of blood in my body instigated quitting. To keep on pushing forward, I knew I had to be actively involved with the game. The NBA Jam Session, a free, interactive basketball festival that travelled to six Canadian cities and was affiliated with NBA Canada, had arrived in Calgary at precisely the right time. It was a weekend filled with basketball-related activities, including a slam-dunk contest, a three-point contest, and an NBA player appearance. My eyes were on the main prize—an all-expenses-paid trip to Toronto, which would be awarded to the champions of the 3-on-3 tournament. The champ would advance to face the other winners from the other cities for the national title. With my new-found basketball associates, Ryan McGavern, Sean Landry, and Moe Abdallah, I put together a powerhouse team to win it all. We were allowed one substitute.

On Saturday, I partook in the slam-dunk contest, judged by NBA player Glen "Big Baby" Davis, who, at the time, was playing for the Boston Celtics. I placed second. On Sunday, my teammates and I were ready to be challenged. After a long-winded day of basketball, we proved to be the undisputed champions of Calgary.

A few days later, my team was Toronto-bound to compete for the national title at the Toronto Raptors' training facility in the Air Canada Centre. The national championship game would take place at the pre-season halftime game between the Raptors and the Phoenix Suns. At one point during the preliminary rounds, Jay Triano, the former head coach of the Toronto Raptors, briefly walked into our closed-door tournament session. An airstream of whispers circulated the room, and every player acted as if the tournament was an open tryout for the Toronto Raptors. If it were that easy to be recruited to an NBA team, the happy ending to my basketball story would have happened then. At the end of the tourney, my team suffered two losses, and the team from Montreal won the 2010 NBA Jam Session national championship.

In spite of our devastating losses, my teammates and I looked at the trip as a weekend getaway. We took the opportunity to explore the city and its nightlife scene. The following day, all of the players who participated were invited to attend the pre-season game between the Raptors and Suns. We sat in box seats and were provided food and drinks. While watching the NBA game, I reflected on my chances of playing in these professional players' sneakers. It was a mesmerizing experience, as I thought about the decreasing likelihood of stepping foot onto centre court and being surrounded by such passionate fans. Then again, as I thought deeper about the possibility of achieving my dreams, my mind slipped back to the bad memories of Dec. 13, 2004. I was still working on expunging my past.

Chapter 34

Hurricane Tomas

"Baby, I'm so scared," my mother wept over the phone. I squeezed my cellphone tightly and clenched it to my ear.

"Where are you?" I asked.

"I'm at the back of the house, in your room." The frightened sound in her voice had me overly concerned and distressed.

"Are you safe? Where's Marva? What's going on with the house?"

"Water is coming inside from the roof at the front of the house. There is water everywhere. Marva is at her boyfriend's house." From the numerous overwhelming posts on Facebook, I could only imagine the damage being caused to my childhood home. "There is no electricity and no water. Mario, I'm so scared," my mother bawled.

In times like these, I never seem to be able to find the right words. I wished my mother had somewhere better to stay, or, better yet, I wished she had come to live with me in Canada. As a kid, I remember promising to buy her a new home. I still aim to keep that promise. My mother has lived in the same green wooden house since her birth. *If I had been able to buy her a house, she would have had fewer worries.* My promise was overdue, and the quick intensification of Hurricane Tomas reminded me that I needed to gain success at a quicker rate.

"Mummy, I am so sorry to hear that. I see everyone posting about it on Facebook. It looks so scary. The hurricane will pass. I will continue praying for you, asking God to guide you through this," I said, hoping she would find my words heartwarming. A minute later, she gained some strength to hang up the long-distance call to save on her cellphone battery life.

There was an instant panic from the Saint Lucian foreign-based communities that still had family and friends living in the Caribbean. Thanks to social media and the uploading of videos and pictures by the locals, we were getting live updates of the devastation happening on our island. Rooftops were being torn off as if the Big Bad Wolf had huffed and puffed and blown them away. A number of homes were demolished and completely flattened to the ground. Certain areas were impassable due to collapsing roads and bridges. The city's streets had transformed into a river with water above waist level. Winds of up to 100 miles per hour were knocking down trees and power lines.

After the hurricane, the death toll was said to be a total of 14 people. The estimated cost of damage was about $100 million US. If there was a good time for Saint Lucians to unite, the aftermath of Hurricane Tomas was it. I did my part alongside other Saint Lucians in Calgary by buying and donating non-perishable food items.

While my people were strategizing on ways to restore their homes and properties, Cho and I were finalizing the submission of my application for permanent residency. The application was very time consuming because of the amount of required information and forms needed for submission. We also had to make sure we had ticked off everything on the document checklist. This included enclosing copies of our marriage certificate, birth certificates, FBI and Saint Lucia police records, proof of medical exams, and a three-page letter happy relationship. I realized later that this letter was just a pack of lies. After checking off all the items on the list, Cho decided to go above and beyond what was required by adding a photo album of our most unforgettable experiences over the past 10 months, which highlighted pictures from our late-summer honeymoon to Nanaimo, British Columbia, on Vancouver Island. Although the 12-hour road trip was supposed to be our honeymoon, Cho brought her 17-year-old son, Blake, who was visiting from Winnipeg.

I felt a bit awkward when Blake arrived at the house in Calgary. Knowing that I was only six years older than him, I was a bit nervous. *Is he going to have the same reaction as his older sister?* If he were uncomfortable with the scenario, I would have completely understood. I was once in a similar position when I found myself in the presence of a bearded, muscular, over six-foot tall, stepfather who loomed over me. And since his sister wasn't too fond of me, I expected a similar reaction from him. Cho's wish was for everyone to get along as one happy family, so I tried my best to keep the peace.

Blake was a quiet, innocent-looking boy who looked more Caucasian than Asian. I didn't want him to hate me, so I treated his space with respect. After all, I had first-hand knowledge of how a man can ruin a relationship with his stepchild. There wasn't much conversation between Blake and I, except for a little—how you doing, that kind of thing—here and there. Nevertheless, I'll always remember the day when we were tossing his football back and forth on the beach on Vancouver Island. He seemed comfortable and he often smiled at my awful attempts at playing quarterback. That sense of acceptance was something I always wanted from my own stepfather. Throughout my life, I often wished I had been raised with better stability in the home, or at least with no domestic violence. No matter how hard I tried, I was still having a hard time erasing these memories of my past. Countless times, I've told myself that I should let bygones be bygones, that there was nothing I could do to change the unchangeable. This was easier said than done, though.

Before mailing my application for permanent residence, I had high hopes that Canada would be my new home. When I logged into my online account on Nov. 8, a message from the Government of Canada read: "We received your application for permanent residence." A little more than a month later, there was an update: "We started processing your application on Dec. 17, 2010. Medical results have been received." If I got approved, maybe, I can move my mother to Canada so that she wouldn't have to worry too much about hurricanes in the Caribbean.

Chapter 35

The Boy Staring at a Glass Window

Dear Diary,

Who knows the person everyone criticizes better than the eyes of the onlooker? Are we going to allow doubters to determine our true potentials or fortunes? For one minute, let's pretend that we live in a flawless world, where our lives are perfect with sunny, blue skies hovering above our smiling faces. Just think about it—your expectations for life would be stagnant and you'd never encounter any inconsistencies. There would be no ups or downs, sort of like a flat line, which, to me, reads: dead. Don't you love that self-confident feeling of conquering life's challenges? Only the being within your mind, body, and soul is capable of defining your outcome. Now, let's snap back to reality. We are an illimitable living breed. We can surpass our own strengths and seek beyond our boundaries by revolutionizing our regularities to discover the endless possibilities.

The willpower to pursue your yearnings is hidden beneath your fears. No matter where we are in life, regardless of age, we can always make a change. No matter your background or origin, we can huddle together over anything that seems unreachable. Our defeats are possibly our success stories. Our victories are always one step ahead. Dreams are achievable; we just have to be enthusiastic enough to claim our visions. We all have a purpose, and no one knows you better than you know yourself. But before moving forward and never looking back, I had to backpedal to learn from what I was giving up.

I was the boy staring at a glass window, looking right through myself, as opposed to, a man standing in a mirror who was willing to make a difference, starting with what he saw looking back. The more I rubbed away what was in front of me, the less aware I became of myself to this reality. The more fog that clouded my dreams, the more obscured the sight of what I could have. I wanted to become a better man, but I needed to let go of my past in order for me to greet the future with a healthier, more substantial soul. Lord knows I was a bad boy. Will I be forgiven? After confessions, are my words going to affect my future relationships? To make the necessary changes in my life, I was obligated to be honest with not only others, but with myself.

Not even promises kept their promises. What good is a man to this world if he can't keep his word? I knelt before the Most High, asking

REBIRTH

for forgiveness for the sins I was about to commit. Will I still make it to Heaven?

As humans, we are equipped for survival, but, then again, only for a short period of time. That is, for however long we are destined to breathe. Sometimes I wonder if statistics can prove a short life lived was greater than a long one. Really, do all the good men die young? If so, why shouldn't I live my life in evil? Surely, goodness shall follow me all the days of my life. After all, I live by faith, not by sight. I chose to be an angel before I'm gone. Either way, the society that raised me had already proven there is a God in control of my stopwatch.

I know I'm not perfect. I never expected to be. My intentions were to inspire others by the way I dealt with my imperfections. There are so many lessons to be learned before reaching the level of maturity where one deserves to be called a man. At times, my thoughts shouted at me, asking, what is wrong with you? Why can't you just man up today? But, really, who, when, and what defines a man? By now, we all know that I've never had many male influences to help me answer these types of questions. Am I entitled to grow in or out of my childhood experiences? An ultimate goal for me is to live the rest of my life being referred to as a real man. But who knows when I'll be ready? Maybe I'll be ready on my 30th birthday, or the day when I realize that I am not only living for myself but for someone else. I was the boy staring at the glass window, as the world was staring right through me.

There are confusions from my past that make it difficult for me to define the true meaning of my life. I once spoke to a wise, blind man, who showed me how to see with my ears. I haven't been deceived ever since. I've met a survivor of a near-death car accident—he now rolls himself in and out of the gym in a wheelchair—who told me that being alive is the most beautiful thing. I wish for everyone to see how beautiful life can be.

I was a boy staring at a glass window, and it was about time that I faced the mirror so that I could move on. I want to be better than the man I was yesterday.

Chapter 36

Hanging On To My Dreams

Hanging on to my dreams till the day I die
Hanging on by a thread, just to get by
For every failure, my successes multiply
With every vision, my fallen tears seem to dry
Can't stare any longer, cockeyed
My mother needs a new life, paradise
So I keep striving to the mountaintop
And I won't stop like green lights till my ears pop
Or till my nose bleeds
I'll plant my seeds and grow higher, higher than any tree
Keep my mind on the goal, like a penalty
It's my destiny, conquering all my hardships
When you take certain risk a child is born
I was never a wish, but I was born a star
You can see it through my eyes, so take a look
You can feel the pain on every page in my book
And now I know what's best, you can read the prints
A quarter of a million words couldn't explain every single scene
Flip through every chapter, yeah, life's a struggle
I'm a keep that hustle till I win all my battles
So close to victory, feeling like a battlefield
Bouncing back from all rejections
All I need is heartbeats
Keep my feet off the ground, like levitation
In this world that I live, there's no limitations
I'm on the flipside, looking like I'm disguised
Overcoming storms like I'm looking down the landslide
I've made it this far, evolution of a star
Out of this world in space shining with the sun
Still, not even close to the finish line
Never in my radar, every day is my prime time
Yeah, it's grind time, so I'm looking at the sky
And as the rain stops, I feel like it's my turn to shine
I stay busy, man, like a businessman
Reaching for the heavens, like I took off with my wingspan
Yeah, I see a better me looking at the mirror
Gotta stay above the line, like I'm a numerator

REBIRTH

Hanging on to my dreams, I'm a strong believer
Burying all the doubters, haters, losers, like the undertaker
Never give up on your dreams, be inspired
It's your call to make, umpire
It has to come from your heart, desire
Live and breathe it through your blood, vampire.

Although I started documenting my journey since before I became a teenager, it took me two solid years of scribbling my life away to have a completed manuscript by December, 2010. By then, my therapeutic phase had ended. The soothing powers of writing had led me to self-discovery and had allowed me to accept a past that I could never change. Reliving these moments encouraged me to believe that I am stronger than I thought I was. I also realized when it came to fighting for what I believed in, my character symbolized strength, courage, willpower, commitment, and focus. I basically needed to remind myself to always have faith while hanging on to my dreams, despite the hitches thrown by life.

The entire writing process was time consuming; however, every hour, day, and month that I spent trying to overcome frequent writer's block was worth every effort. I was a newcomer to the writer's world, so I had to learn quickly. Google was my No. 1 source for increasing my knowledge about becoming an author and for connecting with writers' groups in my community.

How was the world going to react to my story? Are they going to feel inspired? Will someone tell me that I shouldn't quit my day job? Is it all a waste of my time?

With the release of my autobiography came a few anxieties. My top concern was that my mother and siblings would be reading my confessions. I was disappointed that my father never had the chance to read my perspective on life. It was a pity for me.

I was ready to share the first 23 years of my life with the world. It was never about the possibilities of becoming rich and famous. Instead, I felt like I had an inspiring story to share. A story for those who needed to be uplifted, or doubted themselves, or had given up on their visions because of life's hardships. If my words could change just one life for the better, then my work was done. I was inspired to make a difference.

I understood that writers no longer needed the approval of big-name publishing companies in order to publish their work. I had the mind of an artist on the verge of creating a masterpiece, so I contacted and hired some locals to be part of my book's production. I hired a photographer for the book cover and two editors to get the book ready for print. To save myself money, I did whatever I could on my own, such as designing and typesetting. A small publishing house out of Texas handled the rest. It took about five months to get the first physical copy of my book into my hands for review. I used to think the scent of women's perfume was the best. That was, until I held a copy of my book, *Hanging On To My Dreams: An Autobiography of Bouncing Back from All Rejections,* in my hands and smelled the crisp aroma of new paper and freshly printed ink. On May 11, 2011, I was proud to say that I was a published author. But that was only the beginning.

The process of releasing and promoting my book was not as easy as it was written on the blogs I read. One of the issues I had to constantly deal with was Cho's insecurity, particularly with my writing about ex-girlfriends. Would you believe that Cho secretly advised one of my editors to remove the sexually explicit content from my book? I'd later found out after creeping through the private messages on her Facebook account. Because the book was going to be marketed at a younger audience, I reluctantly agreed with my editor's suggestion, when really it was Cho's instruction. It wasn't Cho's decision to make, and I felt like she was limiting my potential as a writer. Why couldn't she understand that the exes were all in my past? Cho acted like I was still in love with them. But since Cho funded the expenses of my book, it was a fight I couldn't win.

My first book was dedicated to my mother, who gave me the strength to hang on to my dreams. Before the book's official release date, I told myself that my mother would be the recipient of the very first copy. Or, so I had hoped. I chickened out and didn't send her a copy because of the contents pertaining to my mother's domestic abuse experiences and my feelings about the absence of my biological father. I just didn't want my mother to disown me; I was afraid of her reaction to the book.

Eventually, Marvin purchased a copy on Amazon.com, and, after reading it, he sent his copy to our mother. I didn't know he had done that, so I wasn't expecting a review by my mother.

"Mario, you bound to put out my business like that," she said during a rare incoming phone call. I was silent as she ranted. "Mario, why was it so hard to talk to me about your feelings?"

"I don't know," I replied, shying away from the awkwardness.

"Overall, I am proud of you, my boy, for publishing your first book. I laugh, I cried. I really enjoyed it," she continued. "You've come a long way, and I love you, my son."

REBIRTH

I couldn't help but smile. My mother's approval made me feel like I was on top of the world. The concern I had had about destroying our relationship because of the words I had written had vanished. However, I still had to deal with the ramifications from my younger siblings, who had briefly stopped all communication with me after reading about my version of their father. I am a believer in the notion that time heals all wounds, and they eventually accepted my work as a non-fiction author.

On July 27, I held the official release of my first published book in Toronto. Not only was it the first work in my series, it also signalled a way for me to live the life that I preached.

I honestly never thought that my story would be read by people of all ages around the world, let alone be inspiring to others. One of the biggest surprises since it was published was a message I received from Ian McCarthy, president and general manager of the Saint John Mill Rats—a Canadian professional basketball team of the National Basketball League of Canada (NBL Canada).

"What's up, Arnold? I finally had a chance to read your book on our recent road trip to Quebec," Ian wrote. "I really enjoyed it. Small world—I actually played for Champlain College in Burlington in 1991-1992. I met Mike "White Mike" Cayole at a recent Champlain basketball reunion. His younger brother, Chris, has been an opponent of my teams in the ABA, PBL, and now NBL Canada. I was curious how you came to settle out west in Canada? You should consider trying out next year for the NBL Canada draft."

I had to wait until the summer draft of 2012 to take his advice. Here was an opportunity presenting itself when I least expected it. I had a year to prepare myself to seize that break, and I was prepared to lose sleep to make my dreams come true.

In my basketball world, whenever there was a chance to fulfil my pro hoop dreams, disappointments were never far behind. A recorded message said it all.

"Hey, Arnold, it is Greg Smith with the Calgary Crush. Um, I'm just calling to let you know, I didn't really want to leave this on a voicemail, but I wanted to let you know before tomorrow, we are trimming the roster down to 12, and, unfortunately, we are not going to ask you to come to tomorrow's practice. Uh, I'd like to keep your contact info, so, if we do have an injury or anything like that, hopefully we can ask you to step in. But, unfortunately, we are not going to ask you to come to tomorrow's practice. Thank you. Bye."

Fittingly and understandably, I felt crushed.

Calgary Crush was a brand new basketball organization formed under the American Basketball Association (ABA). When rumours

181

started spreading amongst the basketball community about a franchise being established, my basketball associates thought of me as being part of the team; the owner himself had foreseen my dreams coming true. Somehow, after making the team and going through a number of hours of practice, I was cut for reasons only the coaching staff knew. I heard gossip that the head coach wanted to focus on those players who once played for him at the college level. That would have been a great opportunity for me to stay in shape until my tryouts with NBL Canada draft. Still, I held no grudges, and, whenever I had the time, I supported them at their home games.

Francis Tobias a.k.a. My Father

Fourth Quarter

Tendency

Chapter 37

I've Become That Monster

I'm the first to admit that I was a dog—a good guy with bad habits. The two early male figures in my life, Tobias and Lucius, who I was striving not to become, were involuntarily present in me. It seemed as if I was the reincarnation of them in their younger years. As I continued to write my life away, I found myself staring at a documentary about my father's life. And then, I saw flashes of my stepfather striking my mother with the wire from our house's telephone. I was becoming that monster.

I tend to believe that partners can bring out the best, or the worst, in each other. The couple that Cho and I had become was not even close to bringing out the best of me. There were more issues arising in our home than on the TV at news hour. I constantly felt like I was just not good enough.

While waiting for the results from my application for permanent residence, I decided to search for a few under-the-table job opportunities. I was getting an intense amount of pressure from a financially frustrated Cho. Even though she was making a six-figure income, she was feeling the constraints of supporting a grown man and being responsible for paying all the bills.

Cho had once cried out to me that she would have been in a better financial position if she hadn't fallen for an African con artist who had scammed her out of tens of thousands of dollars in an online love gone wrong. The ruthless African stranger had led her to believe that he loved her and needed money for family and medical emergencies. Knowing the caring person that Cho was, I know she would have spent her last penny for the one she loved. At times, I would feel the repercussions of the scammer's actions whenever I needed extra funds. She would remind me that she was working hard to pay off the debts from her mistakes. I would say to her, "Never allow someone you left in your past distract you from becoming the better person that you are striving for."

Judging from Cho's past, it was evident as to why she lived independently for so long before she met me. Needless to say, she is a true role model for independent women who won't make the mistake of becoming dependent on men.

Although working under the table was illegal, I was trying to help her out by supporting myself. I hoped that word of mouth and

Kijiji would be valuable sources to finding cash jobs. After weeks of searching, I landed my first job with a furniture moving company. However, that gig didn't last long, as the employer was having a hard time paying me for two weeks of hard labour.

My income needed to continue flowing, so I decided to work nights at a more industrious establishment. After completing an online course, I became a licensed bouncer, a.k.a. doorman, at Soho Bar and Grill, a popular downtown restaurant and nightclub. For a weekend, I made $200, working five hours a night. I didn't consider the job to be work; it felt more like I was getting paid to party. Fridays were known as hip-hop nights, attracting an urban crowd that I could relate to. Saturdays featured a disc jockey who played Spanish music for the Latin crowd. Working at the club brought entertainment to my weeks and a break from clingy Cho.

Looking back on the days I worked at the club, I would never recommend this type of setting for a married man. First of all, a few lunatic patrons would sneak in with lethal weapons and use them to settle simple disagreements. This can quickly escalate into a dangerous setting if you're not alert. Secondly, it can be a major distraction for a man who has a weakness when it comes to remaining faithful. Women of all ages, commonly known as bad bitches or whores, would easily throw themselves at the bouncer, especially to the head doorman in charge of entrance. It was hard to keep my hands to myself because they would be dressed in short, tight, slutty outfits that exposed plenty of cleavage, and they were seductive with their sweet talk. They looked at me as fresh meat, and I was getting so many new numbers, it was as if they were confusing me for a tall, dark version of the Whitepages. For the most part, I resisted the attention, but I occasionally quenched my thirst. I had no one to blame but myself.

I could write chapters of stories about how infidelity infiltrated the nightclub and how mixtures of alcohol and drugs made it so much easier. I remember walking in on girls sucking off, not one, but two guys, at the same time in the bathroom stalls. I've seen girls getting fingered on the dance floor by complete strangers. To top it all off, I've witnessed unprotected intercourse in dark corners of the club. I could go on writing the details of some stimulating stories, but I don't want to expose all the secrets of being a bouncer.

Who am I to judge these people, when I had fallen into that same trap? I was the husband of an unhappy home, and, outside that home, I had the intentions of a bachelor. Before leaving my car to start a nightshift at the club, I often left my wedding ring in the glove compartment and I did so without feeling any guilt. Returning home to Cho, I ensured the ring was back on my finger. If I forgot to grab the ring, I would hide my hand until I retrieved it. I just wanted to do single things before dawn. To a persistent woman, the band around my ring finger wouldn't even matter. Some wanted love; others just wanted to fuck a black Caribbean man. I treated them like worthless side chicks that were only convenient for my sexual needs. In their eyes, I was probably viewed as a newly available man who was tall, dark, handsome, and career driven—I guessed I just had that look to them. Truthfully, my deceitfulness was selfish and heartless. I knew exactly who I was—a man who was emotionally unavailable; in more familiar terms, I was considered to be a womanizer. *Was this all due to patterns of dysfunctional love?*

I tried my best to prevent any broken hearts, but Cho was just too intelligent for my lies. When I wasn't home by 3 a.m., I would notice more than 20 text messages and/or missed calls. I knew she would be hurting, so I constantly lied about my whereabouts to protect her from additional pain. My truth was never the convincing truth. When I got home late because I was with another woman, I would say that I was still at work. If I never came home, I would say that I was too drunk, so I slept on Zaine's couch. I knew if I continued with these deceptive ways, it would soon catch up to me. Still, I lied.

Out of all these sexual encounters, there was one incident that Cho needed to know but I never had the heart to tell her. Without mentioning names, this particular woman was the photographer who captured the images for my first book. It all went down at her parent's house while they were away on vacation in Europe. At that time, she was married, too. Despite knowing what we both know, she remained friends with Cho. *Who is the bigger hypocrite?*

A few weeks after my first wedding anniversary, I came home to one angry wife. It was a Tuesday evening, so I was supposedly returning home from my weekly writers' group meeting. In fact, I had been on a date with a new girl and then visited a mistress of mine. I parked the car in the garage and then placed my wedding ring on its rightful finger. Before stepping outside of the car, I double-checked the quality of the bouquet of flowers that I had just bought for Cho. They were guaranteed to put a smile on her face— just like all the other times—or, so I thought.

I heard the sound of loud footsteps approaching as I tried to enter the house. It was strange because she was usually preparing dinner. *She must have heard me coming from the sound of the opening garage door,* I whispered to myself.

"Where were you?" she asked as soon as I had one foot in the door. The aggressive tone in her voice reflected her facial expression. I remained calm, while my thoughts were trying to trace where I'd messed up on my trails. *Does she know?* I always told myself that I was a professional when it came to covering up my dirt.

"Where the fuck have you been?" she repeated, making me feel small. I stared at the floor, thinking of ways to escape this confrontation. So, I decided to stick to the script.

"I told you I had a writers' group meeting today," I said, walking toward the kitchen, not even bothering to hand her the flowers.

"Who the fuck is Brenda?" she asked, following my every move. By the stomps of her feet, you would have sworn she was a giant.

The name momentarily caused me to be in disarray. *How could she know?*

My first response was reactive. "What the fuck?"

"You were on a fucking date with her," she shouted. "I saw her Facebook status, and she tagged you in it! You went to see *Scream 4* with her at the Chinook Theatre!"

Fuck! I fucked up! Fucking Facebook again.

From that point on, it was a battle of who could yell the loudest. It was a scene we had played out many times before that usually ends with me punching a hole in the wall, some physical restriction getting in her way, or the police showing up because of a neighbour's noise complaint. I immediately searched for a backup plan, which was to lie some more to save my ass.

"OK! Nothing happened," I said, trying to prevent her from putting on her coat. "Don't go! Nothing happened. I swear. I know you don't like scary movies, and I really wanted to see it. She is just a friend." I shoved Cho aside so hard that she collided with the wall. A few seconds later, a quick, sharp, stabbing pain in the top of my head disrupted me from locking the doors. Blood started gushing down my face as swiftly as water flows down a mountain on a stormy day. Initially, I didn't know who or what hit me, and, frankly, I didn't think Cho had it in her to take a swing at my back.

"Fuck! What did you hit me with?"

Cho said nothing but kept her distance to avoid retaliation. As I sat down to settle my dizziness from the impact, I noticed some sort of spray can rolling to a halt at my feet. When Cho noticed I was in pain, she showed empathy by nursing my wound. The fight had ended, but the war had just begun.

A liar will always be a liar; a cheater will always be a cheater— two of Cho's favourite lines whenever she suspected me of wrongdoings. I wasn't man enough for such an amazing woman. Any smart, loyal man with a good heart would die for the love of someone like Cho. While it almost seemed like I needed her, I wanted more. It was as if the love I had to give was waiting for its lawful owner. Almost doesn't exist. Multiple beautiful women were my fixation. I guess they made me feel manlier—and I was a sucker for that. I had a *fucking* problem. Numerous apologies, better excuses, less frequent time away from home, and lots of makeup sex helped me get on better terms with Cho. As a matter of fact, more sex always resolved my fuckups. If I had wanted to, I could've ordered Cho to buy me a brand new car after we made love. For the record, there wasn't much to tell about the situation with Brenda; it really was just a movie date. OK, I may have French-kissed her goodnight, but that was all. Nonetheless, I was on Cho's radar, and it seemed as if I would be on probation for the rest of my life.

Instead of learning by my slip-ups with Brenda, I seized that moment to be more careful with other prospects. For starters, I made a strict change to my Facebook's privacy settings that would restrict anyone from posting to my wall without my permission. Still, that wasn't enough. A few weeks later, Detective Cho caught me in another case of cheating.

It was a blurry night after the Lil Wayne concert in April, 2011, that led me into another quandary with the woman I married a year ago. I'd attended the show with my basketball associates, enjoying the performances by the headliner and his special guests, Nicki Minaj and Rick Ross, from the front row. By the time the show ended, I was so drunk that all I could recall later was getting into a limousine outside of the Scotiabank Saddledome. Vodka was not friendly to me on that Friday evening.

The following morning, I woke up on a concrete floor, feeling as if I had just been defeated by a technical knockout in a 12-round boxing match. I didn't know which hurt more: my numb upper lip, or the hangover. As my vision gained light, shadowy, metal bars became clearer.

"Arnold Henry!" shouted a police officer, who suddenly appeared from behind a closed door.

"Yes," I answered, slowly recovering on my feet. "What happened? Am I arrested?"

"You're in the drunk tank for being too intoxicated outside of Flames Central."

"So—"

"You're free to go now," he said, unlocking the cell.

"I am?" I asked with embarrassment, attempting to retrace last night's outing. All I could remember was pre-drinking and chugging vodka. My head started to spin just thinking about it. *I'm never drinking again,* I lied to myself.

After assembling all of my belongings from the officer, I left the station in hopes of a five-minute taxi ride to Katherine's house on 17th Avenue Southwest. *What happened? What did I do?* I asked myself on the way there.

"Arnold, what's wrong with you?" Katherine asked. "Where were you last night? I've been calling you all morning."

"I don't know, but my lips hurt like shit. I feel like vomiting." I rushed to the bathroom to observe the damages in the mirror. Katherine was just as surprised as I was to see the size of my swollen upper lip. "I think I was in a fight." She brought me a bag of ice and a bottle of Gatorade. That minor cut was the least of my worries, though. Like my wife at home, Katherine, who was my mistress, was expecting my presence in her bed after the concert. I fucked up double time.

Just like in previous incidents, the plan was to tell Cho that I was too drunk to drive home. I pulled my dead cellphone from my pocket and instantly remembered ignoring all of Cho's calls and text messages throughout the night. I knew then that I was going to be in big trouble. "I have to go home," I told Katherine, who knew my true feelings about my marriage. I hid nothing from her. She knew exactly what was at home waiting for me. Cho only saw Katherine as my public relations officer for my book, but she had her doubts.

Speeding my way through traffic, I felt like my life was on the line. My shirt was drenched in sweat. When I arrived home, I pushed the button on the remote control for the garage door opener. The garage door did not react to my command. *That's weird,* I thought after countless attempts. I parked the black 2008 Honda Civic out front and proceeded to key my way in through the front door. Access was denied. It was as if I was using the wrong set of keys. Ringing the doorbell didn't help either. I circled the house about three times, searching for loose windows and doors.

"Cho!" I screamed, pounding my knuckles on the front door. Nothing but silence responded to my cries. I ran out of patience. I desperately needed to use the bathroom. I proceeded with drop kicking the front door. The power of all the might that I could muster instantly unhinged the door from its frame with one blow.

"Cho?" A quick walk-through confirmed that no one was home. I wasn't expecting to find all my clothes bagged up in a black garbage bag. *Oh my God. I truly messed up this time.* I stomped my way to our bedroom to find the home phone. I needed answers.

"Cho, what's going on?" I asked when she answered her cell.

"Arnold, fuck you! How did you get into my house?" she screamed. "I hate you! I don't ever want to see you ever again!

"What—?"

"Get out of my house! I'm going to divorce you!"

"What's your ...?"

"I'm calling the police!"

"Why you calling ...?" I tried to get a word in, but I was stopped by the dial tone. She had hung up on me.

Police? I wasn't convinced that she would call the police because I had heard these threats on several occasions, and, nine times out of 10, the neighbours were the ones who called the cops.

I quickly plugged my phone into the charger, feeling optimistic about finding some clues or reasons why Cho lost her cool with me to such an extent this time. *She knows something that I don't know,* I thought while gathering some ice to place on my lips.

My concentration was broken by a knock at the front of the house. "Cho!" I shouted. To avoid any further damages to the front entrance, I decided to open the garage door.

"Hands up where I can see them!" shouted two police officers as they drew their guns out of their holsters. "Get down! Get down! Get down flat on the ground! Don't move! Don't move!" I was literally kissing the dusty garage floor before the officers were able to finish their orders. The only thing moving was the tightening of my butt cheeks. *Damn, I should have used the toilet.*

"Who are you?"

Scared for my life, I shouted, "I live here! I live here!"

Chapter 38

Peace Bond

"Are the cops coming for me, Cho? I'm going to end it all."

"What're you talking about, Arnold?" Cho asked harshly. I contemplated whether I should take a dive into the river. Then, I shook my head. *Why should I end it all? I have so much more to gain in this world. This is stupid. I can make things right again.* I cautiously retreated into the silver Honda Civic, staring down in the direction of the sirens across the Bow River.

"Cho, did you call the cops on me again? I see the police cars. Cho, are they coming for me?"

"Arnold, I don't know what you talking about. I don't even know where you are," Cho replied.

I used my free hand to turn on the car's engine. My heart raced as a series of flashing blue and red lights approached me. *I gotta get out of here,* I thought as I shifted the car into reverse. "Cho, they're coming for me!"

"Arnold, I didn't call the cops."

"So, why're they coming for me?" Seeing that I was cornered, I thought of running away on foot. *I didn't want to spend another night in jail.* I shifted the car into park. "Oh wait, they're not coming for me," I said with a sigh of relief.

"Why don't you come here and take a shower? I'll make you some soup," Cho suggested.

Wow, is she serious? She still wants me to come over after everything she's put me through? What the fuck is wrong with this woman?

Knowing that I had no money and nowhere to go, I responded, "Um, sure. OK. I'm downtown. I will see you in 20 minutes."

I've been here before, and, clearly, I hadn't learned from my past. Before I drove off, I took one last look at the most recent photos that Cho had posted on her personal Facebook page. *Can I trust her? Is this a set-up?* The answer was staring me right in the face, saying, *don't trust her. She's a mean bitch.* Her Facebook photo album, entitled *This Is From My Husband*, featured half a dozen pictures displaying black-and-blue bruises on parts on her body. *If Cho was so frightened for her life, then why was it so easy for her to accept me back? If she wanted me out, then why was she inviting me back so easily? Was her love that blind?* I couldn't believe that she was accusing me of hitting her.

REBIRTH

Two days ago, she went so far as to involve my mother—the same woman she had called a bitch on numerous occasions— in our crossfires. In the past, Cho had even complained that my mother didn't raise me to be a respectable man.

"Mario, what is going on? Why your wife calling me and tell me that you beat her up," my mother cried out over a long-distance call.

"Mummy, don't worry. Nothing is happening. Cho just wants attention and is playing victim again. I didn't touch her."

"Be careful. You don't want to end up back in Saint Lucia."

Four days earlier, on Sept. 5, an emergency protection order had been granted after police detained me. The morning following my arrest, the conditions set on my bail were revised after I appeared in front of a judge. Cho and I were both made aware that we were not supposed to contact each other—directly or indirectly. In addition to that, I was banned from going within a three-block radius of her house, the place I called home in Canada. To grab a few of my essentials, I was provided with a police escort for a brief visit to the house while Cho was away. I only grabbed some changes of clothes and the silver Honda Civic, which I slept in for a few days.

Driving southbound on Macleod Trail, I was on a course to a restricted area; it was a mind-boggling drive from Point A to Point B. The last year and a half of my marriage was playing back in my mind. *How was I able to trust someone who tried her best to see me fail? Who else was I supposed to call?* Random thoughts were circulating in my brain. I was thinking especially about all the times Cho had dialled 911 for alleged abuse. It was only about five months ago when police held me at gunpoint in the garage of my own home. My ignorance for the Canadian laws initially had me believing I was going to be arrested for burglary. After handing my Alberta's driver's licence to the police officer, he advised me that no crime had been committed.

"Why did you kick in the door? Next time, just use the keys, and, if you don't have a key, just wait for someone to let you in," the officers joked. I almost shit my pants that day.

That same day, I learned Cho's reasoning for changing all the locks. She found out from a friend that I had been picking up girls after the Lil Wayne concert. Apparently, I had gotten into a fight with one girl's boyfriend at the club—which explained my busted lip. I was too drunk to recall these events. Either way, the immature version of me felt like Cho should have at least waited for my return home to hear my lies about the story. Proceeding to take revenge was uncalled for. Although she had expressed all that pain, she then let me back in the house as if I had never left.

193

I was only a few kilometres from the house. The closer I got, the slower I drove, keeping an eye out for anything suspicious. I felt like this was a set-up by Cho and there were police officers on the lookout. *Why did I trust Cho so easily?* Only a few days had passed since Cho called the police on me again. I had just had my wisdom teeth removed, so I was resting in our master bedroom.

"Cho, can you please shut the door?" I asked her after being awakened to the commotion in the kitchen.

I overheard a voice saying to Cho, "Don't do it." That response had come from Cho's no-good friend—an Asian woman who seemed like she was just there to cause trouble. I had no idea who she was or why she was over. I just wanted to rest.

"If you want the door closed, you come do it yourself," said the unfamiliar Asian accent.

What the fuck? Who the fuck is that?

I became enraged. "Don't come to my fucking house and start shit," I screamed at Cho's friend after stomping my way to the kitchen.

"Who the fuck you think you are?" she replied, stepping up to me like a bodyguard.

"Get the fuck out!" I pointed to the door. Before I could say another word, she grabbed Cho and fled through the back door as if they were being chased. *What the fuck just happened?* I suspected Cho must have been telling all her friends about our relationship, while, at the same time, making me out to be some sort of abusive husband. *Cho was playing victim again.* A few minutes later, two police officers were inside the house questioning me like a criminal. Once more, it was a waste of a 911 call because no crimes had been committed. It seemed to me like Cho and her friend were being immature drama queens intentionally playing the victim card to cause problems. I really felt like Cho's mission was to bring me down to the ground, to have me deported. To accomplish her goals, it seemed as if Cho was auditioning for a role to replace Maggie Wilson. After all, she once told me that she believed I beat up Maggie in a fury on Dec. 13, 2004. Even though I felt so much hatred toward Cho, I stayed. I was tempted to leave, but I had nowhere else to go.

"I'm here," I whispered through my cellphone. Before I drove the car into the garage, I scrutinized my surroundings to ensure no neighbours were in close proximity. Although I knew I was breaching the conditions of my bail—and I knew the consequences for that could be jail time or a fine—I needed Cho by my side to make things right because I was not prepared to be alone in Canada. I had no money, no job, and no shelter. I sat in the car for a moment to rethink the situation.

REBIRTH

I figured there was nothing new about this situation; the cycle had repeated itself, and it seemed like I was reliving my freshman year at the University of Vermont. Since I had overcome this cycle in the past, I believed I was stronger and able to do it again. All these deep thoughts intensified the throbbing in my head. The Crown prosecutor had threatened me with the possibility of deportation, and my application for permanent residency was now in jeopardy.

Upon facing Cho inside the house, I was tempted to show her real physical reasons why she should press charges against me. I tried to mask my aggression with a cool, calm demeanour because I knew everything was on the line. For someone who was terrified for her life, Cho seemed pleased to see me and acted as if nothing had happened, as if I hadn't been charged for alleged domestic violence with her as the only witness and victim.

The late-night sounds invaded the awkward silence in the living room. Our exchange of words was down to a minimum. A bowl of soup was set at the table to satisfy my hunger. My unpleasant body odour reminded me that I needed to freshen up. For the past few days, I had been sleeping uncomfortably in the cold car, with no means of showering and no access to clean clothes. I could have called a few people, but I was just too embarrassed to share with my few friends in Calgary the reasons for my circumstance. They had read my story, and I was fearful they would judge me for putting myself in the same situation that had derailed my American hoop dreams.

Break up to make up. That infamous love song had replayed in our relationship way too many times. As if sex was the solution to all of our issues, Cho and I slid underneath the bedsheets exchanging affection. The situation felt so heavy that it ended with Cho in tears. "Why are we going through this," she cried. I truly wanted to slap some sense into her to remind her that she accused me of a crime I did not commit. But I showed my concerns by enveloping her naked body in my arms while fondling her straight, long, black hair. We spent the rest of the night discussing how we were going to make things right again. Lord knew I was concerned about my future in Canada. I really couldn't care less for Cho's feelings after she lied to law enforcement. Things had to be corrected immediately.

The following morning, after packing a few items, I discreetly left. I knew I needed somewhere to sleep, so I reached out to Zaine. After explaining to him the events that had taken place, he provided me with a sleeping area on his living room floor. It was convenient living at Zaine's home because he lived a few blocks from the courthouse, where I needed to be for my hearing on Sept. 13 at 9 a.m.

I didn't have support in Calgary like I had in Burlington, Vermont. This made it a lonely road, as I dealt solely with the false allegations. Before going in front of the judge, I was represented by a duty counsel—a free lawyer who provided legal advice and ran around assisting others on a first-come, first-served basis. I sat with him at an empty rectangular-shaped table inside a private room. He was an older, chubby man, who looked dismayed, as if he had just finished a stressful day at the office. "What are you charged with?" he asked, adjusting his glasses while steadily flipping through my paperwork.

"Domestic violence," I replied, drying my sweaty palms on my dress pants. I constantly caught myself with shaky legs.

"Your first offence?"

"Yes, sir."

"OK, Mr. Henry, here is what we're going to do," he said, gathering his things as if he saw these type of cases all the time. "Since it is your first offence, we are going to aim for a peace bond."

"A peace bond?" I asked.

"Yes. It is basically an agreement for you to keep the peace for a period of time with some conditions. And, at the end, you will not have a criminal record."

I nodded with a sigh of relief, "OK, yes, yes please."

The peace bond was granted and became official after signing a few documents. The conditions were that I had to keep the peace in my relationship with Cho and be on good behaviour for the next 12 months. It was going to be a long process, but I finally felt as if I was able to breathe again.

I was given a few pieces of paper with the following conditions:

1. Within two business days, report in person to a probation officer.
2. Live where approved by probation officer or at Zaine's apartment.
3. Have no contact or communication whatsoever, either directly or indirectly with Cho Kim Wang, except as approved by your probation officer in advance and with consent of Cho Kim Wang.
4. You are banned from going to your home, except as approved by your probation officer in advance and with consent of Cho Kim Wang.
5. You will go for assessment and participate in and complete any counselling, treatment, or programming directed by your probation officer, including:
- Domestic Violence
- Alcohol/Drug/Substance Abuse
6. You will sign any release or waiver of information as directed, providing access to information required by your probation officer.

7. You will provide your probation officer with proof in writing that you have followed through and completed any treatment or counselling you have been directed to take.

Chapter 39

Path of Change

In the neighbourhood of Chaparral, about a 10-minute drive from my estranged wife, was my new place of residence. My roommate was a short, scrawny, Caucasian man who I rarely saw. Although I lived with him, it felt like we were neighbours, each renting a one-bedroom condo. I think I needed the peace and quiet that the unit offered, or maybe I just needed a break from the commitments of being in a marriage.

Many nights, I sat alone on the seemingly more spacious bed, as I realized that my wife and I were better off being friends than lovers. The two of us being together in the flesh was only tearing us apart. I was Mr. No Good for her, something I had known from the start. Still, I was on the edge of being optimistic about our future; I had always thought that I would change my ways and eventually fall deeply in love with Cho. It just wasn't happening. And even if I decided to become a better man for her, Cho was never able to conceive one of the greatest dreams I've ever dreamt—a child.

Despite the conditions of the peace bond, Cho remained my go-to person. I visited her whenever she was horny, and she brought me money or groceries whenever I was hungry. We were both aware that we were breaking the law. With me out of the house, Cho decided to rent the basement to Laurie, the first lady who had responded to an online advertisement. We agreed that Laurie's rent money would be used to pay the rent for my new condo. That plan only lasted for a month because Cho found every reason to hate the poor lady. She ended up kicking out her tenant without a month's notice. I never understood why, but I was visiting when everything went down.

"I don't know what I did to her," Laurie complained to me. "She always complains. I just stay downstairs and I try my best to stay away from her. I am so scared to live here. When I come to the house, I always have to creep inside. She scares me. Please talk to her. Tell that I need a month to find somewhere to rent."

Laurie's shaky remarks had put a smile on my face because I could relate to her situation. I knew then that I wasn't always the cause of the problems. Cho had some real issues living with other people.

It was going on two years since I moved to Calgary, and Cho and I were slowly resolving to become strangers. At 26, the man in me just wasn't ready to act accordingly with the maturity level of my 45 year old wife. I still had a boyishly irresponsible state of mind. Recognizing some of my unhealthy behaviour, I knew this was the time when I needed to simply grow up. I did not want to live in my 30s with haunting memories of my 20-something self. Serious and convincing actions needed to take place. I needed to change, not for anyone else, but for myself. I wanted to see growth in myself where I would be the best man I could possibly be. I wanted to change.

In September, I was ordered by the court to attend counselling at the YWCA Sheriff King Home in Calgary's historic Inglewood neighbourhood. Even though it was a condition of my probation and peace bond agreement, I was more than willingly to comply and make some positive changes.

On the evening of my intake appointment for the men's group counselling program, I inadvertently caught a glimpse of myself from an outside perspective. I was about to get into my car when I was distracted by an uproar coming from one of the condo units above.

"I hate you, Mark!" a woman shouted.

"If you hate me so much, why don't you pack up and leave then," said a guy with a low voice.

"I leave? I leave, Mark," she responded with annoyance. Watching the entertainment through the balcony doors, I could see someone pacing around the living room. She continued yelling at him, "You don't do anything around here. I come home from work and the house is always in a mess! So, fuck you!"

"How about you clean it then!" he demanded.

"I ...," the cries of an infant kept the woman from finishing her statement. I shook my head at the scenario with pangs of guilt. *Was that how bad Cho and I sounded when we fought?* I thought about it from the neighbours' perspective, hearing life-threatening sounds coming from a home. No wonder people are so quick to call the police to report suspected domestic violence.

"Abusive behaviours and attitudes are a result of many years of learning and can be replaced with healthy behaviour and attitudes. Power-and-control attitudes, responses to anger, communication skills, self-awareness, empathy for others, and self-control, will be emphasized in this program."

As much as I felt the need to be part of the Path of Change Counselling program, I believed that Cho should have undergone a similar program for women. She needed some serious help, too. We both needed to learn how to become better partners in a relationship. As a couple, we once tried to seek professional assistance from a marriage counsellor. A few months earlier, we actually attended one session, which amounted to a 60-minute yelling match to determine who could successfully talk over the other. We never went for a follow-up session. I'm sure the counsellor was grateful for that, too, as she probably foresaw there was no point trying to fix our marriage.

For the next 14 weeks, I was seated amongst an open group discussion with random men who were in the same boat as me. I've taken part in many one-on-one counselling programs before, but never openly. Christine, our counsellor, sat at the front of the square room, with her assistant, David, at her side. Christine was a lean, young lady with brown hair, while David was an older, balding, grey-headed man. "We will be going around the room," Christine instructed. "I would like for each of you to introduce yourself. Tell us about someone who is close to you, and something that made you happy over this past week."

Since we were going around the room counter-clockwise and I was seated closest to her right, I was the first to answer. "My name is Arnold Henry. I have no family here. I'm just happy to be alive," I replied, barely able to keep my head up while staring at my shoes. When I did get a chance to scrutinize the room, I saw about a dozen men of every background with name tags pinned to their shirts. Their ages ranged from 18 to 50-plus. While everyone introduced themselves to the group, I got a brief insight of their reasons for what led them to this program—drugs, money, alcohol, and whatnot. They each blamed others for the reason they were here, but none blamed themselves.

The entire process was an invitation to change. I had open ears, and I was willing to learn and apply this new knowledge in life. Every Monday, we learned a new lesson. While Christine and David took turns demonstrating their support toward the group, it was voluntary for us to share our experiences. Hearing similar stories of what the other men had to deal with in their relationships had somewhat helped to generate comfort and familiarity among the group. It definitely encouraged us to talk about sensitive subjects. We didn't have to worry about details of our personal lives being repeated to any outside sources because every word shared amongst the group was strictly confidential.

"One in eight women in Canada is physically abused by their partner," Christine read from the sheet of paper in her hands. "The four basic types of abuse are: psychological abuse, also known as emotional or verbal abuse; sexual abuse; economic abuse; and, physical abuse." As she gave examples from each category, I recognized that I was accountable on a few offences. Every time Christine or David described real-life scenarios, I remembered all the times I had been in similar situations. Back then, I only knew one way to deal with conflicts in a household, and that was with retaliation. During my weekly counselling sessions, I learned a number of skills that can greatly impact how to cope with aggravation and perceived provocation. As a group, we were "safety planning" around our anger. We learned that it was just as important to admit to, and accept, when we are angry or in the wrong.

On one of those evenings, the most imperative lesson I learned was the power of "time outs"—and I'm not talking about a short break in basketball. Time outs are an opportunity to exert control over oneself to avoid becoming aggressive. It is useful when there are early clues of anger. When anger is identified, it is an indication to the parties involved that it's best to take a break to cool down, and provide an estimated length of time needed. For example, "I am getting really upset. I need some time to calm down. I will be back in an hour." Upon returning to your partner, talk about how your feelings in a healthy, constructive manner. *Why wasn't I taught this method in the past?* If I had been able to draw from this knowledge in previous encounters, I would have saved myself from a lot of trouble. Anger was my weakest trait.

In an exercise titled *Change Wheel Model,* I found the courage to share with the group the incident that led to my arrest. Before I began, David said to me, "Think of a recent situation where you got angry with your partner. Think about the situation, your thoughts about the situation, your feelings, and then what you did. Think about the affect your behaviour had on others and yourself."

We were already halfway through the 14 weeks. For the first time, I removed my winter jacket to speak. Without looking, I sensed all eyes were on me, as if I were the headliner onstage. I took a minute to clear my throat. "It was on Monday, the September long weekend of 2011, when it happened," I finally said. "My wife and I were driving around the Forest Lawn area looking for a new place for me to rent. We had both realized that it would be best if we lived in separate homes because of all the disagreements we had." I briefly started to connect with everyone's stares.

"Take your time," Christine said when she spotted a tear dripping down my face.

"I—I, wasn't sure if I was ready to live on my own without a job. My wife said that she would pay for everything. My rent, my food, and give me money, but I was scared," I continued as my eyes dropped to my trembling finger lying on my shaky knees. "We returned home that day and sat inside the parked car. I told my wife how I really felt about moving out of our home. I told her that I don't want to move out now. She reconfirmed with me that she really wanted me to move out. The tone in her voice sounded assertive, and her mind was made up. That led to absolute chaos for the next few minutes. We exchanged fighting words like two territorial dogs meeting head-to-head."

David asked, "At the moment, how did you feel?"

I sighed. "I'm not going to lie, I was a bit angry, but I swear to God that I did not mean her any harm. I just wanted to be out of her sight. I wanted to leave, like a time out," I replied, shaking my head. "She was in the driver's seat, so I told her that I needed the car. But she didn't want me to leave. She said that it was her car. Whenever she gets mad at me, everything she ever gave me is no longer mine. It is like a form of punishment. I used to hate that. That's when I decided to force myself in the driver's seat. A few seconds later, my wife called her friend, Lisa, on her cellphone out of distress. At this point we were sharing the same driver's seat; it was a tight fit."

"So, do you share the car with your wife?" Christine asked.

"No!" I replied. "When I first came to Canada, she told me I could drive that black car. There is silver Honda Civic that she uses. But it was in an accident, so it looks in bad shape. It can be embarrassing to drive. Plus, it was too small for me to drive."

"OK, so the two of you were in the driver's seat. What happened next?" David asked.

"Well, I reached across her body and I opened the driver's door. She was talking with her friend on the phone, saying how much of a bad person I was. So, I decided to scoot over in order for me to gain access to the wheel and gas pedal. She put up a fight to push herself back in the car, but she landed on the concrete driveway. I didn't hit her. I swear I didn't take a swing at her. I pushed her out the car so that I could leave."

"OK. Do you believe that there was a better way to resolve that situation?" Christine asked.

"Yeah, I guess," I replied. "I guess I should have just taken a *time out* without the need to use the car."

"Did she call the police?"

"Yes, later that evening, I received a text message from my wife saying that the cops are looking for me. So, I dialled 911 and the operator said that I should return home. On arrival, the house was in complete darkness. Shortly after, two police officers were knocking at the front door. I was arrested on the sight for domestic violence."

"How do you feel about the whole situation?" David asked.

"I felt like I was set-up by my own wife. It seems like she was trying her best to get me kicked out of the country. She used everything she could against me. The day after my arrest, she put up pictures on her Facebook saying that I beat her up. I don't understand how she got the bruises. Maybe she got them from the pavement. But the stupid cops believed everything."

"I understand, but are you accountable for any of your actions? Did you learn anything?" Christine asked.

"I feel like I should have called the police to inform them that I had a fight with my wife and I didn't hurt her. How do I stop her from lying? But, to be honest, I've gained some knowledge on ways to avoid conflicts. If I find myself in similar situations in the future, I will just walk away."

"That is good, Arnold. Think about the consequences before making choices," Christine reminded me. "It is easy to allow your anger to get the best of you."

After sharing with the group, I felt good hearing everyone's feedback. It was all for the betterment of my future. I understood that we do not have to go through the hardships of life on our own. There are others out there who can relate to our stories. There are valuable tools available to help people deal with whatever personal issues they may have. If you're a man who's having a difficult time coping with a relationship, or with life in general, I recommend finding a men's program in your community before the situation gets out of hand. You are never alone in this world.

Although I still had to report to my probation officer for at least eight more months, I had completed one of the conditions of the peace bond. On Jan. 23, 2012, I received a certificate that stated: "The YWCA Sheriff King Home Men's Program 'Path of Change' is a group-counselling program for men who have been abusive in an intimate relationship. The program consists of 14 weeks with each week focused on a different topic. You have completed the "Path of Change" counselling program and your file will be closed."

Dear Your Honour,

With the completion of my 14 weeks of counselling, I am writing to you with hopes that the no contact order will be lifted, and I will be able to reconnect with my wife.

The entire process I've gone through was indeed a life lesson and learning experience. The counselling sessions have been taken into consideration and I've learned to respond in an assertive way, rather than in an aggressive way. The counsellors did an incredible job in allowing me to be aware of my behaviours. I've learned to respond in ways where my wife and I won't have to suffer emotionally or physically. One example is taking constructive timeouts; taking some time apart to cool off during a heated argument. I've also learned the different levels of anger and the necessary steps to control myself before it becomes dangerous. With that being said, I am thrilled to have completed these sessions because I believe that it was something needed to save my marriage. My wife will be happy to see the new me.

I am hoping that I can connect with my wife soon so that she can see the changes in me. I strongly believe she'll see the major improvements in me. It is absolutely the best time for us to rekindle our relationship, because I know for a fact we are ready to work on our marriage.

Thanking you in advance.

Yours truly,
Arnold Henry

Chapter 40

Permanent Residence

On the night I was arrested for the alleged assault on Cho, the two officers with British accents who came to pick me up at the house asked me if I was a resident of Canada. Then, they told me that I would be deported. It was a night of extreme worries. My eyes burned throughout the night from lack of sleep inside the jail cell. Settling for the peace bond provided me with hopes for my future. I later learned that Cho had the power to stop my application to become a permanent resident. She spared me, but there was still a chance my arrest had been reported to immigration.

In mid-October, I logged onto my account on the Citizenship and Immigration Canada website. I became concerned when I noticed a modification to the status of my application for permanent residence.

"A decision has been made and you will be contacted." I didn't know what to think. I had everything to lose. Three days later, I saw a new update on the website.

"We sent you a letter on Oct. 18, 2011, to your mailing address about the decision on your application. Please consider delays in mail delivery before contacting us. If we have sent the letter to the wrong address, please contact us."

One week later, Cho called to tell me that I had new mail. I drove to her house as quickly as possible, as if I'd just gotten a call about a matching organ donation. I read the letter from Immigration Canada thoroughly. The next step in the application process was an examination interview, to be held at a federal government building in downtown Calgary. Cho was surprised that a decision had made in such a short period of time; it had only been 11 months since applying. Judging from the experiences of our friends with permanent resident statuses, we thought it would take about three years for a decision to be made. I was sweating balls.

Cho and I arrived to the interview on Nov. 24 at 10:30 a.m. On arrival to our appointment at the Harry Hayes building, Cho paid the remaining $490 in fees. We had prepared for the interview as if we were seeking employment, professional attire and all. The wait time was as nerve-wracking as waiting for the final score of a triple-overtime basketball game that you had $1,000 riding on. An hour later, we sat at a desk in an office with an Asian lady named Rachel, who held desperate information. Cho clasped my hand when she noticed I was shaking. "Can I get your passport, the two passport photos, and the receipt of your payment?" Rachel asked. I handed the documents to her.

Rachel then looked over to Cho. "Are you a citizen of Canada?"

"Yes," Cho replied.

"Can I get a piece of government-issued ID?" Cho complied. Cho and I looked across the desk as Rachel started jotting down information on a piece of documentation. "Do you have dependants in or outside Canada?"

"No ma'am," I replied.

"Have you committed a crime in or outside Canada?"

I quickly disconnected our eye contact. Cho squeezed my hand tightly to set off an alarm and wake me up from my sudden daydreaming episode. I snapped out of it. "Yes! Yes!" I cleared my throat and then re-established eye contact. "Yes, ma'am."

"Is there anything I need to know?"

"No," I replied.

"Cho?"

"No."

"Uh, OK," Rachel said. I continued to look across the desk to catch a glimpse of what she was writing. I was startled when Rachel stamped the paper. I took a few deep breaths in anticipation of her next words.

Rachel stood up from her chair and reached out to shake my hand. "Congratulations, Arnold Henry. You are now a permanent resident of Canada," she said.

It felt as if fireworks were exploding in my head. I wanted to hug and kiss Cho, but I kept it professional. I firmly clasped hands with Rachel. "Thank you."

Chapter 41

Dear Saint Lucia

Aug. 31, 2003, was the day I left my country to pursue my hoop dream in the United States of America. I had told myself that my initial departure was not goodbye forever. It was more like a see you later, or until we meet again. I would never turn my back on my birthplace. I had big dreams for my homeland—big, big dreams. The idea was to go beyond where no man on the island had gone before, to achieve greater successes, to put my homeland on the map once and for all. Despite having to assimilate into the many different cultures and countries over a 10-year span, Saint Lucia will always be home. I also hope for it to be my last home. If I happen to be away when I die, please bury me in Castries, Saint Lucia. I'd like my legacy to end where it all began.

I've come across many Saint Lucian athletes, entertainers, producers, artists, and authors who have one goal in common: using their talents to successfully represent our country. Or better yet, allowing the world to know that we have as many talents as the rest of the Caribbean islands. Saint Lucia, also known as the Helen of the West Indies, has a population of more than 170,000 people. In comparison to the population of top Caribbean island countries, Saint Lucia is in 11th place on that list. Barbados is in the 10th spot, with an additional 100,000 people; Jamaica is fifth with more than two million; and, Cuba tops the list with a population of 11 million residents. Just like every vote counts during an election, every Saint Lucian counts in order for us to make a difference in terms of supporting one another. It is true that Saint Lucia is a small island on the map, but, if all Saint Lucians from around the world unite as one, I believe we can be as big as a continent—that is just my opinion.

As a 617-square-kilometre island in the sun, we Saint Lucians need our turn to shine beyond the Caribbean. *But how can we march forward as one people and one nation when we've had so many alterations to our flag?* Ever since the flag was adopted in 1967, some of the designs have been manufactured in incorrect shades. A quick Google search shows numerous examples. Another observation that shows lack of unity comes during Caribbean festivals such as Caribana in Toronto, the Labour Day Parade in New York City, Miami Carnival in Florida, etc.

In order for us to grow, our ghetto *yutes* need to disarm themselves of deadly weapons and replace them with love and forgiveness. *Are the people to be held responsible, though?* I've heard way too much gossip blaming our leaders for the backwardness of our country; however, like a game of chess, we have had too many pawns awaiting commands, and not enough kings and queens determining their own fate. This has become a natural state of mind. I had to learn at a very young age that I was the captain of my destination on my *dream ship*, regardless of the weather. If I didn't have a course set, I was determined to find a way through the storms and hurricanes. Now, I need my people to get on board.

Countless times, I've seen many scenarios where we are supporting everything else but our own; the numerous posts on social media can testify to that. When it comes to music, for sure, the people are entitled to their own tastes, but why not share music from our own? I applaud the next generation of Saint Lucians who dedicate their time and energy to producing songs, trying to pave the way for others—Mecca, Dupes, Shepp Dawg, MonCherie, Kayo, and Big-C & Chunky, to name a few. For our Soca or Calypso lovers, there's a huge selection of artists from which to choose. My all-time favourites are: Ricky T, Ashanti, and Papa Invader. To me, they are true legends. I'd really like for the local radio stations and foreign DJs to play more local artists on the airways and at parties. Furthermore, let's promote more local music during our annual Jazz Festival. Let's have a Saint Lucian as the headliner, instead of just an opening act. Let's support locals.

One love, one Caribbean, one people? We can share the same love that we give to the other Caribbean islands by promoting their people, their culture, and their products. I rarely ever see them returning the favour. It's no wonder why most of my friends in Canada and America had never heard of the island of Saint Lucia until they met me. For some weird reason, people tend to think that Saint Lucia is a city in Jamaica. As a matter of fact, the majority of people I've come across act as if Jamaica is the only island in the Caribbean.

In my humble opinion, a prime example of negligence of Saint Lucian pride was during the 2012 Summer Olympics, when I witnessed my people supporting Jamaican sprinter Usain Bolt as if he had been born in Saint Lucia, while they neglected our very own Olympians: high jumpers Levern Spencer and Darvin Edwards; sailor Beth Lygoe; and, swimmer Danielle Beaubrun. I've noticed that support from the public only comes when it is beneficial to them; the same applies to our government. It hops on the bandwagon as soon as we are doing well for ourselves.

Some things will never change until we can flip everyone on the same page. I've also learned that some Saint Lucians don't always have the best interest in supporting local talent. When I was seeking blurbs for my book, our very own Derek Walcott, the 1992 Nobel Laureate for Literature prizewinner, turned me down. When I called him, I was thinking it was going to be an honour just to speak with him because I'd read many excerpts of his work as a poet and playwright when I was a student.

"Hello, Sir Walcott," I said with an unpretentious tone. "My name is Arnold Henry, an aspiring author born and raised in Saint Lucia. I am calling from Canada today. I've always respected everything you have done as a writer. It will be a dream come true to receive a review from you for my upcoming book. I'd like to place that review on the back cover of my book."

Before I could say anything further, he cut me off as if I was a homeless guy on the street begging for his riches, or a telemarketer pitching a sale. "I'm going to stop you here," he said. "I do not have time for anything. Goodbye!"

The abrupt hanging up of the phone felt like a stab to my heart. I immediately lost all respect for him as a human being. I was discouraged during a moment of silence as I absorbed the events that had just taken place. I wondered how such a prestigious man could be so self-absorbed. All I was looking for was at least a one-sentence review. I would have been happy if I had at least gotten some words of encouragement from him, or some form of conversation in regards to being an up-and-coming writer. Even that would have been a dream come true. I was having a hard time believing that his was an example of the average mindset of a Saint Lucian. Nevertheless, one thing was for certain, I could only depend on me.

It was at that point that I promised myself that I would always do my part to ensure that I don't fall into the traps of being egocentric. I pledged to myself to always support locals from near and far. I pray one day that we all will do the same.

Chapter 42

The Closure

The two-year wait for my official status in Canada was finally over, and, a few days after my 27th birthday, I received my permanent resident (PR) card. I felt like I'd just crossed a battlefield and set foot on freedom. This was definitely a moment for celebration, as my PR card was set to expire in five years. I was feeling self-determined to venture out and explore the many risks of becoming a professional basketball player. In other words, I was free to travel outside of Canada without any worries about whether I would be accepted back into the country.

Looking back at that day, I wished I'd gotten my PR card sooner. That way, I could have seized the opportunity for a basketball tryout in Germany when I was in the best shape of my life in December, 2011. I felt as quick and powerful as LeBron James. Being professionally ready took great lengths of overpowering triumphs with excess physical activities at the gym. One of my biggest triumphs was having to face the rejections of the Calgary Crush. *But if I could not make a local pro team, then what made me think I could make a pro team in Europe?* I refused to let the rejection of one failure determine the outcome of my future prospects. I also failed to mention that I had to overcome a hyperextended elbow injury that handicapped me for two months. Whatever obstacles came my way, I just kept on moving.

Slammers Basketball, a German-based basketball agency representing men and women in Europe that's certified by the International Basketball Agency (FIBA), had sent out an invitation by email for its 13th annual pro tryout tournament. After reading every detail of the lengthy email, I thought this was my calling. I was also contacted by a basketball agent in Mexico, who had a promising offer. But, as luck would have it, I came across a new roadblock on the path to my dreams. Although I had my PR card, I was still on probation, and that prevented me from leaving the country. My parole officer, Barbie Bryson, stated that if I left the country, she would be forced to issue a warrant for my arrest. No matter how hard I tried to reason with Barbie, she couldn't be swayed. Obviously, she didn't care about my dreams.

Even though Cho and I were on better terms, there were still long-term damages due to her domestic violence accusations. She knew that she had interrupted my pursuit of happiness. Being away from her in a European country would surely tear us apart. Being away for more than a month would have probably increased her insecurities and made it easier for her to proceed with filing for a divorce. She knew that as well, and needed me here with her in order to make us work. But I felt my dreams were more important than a failed marriage.

Everything happens for a reason, I usually say with corresponding expectations of greater things to come, but my bigger picture was shrinking. I was just hoping that my moment of success would unveil itself in 2012, but I was expected to pay for my faults until September of that same year. Again, basketball was put on hold until further notice. I took a time out to breathe a little. Perhaps I needed to focus on other things that could make me happy.

Marvin's college basketball success was coming to an end. Of the two of us, I always thought he would go the furthest. At the start of his career, I considered him to be the next Kevin Durant. They had almost the exact same playing style and physique, but things didn't go according to what I had envisioned. My brother has his own stories to tell regarding the difficulties he faced with college basketball. I will leave them for him to tell.

There were certain events that I didn't want to miss for the world; one was my brother's graduation from the University of North Carolina at Greensboro. On Jan. 30, 2012, I made it my obligation to apply for a U.S. visitor visa. Luckily for me, there was an American Embassy in downtown Calgary. Unfortunately, my application was denied for the second straight year. The first time I applied, the immigration officer told me that I needed to be a resident of Canada. One year later, I was told that I needed more economical ties to Canada such as a full-time job, mortgage, or child. It was a heart-shattering moment for me.

"So, you going to deprive me of attending my brother's graduation," I said, almost in tears, to the immigration officer, an older lady on the other side of the bulletproof window. I was so livid by her rejection that security had to escort me out of the building. Later that day, I sincerely apologized to Marvin for missing his graduation in May. His biggest accomplishment was coming up, and I felt bad knowing he attended my graduation, but I was unable to attend his.

The new year had also started with new beginnings for Cho and myself. The judge had granted our request to remove the restraining order. We were now back in the same bed, although the plastered walls in our home were a constant reminder of the hardships in our marriage. Since completing the men's counselling program, I was slowly learning the responsibilities of becoming a man. But I still had a long way to go. I was learning that loving her meant never being the reason for her pain and suffering. Instead, I needed to be the man that sought ways to put a smile on her face. Two lovers on the same journey can conquer anything. *But was Cho's heart really the one that I sought? How could it be when her oldest child despised me?*

Cho constantly reminded me that I was the reason she no longer had a relationship with her daughter. Kris, who had recently broken up with her boyfriend in Australia, had returned home to her Mummy. I guessed they had somehow patched things up. However, I was bothered by the sudden changes. First of all, Cho never consulted with me about Kris moving in with us. She didn't care to hear my feelings about the situation, which made me feel as though I didn't matter. Secondly, I never had Kris's blessing on our wedding day, and, for all I knew, she judged me before meeting me. I had a sour taste in my mouth when it came to Kris. Thirdly, Kris was almost my age, and I just wasn't comfortable with being a stepfather to someone my own age. I was worried.

In the past, I had preached to my brothers who were interested in single mothers. I told them that they had to be willing to commit to, love, and care for both the mother and all her children; otherwise, don't be wasting no one's time. I didn't practice what I preached. After numerous pointless arguments with Cho, I had no choice but to accept the fact that Kris had moved in with us. It seemed that I had no control in a house that was supposed to be my home, until one night when I flew out of control.

I was out and about one evening when I came home to the sounds of giggling from downstairs. Cho was in our room watching television. "Who is downstairs?" I asked her.

"Kris and her friend," she replied.

"Her friend?" I asked. "So, you weren't going to tell me that your daughter is bringing her friend over?"

"My house, I do whatever I want," Cho screamed at me.

I felt disrespected and hurt as Cho constantly reminded me that I never contribute to the marriage. "Wow, your house?"

My concerns set off a squabble between us that led Kris to storm upstairs with an iron rod. She hesitated to take a swing at me in her mother's defence. Like mother, like daughter, they both had the same feistiness, but Kris was bigger physically. "Get the fuck out!" I yelled at Kris's friend when I noticed an innocent, slim Caucasian girl standing in the background. The fear in her eyes was exactly the reaction I expected. I intended to re-enact scenes from my childhood of an abusive stepfather, so that Kris could hate me enough to dismiss herself from my space for good.

"She's not going anywhere," Kris yelled back.

I proceeded to physically force the friend out of the house, but Kris grabbed her friend's hand and they both ran into the downstairs bedroom. "Open the door and get out now!"

"Arnold, don't. This is my daughter and her friend," Cho said as she tried to push me away.

I banged on the door. "Open the fucking door before I break it down."

"Leave us alone! I'm calling the cops!"

That horrifying night de-escalated with the arrival of the police. By then, the police were very familiar with our address. I gave Kris real reasons to hate me. In the end, Cho had to make a choice on who got to stick around: her husband or her first-born. I held my ground and wasn't going anywhere. The next day, Cho's daughter was on her way to Winnipeg to live with her father. Before Kris exited the house, she left a note on one of our wedding pictures. She wrote, "Have fun with your abusive husband." I threw it away before Cho saw it to avoid any further pain. I was happy with the outcome, but there were going to be consequences. Cho was outraged and blamed me for driving her family and children away. It hurt me to know that I had caused her so much pain. Since Cho's son and daughter were never around, I never knew how important her children were to her. Six months later, Cho was still shedding tears.

Both of Cho's children disowned her. I took full responsibility. Despite our rocky love boat, it seemed like Cho was waiting for the day when we could sail away to calmer seas. On the flip side, I knew a day would come when we would be nothing more than a bad memory for each other. My heart aches knowing that I brought her down to the ground when she had expected me to sweep her off her feet. I was just a young man, still seeking to find a better pair of feet to sweep. Or maybe I was still in that phase of exploring my many options. Whatever it was, the fact remained that I wasn't happy in our relationship. I just needed to find a way out, without having to shatter Cho's heart. I did not know how. Walking away meant I would be leaving behind a comfortable life and a wife who did everything for me. I wasn't ready to face the real world.

To rekindle the spark in our relationship, we took an all-inclusive trip to Puerto Vallarta, Mexico. The trip was a few days after my book signing in London, England, in late-February. Our weeklong vacation was intended to rebuild and strengthen our marriage, a sort of overdue honeymoon. We needed to create happier moments. Instead, I fucked up again. On our last night in Mexico, I got so drunk that I ditched Cho at the hotel and took a taxi to a nightclub, where I met two random girls from Saskatchewan. Ten minutes later, I went back to their hotel room and the only thing that I can remember is that I was with the two girls at the same. During the wee hours of that morning, I took a taxi back to my hotel room where I found Cho all fired up. She was so furious that I think she was ready to kill me with her bare hands. I was too wasted to remember the details of the evening and my drunken episode. Cho claims that I smacked her and choked her to a point where it ended with the presence of three Mexican security men. Knowing Cho, she would say anything to make me look bad. I still deny any wrongdoings. She still believes that I got lost while helping a drunken guy to his room—a guy from Calgary who I was drinking with all night before escaping to the nightclub.

Despite that one incident, Cho and I had some memorable moments in Mexico. For the first time, I got to meet and swim with dolphins—my favourite animal. We also had a chance to experience Rhythms of the Night, which I highly recommend to couples who want a relaxing, romantic evening watching the sun set into the horizon. The exclusive voyage began with a picturesque ocean cruise from one end of the shores to a dark, isolated, mysterious island. From out far, the lush and mountainous island looked like it was on fire. Up close, you could see that torches and candles were lit along the coastline. Locals entertained us in an outdoor theatre performance. For the remainder of the night, we enjoyed a buffet-style dinner on the paradisiacal shores of the Pacific Ocean.

While we're on the subject of paradise, a week later, I booked a much-needed visit to Saint Lucia. Even though I didn't tell Cho directly, she wasn't allowed to come with me. Any break from one another was going to be best for both of us. My whereabouts were never reported to my parole officers, and I really didn't care if I was continuously breaching the conditions of my peace bond. If I made it back in time for our monthly meetings, I had nothing to worry about. I left Canada for the third time while on probation. I had to continue living my life, and that is exactly what I did.

On Sunday, March 11, 2012, I reunited with my birthplace for the first time in two years. But before landing in Saint Lucia, there was one thing I had to take do: meet my older sister, Heidi, for the first time. Since I had a layover in Bridgetown, Barbados, we made plans to meet up at the Grantley Adams International Airport. Not only did I get to meet Heidi, I also met my two-year-old niece, Jazara. Our time together was brief. Nevertheless, it will not be forgotten because family is forever.

REBIRTH

While the main reason for my return to my homeland was to attend my book signing on April 2, my goal was to make a difference on the island. I especially wanted to inspire the youths through my new work as an author and motivational speaker.

During my book signing at the Bay Gardens Inn, I got some overdue answers to some of the questions I've been asking. For the Q&A segment of my presentation, my mother surprised me by standing up in the audience to speak. The audience was a true reflection of my life that featured my close family and friends, including my godfather, Peter Flood; my former principal and head basketball coach at Entrepot Secondary School, Dexter Cumberbatch and Augusta Ifill; and, my good friends, Dudley and Ali.

I dropped my microphone as she began to speak. "A lot of people were saying that I was in denial with the things he was saying in his book," she said, choosing her words carefully. "I just want to clear the air. When I was pregnant, Toby did not want anything to do with Mario. He wanted me to have an abortion. But I wanted to keep my baby. I knew Toby had a family and I did not care. I wanted to have my son."

Hearing these words from my mother was the ultimate closure to my family matters episode. If I had not been the centre of attention that evening, I never would have been able to hold back the tears. *I'm not even supposed to be alive,* I thought to myself. My mother was wrong; my father was wrong.

After my mother spoke, sharing the stage with me for about 10 minutes, she concluded with: "I'm proud of you, Mario. Despite everything, you know I'll always support you."

As long as my books lasted on the shelves at Sunshine Bookshop—the leading bookstore in Saint Lucia—I tried my best to enhance my marketing strategies. I was featured on several radio station talk shows and television programs. I gave copies to the Prime Minister, Dr. Kenny Anthony, and the Governor-General, Her Excellency Dame Pearlette Louisy. I hosted many motivational speaking engagements and school author visits at secondary schools, including my alma mater. Of the places where I held motivational events, my favourite was the visit to the Children's Home because I felt like these brave kids needed the most inspiration.

Chapter 43

An Old Crush

In my younger years, I had a crush on a tall, slim, brown-skinned girl who used to visit her family in the two-storey pink house opposite my home. I sat at a coffee shop in Castries, working on my second book, when I felt on my lips, a quick, innocent kiss that we shared as kids. She stood before my eyes today, transformed into a gorgeous woman, with curves that would fulfil all my desires. My jaw dropped to the floor and my tongue rolled down to her feet, desperate for a taste. I swallowed saliva, almost drowning myself. *Damn,* she had grown up to be the voluptuous type of woman I only dream of having by my side. There was no doubt in my mind that destiny was trying to reintroduce Abigail into my life. I never thought women like this existed in Saint Lucia.

"Hey, Shaye, you have Abigail's BlackBerry PIN?" I typed on my BlackBerry Messenger to the only family member of hers I knew on my contact list.

"Yes, Mario," she replied. She added a curious emoticon to indicate she was wondering what my reason was for wanting her cousin's contact information.

"I just need it," I replied.

I hadn't felt so passionate about a girl since Becca. I was still married, but I desired Abigail the most.

After a night of messaging with Abigail, I knew that I was ready to forget all about my wife. My wedding ring was displayed on my right hand as part of a fashion statement. In fact, the only time someone from Saint Lucia knew I was married was when they read the biography on the inside jacket of my book.

I learned that Abigail worked at Lime, a telecommunications company in the same mall where I did all my daily writing. On April 11, Abigail and I met at the coffee shop. I felt like we had the perfect history to create a promising future. We knew from the start that we were right for each other. We were feeling fortunate that destiny had reconnected us.

It wasn't hours later when word had reached Abigail that I was living a secret life. Saint Lucia is a small island where gossip spreads faster than it does on Twitter and Facebook. In our community, there were girls prior to Abigail but after Cho who hated the fact that I had fallen in love with Abigail. I'd even received a four-page letter from one of my one-night stands who thought it was degrading that I chose Abigail over her.

One day when Abigail was feeling under the weather, she sent a message to my cellphone. "Dude is calling my phone, saying that he can't believe that I would completely end what we had for a married man," she said. After reading that message about the man she had been dating, I thought I had lost her forever. My heart was racing as I anticipated her thoughts. She continued, "I honestly don't give a fuck what nobody thinks or says about us because people will talk." Seeing this gave me a better perspective of her loyalty to me. Our dating life was now part of another secret life since Cho was back in Canada still hoping for our future. However, I didn't want Cho—I needed her. Looking back at my affairs, I realize now that I was an asshole. Cho didn't deserve this. I was not a man.

But I felt like I had found happiness. Abigail and I had a mutual love for one another. To me, it felt like we were catching up on a missed opportunity of being childhood sweethearts. Our families were like family—there was no need for introductions. My mother loved Abigail for me, and Abigail's mother, Ruth, felt the same way about me for Abigail. I'd never had such a likeminded lover. One of the moments that kept replaying in my head was a Sunday morning when we woke up in each other's arms to a beautiful sunrise above the beach's shore. We appreciated the horizons of the deep blue sea together. It was just one of our many spontaneous nights of mingling and fulfilling our desires for each other in the presence of Mother Nature. I've never felt anything wetter than when I was inside her.

We both knew that my time in Saint Lucia was limited, so, for the rest of my stay, we seized every moment. One month passed, and it felt as if we had been dating for as long as we've know each other. Since I was jetting back to Calgary soon, Abigail and I promised to wait for each other. We wanted it all—children, marriage, and a future. On May 18, Abigail watched with a pool of tears as I said my final goodbyes. I wished I didn't have to go, but I didn't want to miss out on better opportunities in Canada. Furthermore, my return to Calgary was not by choice.

I had to depart suddenly, and no one, except Cho, knew why. Cho had informed me of my probation officer's concerns for my whereabouts. I was so caught up with love that I had forgotten about my scheduled meetings with my probation officer. When I realized this, I immediately sent an email to Barbie stating that I had returned to Saint Lucia to renew my expired passport. She replied with the following warning letter:

Arnold,

It is April 27th and you have not been in touch with me. I am giving you until May 15th at 9 a.m. to be in office. If you fail to report on this date, in person, I will have no choice but to breach you. You have not reported as directed in months, left the country without informing me, and are not maintaining contact through this situation.

I made it very clear that you not having proper identification won't absolve you from your responsibilities of probation. I also told you I was not going to be the one to keep in contact with you. You are not taking accountability or responsibility for this situation.

Again, on May 15th at 9 a.m., you are required to be in my office in person.

Barbie Bryson
Probation Officer
Calgary Central Office

Chapter 44

Separation

I began to make it a priority to report in person to my probation officer, who had given me a chance to redeem myself. Four more months, and I would no longer have to serve my punishment for Cho's allegations.

While Abigail was making plans to move to Texas to pursue a few of her own dreams, I was back in Calgary living with my wife after three months of promoting my first book. I'd never had any luck with long-distance relationships as evidenced by my previous relationships. I've always had a hard time with commitments because there was always someone else out there to pique my interest. I was willing to make a change, though, by waiting for the day when I could pick Abigail up at the Calgary airport. Abigail and I would talk for hours about finally being reunited. We usually concluded that we would end up spending a whole day in bed. We discussed many plans for the future, but having a baby was our most-talked-about topic. I looked at her as the perfect mother to raise my child. She was a loving, caring, goal-oriented woman, who was raised by a respected mother. The way she treated me was everything a man could ever ask for.

To ease the emotional pain of being apart for so long, BlackBerry Messenger and Apple's FaceTime were our best forms of communication. Of course, I had to be secretive about my new lover because I was still living under the same roof as my wife. Moving back into a lost and forgotten married life wasn't easy. Living with Cho was like living with a roommate. I was never above suspicion with Cho. Her allegations about my behaviour never broke my silence, though. Even when she threatened to report me to immigration, I acted like I was the perfect man. She would have claimed that I married her for papers, but deep down, I knew that we were two hearts that were never meant for each other. I just wanted to play the game until I ran out the clock. To be completely honest, I was in a vulnerable position because, without Cho, I had nothing in Canada—that was, until I became a permanent resident.

In the summer of 2012, I landed a job at Shaw Communications Inc. in Calgary as a technical support representative. That was probably the most stable job I had had since graduating from college. After eight-hour days of troubleshooting customers' internet, home phone and cable issues, I began working twice as hard toward my overdue dreams. I remembered telling myself, *the only thing stopping you right now is the road you left behind. There should be nothing else obstructing your road ahead. You've been through it all.* Upon completion of my probationary period with the telecommunications company, I had thought about the tryouts in Germany, but I decided to pass on that because I had only heard bad reviews from a few European coaches and North American basketball players. Apparently, it was a money-making scheme for the organizers. A local teammate from the Calgary men's league, who I thought should have gotten a contract easily, was unsuccessful at the Slammers Basketball tournament tryouts. In addition to that, coaches I knew personally did not recommend the journey and investment, which would have been more than $3,000 for flights, accommodations, and registration. Instead, I put all my devotion to the combined draft of NBL Canada.

And I wasn't the only one in my family pursuing his hoop dreams: Marvin was, too. After graduating, he was on a mission. I've always said to myself, if my brother made it, I would feel like I had made it, too. Throughout the summer, we encouraged each other. Luckily for Marvin, he was still living in the U.S., the basketball land of opportunities, and I was living in a winter land of hockey. I fed off Marvin's will to continue pursuing the sport we both loved.

Finally, I was more than ready to close the deal on a professional basketball contract. The ball was literally in my court. I was playing basketball at every men's league in the city. Not only that, a few weeks earlier, I played up until the quarterfinals of the men's basketball league in Saint Lucia for my old team, Courts Jets—the undefeated champions on the island. Now that I was back in Canada, there would be no days off. Ian McCarthy, who had personally invited me to the NBL Canada tryout, was well aware of my preparations. We were friends on Facebook, where I posted daily updates about my successful workouts. On May 19, I sent Ian a private message.

"Good morning Sir, how's it going? I've now returned to Canada to start training towards the NBLC tryout. Have you come to a conclusion for the tryout in Toronto in August? Also, since I'm a resident of Canada, what day are my tryouts held?"

"It's going to be the end of August," he replied. "Players only qualify as Canadian if they are Canadian citizens not just residents."

"Thanks for your timely response. Looking forward to the official date of the tryout."

One month later, Ian messaged me, "Registration is open on www.nblcanada.ca."

I hadn't played basketball at such a high level in more than three years, so I was focused more than ever and my work ethic was in overdrive. Every day, I was strategizing on ways to dominate against the hundreds of prospects who wanted to live my dream. *I'll come to the tryout, and play defensive like no other,* I thought to myself at 5 a.m. as I did defensive slides at the YMCA. *Nah, I'll just dunk on everyone and show these coaches my NBA post moves.* I was so pumped to showcase my abilities that I was aiming to be the No. 1 overall pick.

Everyone who read my story was rooting for me. This was the moment I was waiting for—to no longer hang on to, but to be living my dream. I had it all planned out. For my arrival at Toronto Pearson International Airport, Beverley, a friend who was living in Toronto, had offered to give me a ride to Orangeville, Ontario, where the 2012 NBL Canada Draft Combine would be held. She had read my first book and wanted to be supportive. I was more than ready. However, I would never get on that plane. Exactly one week before departure, I found myself using two of my teammates as crutches to walk off the basketball court during a Calgary men's league game.

It was a Sunday when I saw my entire basketball life flash before my eyes. I saw the highlights. I saw the tragedies. I saw the first time I held the ball. I saw it all. I grabbed my ankle as I repeatedly thought, *Fuck! Fuck! Fuck! I should not have played that second game.*

It was the first time in the Hoopz League's season that we played back-to-back games. We won our first matchup and immediately had to play another one. Within the first few minutes of the first quarter, after a missed shot attempt by the opponents, a loose ball came to a stop near my feet. Normally, I would dive on the floor for the ball. But since the ball was so close to me, I figured I would bend over to pick it up. What happened next was unexpected. A 300-pound opponent decided to dive for the ball as if he was looking into a pool of deep waters. As my opponent grabbed the ball, my left ankle got caught in a tight grip in his arms. Meanwhile, my upper body drifted away from the ball. I blacked out for a split second, and then the sound of my ankle snapping echoed in my ears. I squeezed onto my left thigh as if to stop the pain from spreading through my upper body. It felt like my left foot had parted ways with my ankle. I have never felt anything like it. Inside, I was crying at the idea I had just reached the end of my basketball career. I was stuck underneath the basket with an injury, as if to symbolize the lack of strength left to hang on to my dreams.

Chapter 45

Waking Up

Disappointed wasn't the word I would use to describe how I felt after I rolled my ankle. No, that would have been an understatement. I felt like killing the guy who ruined my chances. Overnight, my ankle had swollen to the size of a tennis ball. Luckily, there were no broken bones, and doctors predicted I would be fully recovered within the next six months. But that was the only good news that resulted from the injury. I was down and out like a crippled man rolling around in his wheelchair. Watching basketball games from the stands made me feel like I was window shopping, like a kid unable to get his Christmas wish. I wanted to kick the basketball with my good foot to get it as far away from me as possible. I wanted to squeeze it so tight, I'd make it pop. I wanted to stab it. I was done.

Who was I kidding? After two miserable weeks of icing and massaging my ankle, I was limping to the gym, looking forward to the following year. I've heard many stories about athletes who called it quits after sustaining injuries. However, I programmed my mind to keep a positive attitude and to keep pushing through.

One month later, on Aug. 12, the NBA 3X (previously known as the NBA Jam Session) was back in Calgary for the third straight year. I find inspiration in the slightest or biggest of things, and being amongst local talented basketball players was no exception. Every year, the NBA invites players to host the event—Brandon Knight, of the Detroit Pistons, and Buckets Blakes, of the Harlem Globetrotters, were among the special invited guests. I was honoured that they each accepted a copy of my first book when I presented it to them. They were also two of the three judges for the Sprite Slam Dunk throw down. With only one fully functional leg and an injured ankle, I was better off being a spectator, as there was no way I'd be able to elevate and execute my dunks. Still, I was determined to play in the 3-on-3 tournament.

The previous year, my teammates and I had failed to defend our 3-on-3 men's championship title, after getting knocked out in the semifinals by a local team that went on to win it all in Halifax. One year later, we were facing the same defending champions—not only city champions but national champions. To get back the title that was lost, I recruited new players who were just as passionate as me about winning. Déjà vu presented itself at the tournament when we faced the defending champions in the preliminary rounds. After an intense battle, we suffered our first loss of the day. Luckily for our team, double elimination meant an automatic withdrawal. For us, losing only helped us to know what it would take to win. We went on to win the quarterfinals and semifinals to face the defending champions again in the finals.

If you're familiar with basketball in Calgary, you have probably already heard of a team called Troybuilt. These veterans never cease to amaze me with their championship mentality. There is nothing fancy about them; they are just very good. The first half of the 3-on-3 matchup had our team down the majority of the time. After a brief rest during halftime, we decided that our key to victory was defense. The clock was ticking away, and we were still chasing to gain the lead in the second half. Out of desperation and pride, we were able to tie the score before the time expired. The audience truly appreciated the intensity of the game.

"Overtime! The first to score the next two baskets wins," shouted the referee. No prep talk was needed. The instructions were made very clear. A coin toss awarded our opponent the first possession. We retook our defensive stance. The ball was entered into the post, where I forced a turnover, and we gained possession. One of my teammates drove to the basket and drew a foul. He went on to score the free throw. "One more stop! One more point," I yelled at my teammates.

From on top of the key, our opponents decided to shoot for a 3-pointer. Our defense blocked his shot from reaching the rim—an "air ball." I rebounded his missed shot and quickly dished it out to my guard from on top of the key. We had no set plays. We just believed in ourselves and played the game like the name of our team—Tru Ballaz. One of my teammates sized up his defender from on top of the 3-point line. We opened space on the court by isolating to the wings. As my teammate decided to drive to the basket, all three defenders collapsed to the zone; somehow, through the traffic, my teammate was able to find me open on the wing.

"Arnold for the win," said the announcer. I perfected my shooting form, and there was no hesitation in my jumpshot as I intentionally banked it in.

"Let's go! Let's go!" I shouted while engaging in celebratory hand gestures with my teammates and our nearby supporters. We shared the grand prize total of $1,000. I needed that victory. I wanted to be reminded of how it felt to win. *Have you ever wondered where you'd be if you never gave up?*

Chapter 46

My Addiction

Life at 27 years old was supposed to be the peak years for living my dreams. At least that was what I had always dreamt. I should've been at my happiest, and I should have been sharing that happiness with everyone else in my circle, especially my mother to whom I'd promised a glamorous lifestyle. I've often wondered if my dreams were her dreams, too. Then, I reminded myself, *if I fail, then we both fail.* I really wanted to make my mother proud.

All I ever strived for was an NBA career, a family, and to become a better man. The fight within me was fighting the fight within me. All of my blessings had seemed to become a cycle of curses. The bigger picture was slowly becoming blurry and fading away. Day by day, it seemed like I was becoming less athletic and less interested in pursuing my dreams. *How long are we to dream a forlorn dream? When is giving up no longer considered quitting?* My clock was ticking, and I sensed game over was only seconds away. *Should I throw in the towel?* But I was at that point in my life when nothing could have stopped me from pushing ahead. I was too motivated to stop as long as I was still breathing.

The first few days of autumn, I was feeling about 60 per cent recovered from my ankle injury. Although I could still feel a sting whenever I pressed my foot toward the ground, I had stopped limping. My weekly routines returned to normal: waking up half of the time by myself, working my two jobs, going to the gym, and then going to bed with the hopes of waking up to do it all again the next day. Sustaining an injury and having to pick up where I left off meant I had to fall in love with basketball all over again. Basketball and I have had many ups and downs, but it felt like a relationship that would never be broken, no matter how much pain it caused.

Four months had passed, and Abigail was still in my heart. We were missing each other more than a blind cupid shooting its arrows. Plans were set for her to visit me in Canada. We talked about it a lot. On Sept. 11, the Canadian government implemented visa requirements for all Saint Lucians who were visiting Canada. This was a huge inconvenience. Abigail immediately filed for a visa at the office in Port of Spain, Trinidad. A few weeks later, she received her passport in the mail with a copy of a temporary resident visa. Nothing would have stopped her from getting to me. Well, I take that back. There was always something that stopped a good thing from getting to me—and, this time, I was the culprit.

I always want what I can't have. The more I can't have something, the more I want it. I get bored of things quickly. Things are easier to get rid of when I'm unable to smell, feel, or taste them. If I can't have it at that moment, I'll try my best to get it into my hands, or I will simply replace it. This is a synopsis of my addictive ways. Five months later, this was the case with Abigail. Not that there hadn't been other women filling my sexual void since I'd left her in Saint Lucia, but, one day at the YMCA, another young lady caught my attention.

I was at the YMCA in south Calgary to work on my upper body when I spotted a new member near the dumbbells rack. It's obvious when someone is new because they usually take more time looking for equipment than they do working out. Normally, I would be so focused on my exercises that I might seem narcissistic. That day, however, I was energetically social and flirtatious. "It doesn't go there," I said with a serious tone.

"Oh, sorry," she politely replied, attempting to pick up the medicine ball again.

I smirked, "I was joking. I was just joking."

She smiled, letting go of the ball, "Oh."

"Hi," I said, as I reached for a handshake, "Arnold."

She clasped my hand, "Kyla."

"Where are you from? You're not from here, are you?"

"Ontario. I moved here a week ago," she replied.

After an evening of working out, our conversation had transitioned to the sitting area on the main floor of the YMCA. For the first time in a very long time, I was attracted to a woman by our conversation, instead of her beauty. She was a slim, gorgeous brunette who had the most innocent-looking smile when she laughed at my jokes. I shared with her my reasons for being at the gym every night. I believed that we had a mutual attraction for each other's perseverance and determination. She, too, was using the gym to help her reach her dreams—to become a world-class fitness model.

That same night, the rain wouldn't cease, so I offered Kyla a ride to her aunt's residence. Before my bedtime, my addiction for beautiful women had gotten the best of me again, and I was intrigued to know what the future held for us. Kyla was the only good thing to happen to me in the last quarter of 2012. And even though I would have rather been with Abigail, I could have held Kyla at any given time.

In my world, I tend to believe that good news only lasts for a couple of hours. My mother, the main lady in my life, had called to share some bad news with me. She told me that she had cervical cancer, and I felt as if I was talking to her from her grave. Tears were escaping from my eyes while I silently listened as she spoke. She claimed that it was in the early stages and she would have to consider surgery or treatment to kill the cells before it worsened. I was so scared; it was as if I had already lost her. Straightaway, I had this overwhelming fear that my mother would die knowing I was a failure at my basketball dreams. During that long-distance phone call, she mentioned that it would cost tens of thousands of dollars to stop the cancer from spreading. In addition to that, she would have to fly to Martinique, since Saint Lucia did not have the medical technology to treat her cancer. I had to figure out a master plan to raise the funds.

My mother could not leave me now. I needed to win one of these Canadian lotteries. Basketball had failed me in my dream of becoming a millionaire. My younger brother had followed in my footsteps, and basketball had given him many difficulties in becoming a professional player, too. In late-October, Marvin was on the verge of making history for being drafted by the NBA's developmental league, better known as NBA D-League. But as our luck would have it, his chances were ruined because he had illegally stayed in America after graduation. All his hard work was suddenly flushed down the toilet.

I needed cash, fast. The only way I knew how to win fast money was at a casino, a place I was only briefly introduced to a couple of years earlier.

On my last hand, I had gone all in with my winnings of $40. "Blackjack!" I screamed after the dealer dealt an ace on my face card. Five dollars had instantly turned into $100 after I won four hands in a row. I was a big fan of the Kevin Spacey movie *21*, so I was on a mission to get rich just like the film's characters. I promised myself that I would only go for three days in a row before calling it quits. This was my little secret. The first day at Elbow River Casino, I cashed out with $1,700, after only buying in with $100. The players at the blackjack table were amazed by my luck. I quickly ran to the bank to make a deposit.

The next day, I meant business. I sat down at the same table and put on a serious game face. The first few hands didn't go as smoothly as the previous day. I had bought in for almost $1,400 before calling my bank to inquire about an additional increase on my daily cash withdrawal limit. The last $300 in my account was equally divided, as I went all in, placing bets in three hands. Approximately three hours later, I had drawn a crowd around the $10-minimum-limit table where I was sitting. Forget about playing by the books, I was playing blackjack like a pro. I was staying, splitting, hitting, and doubling on the most ridiculous hands. I had stacked up so many black chips that I needed a tray to carry my winnings to the cashier. After I cashed out, the workers asked me if I needed security to walk me to my vehicle. That evening, I won an unbelievable amount of $11,945. I had never held so many hundreds at one time before. I truly felt like I had just won the lottery and all my problems were solved. My jawbone hurt from smiling so much.

"Mummy, Mummy, I'm going to send so much money tomorrow. You are going to be so happy," I said bursting with excitement over a rare late-night phone call on my drive home.

Chapter 47

Erythema Multiforme

I felt like God personally hand-picked Kyla for me. She was the most caring, respectful, sympathetic person that I had ever came across, so it was no surprise that she had chosen a career as a registered nurse. She also enjoyed reading, athletics, and fitness. Ever since the day we met at the YMCA, I wouldn't let a day go by without hearing her voice or seeing her beautiful face. Kyla lived about a 15- minute drive away with her brother, Joel, his girlfriend, Ali, and their dogs. I was over at their house so many days in a row that I may as well have been living with them.

By then, I was no longer sleeping in the same bed as my wife. I slept downstairs in Cho's daughter's old bedroom. Even though we had an understanding that we were just living together, Cho was still having a hard time letting go. She would still creep me out on my Facebook page, and accuse me of fucking every beautiful girl on my friends list. She'd still blow up my phone, questioning my whereabouts. All of Cho's friends knew her as the saint in our marriage, and I was the mean, controlling, abusive husband. When enough was finally enough, we decided to officially separate. The lies, the games, and the stress had become wearisome. I found an apartment closer to the new girl in my life.

Kyla knew about my relationship with my wife, and she understood that it was soon to be over. However, she knew nothing about my Saint Lucian lover or the dozens of other women I had on the go in Calgary. Abigail would have been the perfect match for me, but Kyla was accessible. The long-distance relationship with Abigail was not appealing anymore. Eventually, I announced the broken promises to Abigail; though, I did not position it in regards to another woman; I just stopped communicating with her and she got the point. Kyla had, in effect, taken hostage the dreams and hopes Abigail and I held for our future.

My new-found love gave me the strength I needed to, once again, chase my basketball dreams. Kyla and I talked about Europe on numerous occasions. If I was offered a contract, she was willing to fly away with me and find work there as a nurse. The first time she watched me play a competitive basketball game was on Jan. 5, 2013. It was also my first professional basketball game within the ABA. The Olympia Rise, of Washington state, was scheduled to play against the

Calgary Crush. Because a few foreign players on the opposing team were unable to cross the Canada-U.S. border, me and a few other local players were asked to fill up the roster. It was fortuitous that I was able to play against the team that cut me for reasons no one in Calgary understood—a perfect opportunity to show them what they were missing.

The Crush played a well-structured game, and we were a team with a few players on the court together for the first time. I just wanted to help the Olympia Rise to victory. By the end of the game, I contributed 19 points, 18 rebounds, three steals, two assists and one block, to a 130-82 loss. "You should be playing for Calgary Crush," my teammates for the day said to me. I just nodded and then shook my head. "Why aren't you playing for them?"

"I wish I knew," I replied.

Kyla was so impressed with my performance. She reminded me that I had what it takes to play with the pros.

When I won the $11,945 at the casino, Kyla was one of the first people in Calgary to know, followed by my wife. Cho wanted me to buy her a $1,000 ring, which I actually considered. The next day, instead of wiring the money I had promised my mother, I brought Kyla to the casino with me as a good luck charm to try to increase my winnings. This time, I was betting at a high-limit table, and, within the first few minutes, I had a total of $14,000. I was stacking and stacking chips; the money was growing fast, and all I wanted was more, more, more. While at the table, I could feel forces encouraging me to stay longer. So, I did. Kyla was so distraught by the $1,000 bets I was placing that she decided to take a coffee break. A rush of adrenaline took over my mind and it seemed like I was incapable of controlling my body. The good side advised me to leave; the bad side told me that I could go for $50,000. A few bets later, Kyla witnesses my loss. I didn't have a penny to my name. I felt so stupid. I was so humiliated that I remained silent on our drive home. I kept saying to myself, *I should have left when I was up. I should have left when I was up. I should have left when I was up.* I was quickly learning that chasing my losses was a greater thrill than winning.

It wasn't the best time in my life to have gone on a gambling rampage. I'd just financed a brand new 2013 fully loaded Honda Pilot. I was also going through a divorce, so I was now paying for rent. My bills were past due every month, and I was suffering the consequences: threats of eviction, repossession, and suspension of services. *Why did I allow myself to get trapped in this corner?* I was hooked on the casino, like a drug addict desperately craving a needle. I was spending more time in the casino than at the gym. I was broke. Every day, as I left the casino, I kept asking myself, *why do I keep going back?*

I started to live by the famous saying, "For the love of money is the root of all kinds of evil." My greed gave rise to my wicked behaviours. I was willing to do anything to get my hands on more money by borrowing from loan sharks, selling drugs to patrons at the nightclubs where I worked, and scamming friends and family with no remorse or regard for their circumstances. At one point, I even considered robbing the gamblers in the casino parking lots. I was using my mother's illness for my own financial gains. As usual, Cho got the worst of all my lies because I would continually fuck with her mind and blame her for my compulsive gambling. I treated her like a mother, instead of as my separated wife, or, better yet, my bankroll or personal ATM. All I had to do was have sex with her, and I could get whatever I wanted out of her. I actually thought that I had gotten so good at playing multiple women at the same time that Kyla had no clue about my cheating ways. And Cho had never heard of Kyla. For months, Cho bailed me out, even though my gambling debts were putting her in debt. One time, she even saved me from getting killed.

"Arnold, why the fuck three guys knocking on my door?" Cho asked during a phone call. She sounded like her life was being threatened.

"I don't know. Who are they?"

"They say that you owe them money. Fuck you. Are you still gambling?"

"No, I am not," I lied. "I don't know these guys, Cho."

"You are a liar. I know you still owe people money. You will never change, Arnold. I am going to call the police."

Money was now where my heart used to be. The loan sharks who showed up at Cho's front door were ready to take serious actions to get back the money I owed. I was so happy that Cho didn't know the address of my new residence; otherwise, I would have been a dead man.

The first time I acknowledged I had a gambling addiction was on the same day that I used my car to get a $3,500 equity loan and lost the money in a matter of minutes. Only then did I realize that it wasn't worth it for the amount of interest I had to pay back on a two-year term. Life became a very lonely road. I was in the red with a shitload of insufficient funds fees, overdraft interest fees, service charges, and stop payments. To sum it all up, I had lost more than $75,000 of my personal money and I owed more than $30,000. I couldn't pay for a meal, let alone pay back the money I had borrowed. Ignoring calls and hiding from lenders was my only option now. I was ashamed of the devil I had become.

I will make it back. I will make it back. I kept fooling myself. Gambling was not making me happy at all. Depression had washed over every ounce of happiness I had left. *Money will never make me happy. It is just an essential to staying alive—to provide me with food, clothes, and shelter. I need to stop thinking that money will make me happier.*

Kyla was my emotional support and was always there when I needed someone to talk to. She kept me happy whenever stress overtook me. If I needed cash, she would loan me hundreds of dollars without asking me why I needed it. She knew of my losses, but I never admitted to her that gambling was an issue. In her eyes, I was a saint, an author, and a motivational speaker. She thought I was ambitious and would soon be a professional basketball player. Underneath it all, I really was that person, and I treated her like a princess. But the person I saw in the mirror was a deceitful user and abuser, a lying, cheating, confused, lonely and depressed little boy. I needed to change my ways, or else I would lose the one person I could not live without.

In March, 2013, I felt like I was being punished for all the wrongs I had done to my wife, loved ones, family, and friends. It seemed like my God was delivering a personal message to me to remind me that he was still in charge. I hadn't visited with or spoken to Him in so long, and I felt like I was paying for my sins. I had adopted bad habits of only calling on Him during times of struggle. I was no longer thankful for life. *Help me, God,* I whispered. This time, I was truly starting to believe that it was the end to all my dreams.

I found myself lying in bed, in pain from the targeted lesions that were spreading across my body. Small, round, blister-like sores had started on my hands, and were spreading to my elbows, legs, and feet. The pain was so overbearing that it felt like a mole, the small mammal, was burrowing its way through my skin. The burning sensation made me feel like I was burning in an oven. I had never seen or felt anything like it. By the looks of it, it seemed like my body had invented a new disease. On the second day, I was drooling because the sores had spread to the insides of my mouth, my lips, and my tongue. When I was no longer able to withstand the pain, Kyla rushed me to hospital. I felt like death was calling on me.

Chapter 48

The End

"How you feeling?" Kyla asked with a sympathetic expression.

"Am in so much pain," I replied, struggling to pronounce the words from the hospital bed. She kept our conversation to a minimum as soon as she noticed how much pain mumbling caused me. Kyla held my hand and looked into my eyes with winks of hope.

I was high as the sky from the morphine running through my veins. I was also receiving fluids intravenously to keep me hydrated since I wasn't able to drink or eat anything. My skin felt like it was deteriorating and, judging by the way I was drooling, my jaw felt like it was broken. I had a fever, but it was slowly dropping. Every new target lesion that I discovered on my body made me more and more self-conscious. I started to hate the body I was in. I kept on thinking that this was some sort of cruel punishment.

Kyla treated me no differently and reminded me of how handsome I was. I noticed the hurt in her eyes caused by the look of irritation on my face. She was right by my bedside when I needed someone the most. When she was working, she was only one floor above. I would have been so lonely without her because Cho probably didn't care if I was dead or alive. I didn't blame her, though. I wasn't worth her attention for all the bullshit that I had put her through.

After work, Kyla would be seated near my bedside, reminding me that everything would be fine, until she fell asleep. The love I had for her had grown stronger, and I truly felt like she was the one I was waiting for my entire life. Kyla knew how to please me and she was the first woman to ever make me feel like I was making love to myself. I enjoyed watching her as she slept, saying to myself, *Damn, I love this girl.* Kyla gave me new reasons to believe that love was worth waiting for. By April, we had been dating for about six months and I was more than happy to accept her in my life forever. I was convinced that Kyla was made just for me. She was a true angel sent by God.

Finally, the results were in. All of my blood work and urine samples came back inconclusive. During the past five days at the hospital, I must have seen 10 different doctors, and each one was just as stumped as the next. *What was going on with me?* On the day I was released, the pain was less severe and I was able to eat again.

Since the tests at the hospital were inconclusive, I was referred to Dr. Richard M. Haber, of the Diagnostic and Treatment Centre. Dr. Haber was a very knowledgeable man who immediately ruled out every skin disease or virus, except for a rare skin condition called erythema multiforme (EM). A biopsy confirmed his assumptions.

"That's definitely EM," he said, scrutinizing the lesions on my body.

"What causes it?" I asked.

"It can be anything," he said. "Your immune system, infections, medication, stress. Who knows."

"So, are the lesions ever gonna go away?"

"Arnold, it might or might not go away. We never know with this thing. All I can do is prescribe you some medication to slow it down."

I sighed. "So you don't have the slightest clue?"

"I know this can be frustrating for you. The most important thing right now is to figure out your trigger. Once we determine that, we can eliminate the causes, and, hopefully, you won't have a flare up again."

Although subsequent outbreaks weren't as life-threatening as the first, new lesions were appearing on a weekly—or daily—basis. My morning ritual now included taking 50 milligrams of prednisone, at least for a couple of days. I saw results almost immediately. The drug reduced any outbreaks and scabbed away the sores. But I still hadn't been able to determine what was triggering the EM. It seemed like mission impossible.

Erythema multiforme had become my worst nightmare; I wouldn't wish it on the people who had hurt me the most. The sores would start the size of a dot, and then grow into various shapes and sizes with a red centre, pale rings, and dark red outer rings. After the sores scabbed, I was left with dark scars marking my skin in a polka-dot pattern. I was uncomfortable in my own skin. The gorgeous person I thought I had grown up to be was forgotten. I limited myself from any outdoor activities and hid inside my darkened room like a bat during the daylight. I hid my body by wearing long-sleeved shirts and pants. I kept on reminding myself that scars represented victorious struggles. I tried to focus on being an amazing person from the inside to show others how beautiful I was from the outside. However, not being able to put on my basketball shoes turned out to be the hardest part of having this rare skin condition.

"Are you making it to the National Basketball League of Canada draft this year?" Ian McCarthy asked me via Facebook Messenger.

Before replying, I took a glance at the painful lesions on my feet. "It seems like every year, something new pops up. Unfortunately, I won't be able to make it. I am fighting a rare skin condition called erythema multiforme, which has taken over my life since March of this year. Doctors and dermatologists have been assisting with finding out what triggers my reaction. But I'm still hanging on to my dreams. Thanks for reaching out. Right now, I'm just trying to get better."

"Geeze that's terrible. I hope you can win," Ian replied.

"Thank you, sir."

No one will ever know how much I cried on the night I read Ian's last response. Winning was all I ever wanted. But somehow, my never-give-up attitude was becoming a thing of the past. I was ready to tap out. Having one of the world's rarest skin conditions of unknown cause meant all of the hard work I dedicated toward fulfilling my dreams was for nothing. Erythema multiforme had caused me to feel so weak that all I wanted to do was to let go of the ropes. I seriously felt like I was at the edge of a cliff, waiting for one more thing to push me over. I felt I was fighting a battle I had no chance of winning.

Only a handful of people knew about the pain I had to endure on a daily basis. I was too self-conscious about exposing myself. When I contemplated suicide in an online article, a saint replied to my message at a very critical moment. "You are not alone," the lady wrote. "Please join us on Facebook. Search for: Erythema Multiforme Support Group for Suffers and Their Families. We are here for each other." She was right. I wasn't alone. There were about 250 members on the day I was accepted to the group. They offered just the support I needed to get through it. Maybe it wasn't my day to die.

Despite the circumstances, Kyla made me feel alive. Not only was she my personal nurse at home, she was now my financial support. I was missing so many days of work and losing so much money at the casino that I couldn't feed myself. As much as I tried to keep my financial constraints on the down low, Kyla finally discovered that I had a gambling problem. One evening, she drove to every casino until she found me. I was on my way to losing an entire paycheque at the blackjack table. I was so shocked to know that she loved me so much she was willing to come look for me and beg me to leave. She cried to me that night, saying that she didn't want a boyfriend with an addiction. I cried with her, too, promising that I would seek counselling. Still, that did not stop me because I was back the next day, gambling until I was broke.

I wasn't able to pay my $800 monthly rent, so Kyla had agreed to let me move in with her and her brother, who was now single. Throughout this time, we loved each other, but we had a mutual agreement that we were not in a committed relationship. She said she was not my girlfriend, and I was not her boyfriend. Even though we were simply dating with a promise that we were on exclusive terms, we were not an official couple. I had tried to make it official in December, 2012, but when I asked her to be my girlfriend, she shut me down, saying she wasn't ready. Kyla had been in a nine-year relationship with a guy who had a drug problem. Two months later, when her heart was ready, I returned the rejection because I realized that I wasn't man enough for her love. I told her that I would be ready when I was ready.

On the day I realized I had been taking Kyla for granted, I arrived home from work and noticed a letter on the kitchen table. No one was home. "Arnold, this isn't good," she had written. I read the following sentences with an accelerated heart rate. My instincts warned me that it was the end of our dating life. Kyla wasn't happy with the person I had become. I was going down, and she wasn't strong enough to pick me up. I tore the letter into tiny pieces and flushed it down the toilet. I rang her cellphone and demanded her to come home. At the same kitchen table where I found the breakup letter, I poured my heart out to her, pleading for a second chance to prove that I could become a better man. I promised to love her like no other.

I was given that second chance, and we were the happiest couple ever. To prove to her that I was ready for a commitment, we got her ring finger fitted. I had plans to propose on her birthday. I had let go of my gambling habits because I never wanted to lose her again. Kyla didn't want anything more than to be with me, and I had never felt the same about another woman. We had the same moral values. We were planning on setting forth a strong foundation and building from the ground up. We had our future all planned out and written down in our dream journal. I had found the perfect partner, a woman I would be willing to die for. No more games were being played; there were no other women in my eyes but her. I was ready to be faithful to her. I had won myself the championship trophy.

It was a fresh start at love for us. I wanted to come clean and tell Kyla about all the other women, but I knew it might be too painful for a woman's heart. Sometimes, hurtful truths are better left unsaid—or so I thought. As long as I was keeping a smile on her face, I thought that was enough. In June, three days before Kyla's birthday, the sweet, innocent angel I had known transformed into a strong, heartless, no-nonsense woman. It was as disastrous as the heavy rainfall that triggered the catastrophic flooding that was the worst in Alberta's history.

My past had finally caught up to me. All my secrets were being held captive, making me feel as if I was under duress. I was at work for my last hour of the day when I got a series of random text messages from Kyla. From my recollections of that morning, we'd happily kissed each other goodbye; everything was just fine. By the sarcastic tone of her sentences, I assumed her smile had been flipped upside-down.

"So, you're a good man, huh?"

"Yeah, babe," I replied, thinking, *what the hell?*

"You're such a good man, Arnold.

"Um, Kyla, is everything OK?"

"You tell me, Arnold."

"Kyla, I don't know what's going on," I replied. "I'm so confused." *Something is wrong*, I said to myself. She never used that tone with me. I sent about 10 text messages that she never responded to. I sensed that I was in big trouble.

I rushed home, speeding at 140 kilometres per hour on the highway. "Kyla?" I yelled as I burst through the front door. I was so lost in thought that I'd forgotten to look for her car on the street. No one was home, except for the dog. The house was in complete darkness. I was desperate for answers, so I attempted to call her a few more times. No answer. I was so anxious. I was in our downstairs bedroom, pacing back and forth, ignoring the highlights of Game 7 of the Miami Heat vs. San Antonio game.

Suddenly, the doorknob turned quietly, as if a thief were carefully invading our home. I looked through a crack in the entrance to the bedroom. Standing before me was a testament of the boy I was in the past—someone I had deleted from my life about three months ago. I had no choice but to surrender. This wasn't my idea of a threesome. I had basically been caught red-handed. I could only imagine that Kyla would see through all of my excuses.

Kyla had brought home a fling from my past who served as an eyewitness, testifying against me for a full hour. I knew it was the end.

Bonus Chapter

Four Months Later

I have a big heart. I've always wondered what it would be like to be in a polygamous relationship. I truly believed that I could be in an intimate relationship with several women who all devoted their love to me. *Is it that I have no heart? Was the monogamous lifestyle for me?* In reality, I felt like I was living in my imagination, especially while I was lying next to my rebound lover, Lisa—who was keeping me from experiencing the full extent of the emotional pain caused by my recent breakup with Kyla. *Was Kyla the one I had been longing for? Did I allow my soulmate to slip away?* It is funny how love can spread faster than a forest fire but can completely burn out in a matter of seconds.

A loud banging on the walls awakened me.

"Get out! Get out! Get out!" I was confused as I wondered if I had been awakened by the sounds in my own dream. "Get out! Get out now!" The masculine voice was real. All the noise had vibrated to the inside of Lisa's condo while she remained sleeping. The digital clock showed that it was 5 a.m. "Get out of the house now!" I jumped out of the bed and ran through the open door and into a hallway, which was filled with white smoke so grandiose it looked as spooky as scenes from a horror film. I felt like I was running to the entrance of the pearly gates.

For a brief moment, I thought I was sleepwalking. The closer I stepped to end of the smoky hallway, the more I felt like I was going to suffocate—as if I had inhaled smoke with no means of exhalation. A series of shadows on the walls and floors drew pictures of trees being blown by violent winds. The burning scent of wood had invaded my nose as I coughed and gasped. I truly felt like I was walking on clouds to the gates of Heaven. But this wasn't death. My eyes weren't ready for what my mind had conjured up.

As I approached the living room of Lisa's condo, the water in my eyes started to sting. There was no more hesitation in my steps once I realized I was trapped in a life-or-death situation.

I paced back and forth between the bedroom and the sight of a blazing hot patio. In the midst of panicking, I heard a series of coughs. "Get out! Get out! Get out now!" Looking through the double sliding door that separated the living room from the patio, I noticed a shirtless figure. Was that a real fireman or a civilian?

As soon as this horrific reality began to sink in, I shouted, "Oh my God! Oh my God! Lisa! Lisa!"

She turned around in the bed to face me. Her worried stare made it difficult to determine if she had sobered up from her night of partying, or if she could smell the smoke. "What?" she asked.

"Oh my God! Oh my God!" I couldn't stop pacing. "Lisa! Oh my God! Oh my God! Lisa!" She was quick to get out of bed and follow my trail, which hinted at the reason for my panic attack. The fiery orange glow reflected in her eyes as she tried to keep herself from collapsing. "Who did that?" she sobbed, her tears smearing eyeliner down her face. The patio had quickly transmuted into hell on Earth. But if this was a fire that had been deliberately set, that was just cold.

"Get out," the saint from the patio reminded us.

"Who did that?" Lisa repeated.

"Get out," the half-naked man shouted while he fought the fire with his shirt. The blazing flames were thirsty for more fuel and set their sights on the furniture inside the house. For the next few minutes, it was as if someone had pressed the fast-forward button on the remote control. The fire was aggressively aiming to get hold of everything in its path, including us.

Lisa had everything to lose. It wasn't until she ran to open the sliding door when I realized that we were both naked. I left Lisa in the living room and quickly ran into the bedroom to throw on some clothing. While I was jumping into my pants, I heard the loud sound of shattering glass. Lisa screamed.

"Lisa!" My first thought was that the fire had caught up to the gas tank attached to the barbecue. "Lisa!"

My heart was racing in pace with the time it took to attend to the impulsive uproar of screams. "Lisa, what happened?" I yelled, coughing my lungs out. The fear in her eyes answered my question. "I can't get this damn thing to work," she said with a shaky voice while coughing and handing the fire extinguisher to me. She seemed as if she had lost all hope, like the entire condo complex was on the verge of burning flat to the ground. I heard the last of her cries as she fled her home.

Breathing in and out was somewhat impossible. I felt like I was being strangled to death. "Look!" I said to the stranger who was fighting the fire from outside. I shouted, "I can't open the door!" I tried muscling it a few times. "Step back!" I pulled the pin out of the fire extinguisher and squeezed the lever, aiming its hose at the fire. Only 10 seconds of extinguishing power was discharged; the fire was still spreading as it fed on the wooden infrastructure. I quickly imagined the Incredible Hulk, which inspired me to find the strength to open the door wide enough to at least hand the stranger buckets of water. I ran around like a lunatic, searching for a bucket. *Water,* I thought, *water.* I dashed from the kitchen sink to the bathtub, filling two buckets at a time. I lived up to my Aquarian sign, carrying water to the door so that the stranger could dump it on the raging fire in hopes of dousing the flames.

"Get out! Get out! Get out now!" I looked back to witness a stampede of real firefighters with a hose in their hands. "Who else is in here with you?"

"There's a cat and a dog inside. I don't know where they are," I said, sprinting into the bedroom.

A fireman followed me. "You have to get out now!" I grabbed my laptop before being escorted out of the condo unit.

I searched for Lisa in the crowd and held her in my arms, tight enough to soften the shaking generating from her body. Flames running through my mind had burned the motivational words that usually poured from my mouth. Even though it was just a few minutes before 6 a.m., the sounds and sirens from the fire trucks had drawn a crowd from the nearby condo units. Clearly, all the staring eyes assumed that Lisa and I were the ones who were most affected by the fire. Lisa wasn't able to stop the tears from flowing.

I asked myself: *Were we just victimized by some psycho from my past? Did someone want me dead? Am I even supposed to be here? Why would someone target us on the Thanksgiving long weekend of 2013?*

I wouldn't have been here if it hadn't been for what happened about four months ago, which was when Kyla had found out about my love affair, by a woman who I had left in the past.

The Rebirth, November 15, 2014
Time: 5:26 a.m.
Weight: 8.6 pounds & Height: 20 inches

Afterword

Before the mother of my first-born, before the fire that almost took away my life, before I broke Lisa's heart, before I had to live in my car, before losing Kyla forever, before the man I used to be, there were many secrets yet to unfold. Another woman had walked back into my life, reintroducing a past I thought I had left behind. I had already moved on, learning from the actions I wasn't proud of, and I thought I had found my soulmate. I had made a promise to myself that I was going to be a better man. But this woman, this fling, was out for revenge. She took away my most prized reward, and it seemed like I couldn't make it without Kyla. *Why then?* I had made it very clear to this woman that we were nothing more than a casual fuck. Karma was here to teach me that I should have never played with anyone's heart.

I begged for forgiveness, but the woman I thought was the love of my life didn't believe in third chances. Somehow, Kyla thought that our sex life was too good to let go so quickly. She started playing with my heart for her own pleasures. *Did she ever want me back or not? Why did we go from lovers to enemies in a matter of seconds?* I felt so dead inside and on the outside I wanted to live that feeling. The only way I knew how to deal with heartbreaks was to gamble my life away. I liked the idea of having a chance to win back all of my losses. But payback's a bitch.

By the autumn of 2013, I started to become a believer that not every dream comes true. Erythema multiforme had completely taken over my life. The lesions had spread and my unbearable skin condition was uncontrollable. I had another terrible outbreak during the summer, when I should have been going to several pro basketball tryouts but couldn't put on my basketball sneakers. I just didn't know—or understand how—to figure out EM's triggers. I was stressed, depressed, and, to make matters worse, I was fired from my job, my only means of income. I felt so lonely and sad in a country where I didn't belong. *Who could I turn to? Who was willing to accept the person I was?* The bad habits I had adopted had driven everyone away from me. I had no one left, and my marriage wouldn't be dissolved until we had torn each other apart. Cho was so manipulating and she was willing to do anything in her powers to have me deported.

Meanwhile, in Saint Lucia, people I used to call friends had served my mother with a six-month eviction notice. She was being forced to evacuate her own home where she had lived for 60 years. We would have to fight for what was ours, or my mother would have to find a new place to live. Her health was another issue that worried me. She didn't know what to expect with the cancer.

As far as basketball goes, my brother Marvin gave us hope. In September, 2014, he was living our hoop dreams after accepting an offer from KK Pärnu, an Estonian professional basketball team.

"How did you keep yourself motivated to fulfil your dream after not playing competitive basketball in two years?" I asked him.

"My son and my wife," he replied.

I looked up to my younger brother for putting his family first. Seeing him living his dream made me feel like my dream had come true, too. However, as the sayings go, life doesn't always go according to plan and nothing lasts forever.

Before saying goodbye to my 20s and welcoming my 30s, I had to once and for all let go of the past 29 years, especially all of those bad habits that almost cost me my life. I was becoming the man I always dreamed of being, and it was all because of the next chapters.

Acknowledgements

There wouldn't be a second book without the thousands of readers and supporters who've encouraged me to continue writing. I am so honoured and thankful for all the feedback that I've received during my years as an author. I'm also thrilled to know that my storytelling ability has changed lives and inspired others to never give up on their dreams. I am also grateful for the services of all the editors who worked on my second book: Charity Teglar, Barb Howard, and Cindy Kavanaugh.

I would like to take this opportunity to show gratitude toward my Heavenly Father for his continuous guidance, protection, and blessings. His words continue to work in mysterious ways. I wouldn't have lived to see my 30th birthday without my faith in Him. Special thanks to Jo-Anne Sieppert and all the members of our writer's group, Pen to Paper, for their massive contribution towards my development as an author. I've learned so much from our group meetings and author panels.

I also owe a big thank you to all of the volunteers who assisted with organizing and promoting my first book signings: my two Saint Lucians friends, Chevy Eugene and Gilson Lubin, who now live in Toronto; Jerry George, of Saint Lucia; the members of the Saint Lucia Young People's Association, which is based in the United Kingdom; the staff of Sunshine Bookshop in Saint Lucia; and, Brian Lowe, of Mini Hoops Canada. Your efforts and involvements will never be forgotten.

During my last year in college, I was fortunate to have found Kimberly Jordan and Deborah Williams, of Jacksonville, Florida, a sister and a mother who welcomed me into their homes and provided me with food, shelter, and so much more. That generosity and comfort made it less stressful for me to complete my studies. I'm so happy to still be able to call the two of you family.

As I grow older, I have gained knowledge of what true friendship means, and I've also lost a few friends on my journey. I will forever be appreciative toward all my new friends, especially Susana Perez for all the times that you presented me with Christmas gifts knowing I didn't have family in Calgary, and for always being by my side through my rough times. More thanks goes out to the Hector family—of the U.K., but living in Calgary—for always thinking of me when I needed a plate of food. I can't forget Sherwin and Wendell Roberts, the power couple I looked to for inspiration whenever I needed a reminder that love still exists. And to the many other friends and family who weren't mentioned by name, I will cherish our memories forever.

Today, I am blessed with the ultimate prize—a family of my own. To my beautiful, amazing future wife, Stephanie Beninger: I absolutely adore you and appreciate your patience with me as I seek better ways to become the perfect man for you. Thank you for helping to bring into this world the most incredible little boy, our greatest creation, our pride and joy, our son, Amarion Stephen Henry. I'm looking forward to spending the rest of my life with the two of you.

Made in the USA
Charleston, SC
11 September 2015